Vision and Virtue

Vision and Virtue

ESSAYS IN
CHRISTIAN ETHICAL REFLECTION

Stanley Hauerwas

University of Notre Dame Press
Notre Dame, Indiana

University of Notre Dame Press edition 1981

Copyright © 1974 by Fides Publishers, Inc.

Reprinted by arrangement with Fides Publishers, Inc.

Printed in the United States of America

Library of Congress Cataloging in Publication Data

Hauerwas, Stanley, 1940–
    Vision and virtue.

    Reprint of the ed. published by Fides, Notre Dame, Ind.
    Includes bibliographical references.
    1. Christian ethics—Addresses, essays, lectures.
I. Title.
BJ1241.H38   241   80-54877
ISBN 0-268-01921-5
ISBN 0-268-01922-3 pbk.

TO

ANNE AND ADAM

Preface

I have brought these essays together in the hope they will prove to be useful for classes in Christian ethics. These essays develop a perspective that has been sadly lacking in much of recent Christian ethics. I wish, however, to make no exaggerated claims for the importance of this book as it is incomplete in many ways. Important issues concerning the nature of obligation, justification, and value theory are only hinted at or ignored entirely. My hope is, however, that these essays will serve to introduce students to Christian ethics in a manner that makes clear that Christian ethics is a disciplined and serious business. Much I have done here may be wrong, but I hope I have done it in a way that others can learn how to do Christian ethics better than I have.

There are many people that have helped in the preparation of one or more of these essays. I wish particularly to thank Ross Paulson, Frank DeGrave, Jill Whitney, Donald Evans, Mary Jo Weaver, Leroy Walters, James Gustafson, Hal Moore, James Burtchaell, and Elena Malits for their patience in trying to help me think and write better. I would also like to thank the Department of Theology at Notre Dame and the Kennedy Center for Bioethics at Georgetown University for the support of the sabbatical during which this book was prepared.

There are six people that I owe a very special debt. I am grateful to Dr. John Score, my teacher at Southwestern University, for first suggesting to me that it might be useful to bring these essays together. I owe him much more than this as he taught me the difference between being smart and being wise by steadfastly refusing to be more than an honest man. Rev. David Burrell, the chairman of my department, has often taken the time from his busy schedule to read and criticize my work. His leadership is one of the main reasons it is such a joy for me to teach at Notre Dame. Dr. David Harned has given me confidence that some of this may be worthwhile by suggesting that my work has been important for his own. His own book, *Faith and Virtue,* is so good it is a source of satisfaction to know that my work may have influenced him in some way. Over the time I have written these essays, and before as a fellow student, Dr. Jim Childress has been my good critic, provided encouragement when there were few others, and most of all has been my friend. He has had to carry the burden of reading more of my work of anyone and what is good about it owes much to him. It finally makes no sense to speak of debts between friends for friendship is the gift to rejoice in the presence of the other because of their independence for our being. I am extremely grateful I can call all these men my friends.

However my most important friends have been my wife, Anne, and my son, Adam. Together they have taught me most of what I have learned about what makes life worthwhile and joyful. They are gifts I cannot possess and are all the more valuable because of it. I thank God for them.

Stanley Hauerwas
September, 1973
Notre Dame, Indiana

Acknowledgements

The author and publisher are grateful to the following for permission to reprint:

Irish Theological Quarterly for "Situation Ethics, Moral Notions, and Moral Theology";

Studies in Religion/Sciences Religieuses for "The Significance of Vision: Toward an Esthetic Ethic";

Theological Studies for "Towards an Ethics of Character";

Journal of Religious Ethics for "The Self as Story: A Reconsideration of the Relation of Religion and Morality from the Agent's Perspective";

Cross Currents for "Love's Not All You Need," "Abortion and Normative Ethics," and "Politics, Vision, and the Common Good";

The American Ecclesiastical Review for "Abortion: The Agent's Perspective";

Journal of Religious Studies (India) for "The Nonresistant Church: The Theological Ethics of John Howard Yoder";

The Murphy Center for Liturgical Research, University of Notre Dame, for "The Ethics of Death: Letting Die or Putting to Death," to be published in *The Liturgy of Healing and Death*.

Religious Education and *Theology Digest* (edited version) for "Aslan and the New Morality";

Notre Dame Magazine for "The Christian, Society, and the Weak," and to *Theology Today* for its edited version entitled "The Christian Care of the Retarded";

Review of Politics for "Theology and the New American Culture," and to Ronald Weber and the University of Notre Dame Press for this article's inclusion in the collection of essays entitled *America in Change*, University of Notre Dame Press, 1972.

Contents

Introduction

The central intention and unifying focus of these essays is the attempt to do responsible and constructive Christian ethical reflection. There would be nothing remarkable about this except that for many the idea of trying to do Christian ethics has become a doubtful enterprise. Philosophical, theological, and sociological reasons have come together to make problematic the idea that Christian ethics is anything distinct from ethics. Some philosophers for logical reasons have denied that there can be any conceptual relation between religion and morality. Some theologians, embarrassed by the narrow and dogmatic forms of some kinds of Christian ethics in the past, and impressed by the loss of vitality of basic Christian symbols for "modern man," are attempting to work from what they consider to be a broader and more open perspective. Moreover, Christian ethics has become something of an academic embarrassment in departments of religion that teach students of varied religious and nonreligious backgrounds.

This book does not pretend to meet all the objections that might be raised against Christian ethics. Rather, in the first part of this book, I try to develop in a positive way the methodological basis that makes intelligible the kinds of claims Christians do, might, or should want to make about the nature of the Christian moral life. The rest of the book attempts to show the implications of this methodology for some of the issues raised by the "new morality," concrete normative issues, and social ethics. Methodologically, it is my contention that the current difficulty of Christian ethics stems from the far too narrow conception of moral experience accepted by many philosophical and religious ethicists. When ethics is limited to an analysis of the justification for particular actions, then it is indeed difficult to make sense of Christian ethics. The language of the Gospel includes, but points beyond, judgments about particular actions and practices to the nature of the self and how it is formed for our life project.

1

Once ethics is focused on the nature and moral determination of the self, vision and virtue again become morally significant categories. We are as we come to see and as that seeing becomes enduring in our intentionality. We do not come to see, however, just by looking but by training our vision through the metaphors and symbols that constitute our central convictions. How we come to see therefore is a function of how we come to be since our seeing necessarily is determined by how our basic images are embodied by the self—i.e., in our character. Christian ethics is the conceptual discipline that analyzes and imaginatively tests the images most appropriate to score the Christian life in accordance with the central conviction that the world has been redeemed by the work and person of Christ.

I have tried to arrange these essays in a way that makes clear the development of this central theme. The first essay, "Situation Ethics, Moral Notions, and Theological Ethics," shows the significance of directing attention to moral notions rather than decisions. The kind of ambiguity in our moral experience that lends credibility to situation ethics is better accounted for by recognizing the open character of many of our moral notions. The moral life is not first a life of choice—decision is not king—but is rather woven from the notions that we use to see and form the situations we confront. Moral life involves learning to see the world through an imaginative ordering of our basic symbols and notions.

"The Significance of Vision" is an analysis of Iris Murdoch's contention that ethics and the moral life is best understood as a form of aesthetics. The moral life is fundamentally the life of vision, for the task is to see accurately the nature of the world, self, and others without illusion. The ethical problem reflects a classical priority in seeking to know the truth rather than to choose or will the good. Such truthful vision, however, does not come without discipline. The self must be transformed if we are to attend honestly to how we are to live justly in a contingent world. Such discipline is not a code of conduct but rather the willingness to stand and accept the reality of the other without neurotic self-regard or the comfort of convention.

Such discipline is possible only when the self has been rightly formed for we do not see with our eyes but with the self formed by images that truthfully reflect the nature of our existence. Virtue and character is therefore the necessary correlative of our ability to see rightly. "Towards an Ethics of Character" develops an agency theory of the self necessary to understand the idea of character and its ethical significance. Character is the qualification of our self-agency formed by our having certain intentions rather than others. Our character is the orientation that gives unity and direction to our lives by forming our intentions into meaningful configurations determined by our dominant convictions.

The final essay of the methodological section, "The Self as Story," attempts systematically to develop the interdependence of vision and virtue in order to address directly the question of the relation between religion and morality from the agent's perspective. The metaphors that determine our vision must form a coherent story if our lives are to have duration and unity. Such stories create the context of meaning for the concrete moral rules and principles to which we adhere. There is no principled way to separate the "religious" from the "moral" in such stories. Therefore attempts to construe the relation of religion and morality in terms of higher to lower or internal (motivational) to external morality distort the manner in which religion and morality coalesce in forming the self.

The first two essays of the second part are critiques of the "new morality." "Aslan and the New Morality" does not defend something called the "old morality," but rather illustrates the central theme I have developed in the methodological essays. It criticizes the "new morality" for failing to help us see the truth about our existence. What is at stake is not something called absolute principles or inherently wrong acts, but whether our moral rules and notions help us see the world and understand human existence as it is. I am particularly critical of the attempt by advocates of the "new morality" to avoid the judgment, pain, and guilt of the moral life in the name of an ethics of self-fulfillment and understanding. Such an ethic has little use for the basic symbols of the Christian life, as it ignores the experience the symbols of the faith help us to see, embody, and enliven. The result is not only to render unintellligible the nature of faith but to leave us at the mercy of convention. For the break with convention can only come when we have the substance to face the agony of human existence which convention is inherently designed to help us forget.

"Love's Not All You Need," develops this theme by exposing

the simplistic assumptions associated with the idea that "love is all you need" for the moral life. The latter view cannot be supported on theological or moral grounds. Theologically, love as a disposition or norm cannot be abstracted from its Christological context and form. The theological qualification of the ethics of love is moreover necessary if we are to do justice to the complexity of our moral experience. The peculiar commitments that shape the Christian moral life are not "revelations" added on to or above human experience but the skills (linguistic and moral) necessary to understand, face, and properly embody that experience for our entire life project. The reality of Christ and the symbols and stories dependent on his reality help us to face truthfully a world where the legitimate command to love necessarily involves unfaithfulness and injury to others. It is the crucified savior that teaches us to say this honestly so we might also learn the skill to participate in and to become His truth.

The essays on abortion applies this perspective to one of the most difficult normative issues currently faced in the public domain. "Abortion and Normative Ethics," is an attempt to redefine what makes abortion a moral problem through a critical analysis of work on abortion by Callahan and Grisez. Both fail to consider sufficiently the basic question of what abortion is morally as they assume what convention has identified as acts of abortion to be equivalent to a moral description. "Abortion: The Agent's Perspective" argues to the contrary that morally an abortion is not equivalent to the physical act of taking the fetus before term. Abortion can and should in many cases be considered different from murder, not because the fetus is nonhuman, but because the intentionality associated with the notion of abortion cannot always be described as "unjust aggression" but is often an ambiguous response to a tragic situation. The agent's perspective is significant for understanding particular acts of abortion precisely because the agent's intention helps to constitute abortion as a moral notion.

Our tendency to use "abortion" as a class word for a practice allows us, however, to overlook the intentionality of the agent. Many men of good will have felt it necessary to deny the fetus human status in order to account for the permissibility of abortion in tragic and hard cases. In fact, however, abortions are undertaken in human contexts replete with the tragedy and guilt unavoidable in our common existence. Unless we can learn to deliberate about such activities in a language which reflects that human situation, we will lose our capacity for moral discrimination. There are good reasons why a people, and in particular a Christian people, should generally regard abortion to be morally prohibited. The harder question asks whether prohibition enlivens rather than destroys basic commitment of the participants of that community to care for one another.

We cannot sidestep this perspective issue by attempting to apply a deontological or utilitarian theory directly to the problem of abortion. Normative theory cannot substitute for what only a substantive community can provide. My own position on abortion would be classified, broadly speaking, as deontological, but I do not assume that any such theory is or should be necessary in order to justify all that we should and should not do. As I tried to show in "Situation Ethics, Moral Notions, and Theological Ethics," the basic mistake of situation ethics has been the attempt to make one theory, act-utilitarianism, account for and justify every moral act and practice. When this is done, moral reflection is arbitrarily divorced from the historical experience that gives it life. Utilitarians, in their penchant to make every act and rule theory-dependent, fail to do justice to the wisdom of human experience embodied in our inherited moral notions. The strong presumption against abortion suggests that we are less in need of a unified theory to justify it, than we are of learning how to use the notion in a way that does justice to the moral complexity involved in some abortion situations.

Hence I can avoid the language of "rights" in my discussion of abortion, since I assume that obligation is a community bound matter. I am sure that there are some obligations that accrue to us as participants in human community. I am not sure whether or how abortion can be adequately analyzed in terms of these general obligations. But I am sure that Christians have an obligation, given the basic form of their community, to protect the weak. In such a community it is not unreasonable to expect children to be born that have been conceived in less than ideal conditions (although there may be overriding reasons in some cases why this would not be so). Such a community must of course also be willing to provide adequate care for mother and child so that such an expectation will be humane. That such children can be born into such communities depends on the background assumption that life is not an end in itself but exists for ends beyond survival of either particular individuals, that community, or even the species.

"The Ethics of Death: Letting Die or Putting to Death?" directly explores the ethics of survival through an analysis of the issues raised by modern medicine's power to sustain life beyond all reasonable purpose. Material criteria of the moment of death are not irrelevant for the moral meaning of our death, as such criteria can check arbitrary judgments of the worth of another's life. Even though the rhetoric of those advocating a dignified death is excessive, our unwillingness to die well is perverting our living and the practice of medicine. If Christians are a people who have learned to die then they will insist that their medicine be concerned more with care than cure. For caring implies that we have learned to regard and respect the other even though he is destined for a death which no cure is efficacious to prevent.

The short meditation, "The Christian, Society, and the Weak," in many ways summarizes the primary themes of the essays in the second section. The Christian care of the retarded is rooted in the central Christian images of God as we find him gestured in the eucharist. The great affirmation of the Gospel becomes relevant when we face honestly what such care involves—namely, that we can afford to face the truth about ourselves as mirrored in the cross without that truth destroying. A people who have been formed by such truth have the basis to learn the form of care of the weak in nondestructive ways.

Even though the last section is concerned with "social ethics," there can be no fundamental distinction between "social" and "personal" ethics from the perspective of an ethics of vision and virtue. The vision and virtue that forms the self cannot be separated from the community from which the self springs. This last section is therefore an attempt to outline the nature of the good community and its relation to the wider social order.

The canard that there is no specifically Christian ethics is especially prevalent in the context of social ethical concerns. The essay, "The Nonresistant Church," attempts to reopen this issue by analyzing John Howard Yoder's argument that the social responsibility of the church is to be itself. Yoder has been particularly persuasive in exposing the constantinian assumption behind the ethics of "responsible Christian social action." The Christian is not in principle responsible for every aspect of wider society. Rather the Christian must choose his issues in accordance with his primary loyalties. This discriminating social ethic does not justify withdrawing from society, but rather attempts to free us from the assumption that the church's social ethical task is synonomous with compulsive programs for improving society.

For example, "Politics, Vision, and the Common Good" argues that the responsibility of the church is to be first and foremost an honest institution. I am critical of the new "political theologians" who call for utopian visions as if such societies are possible to achieve without facing violence and bloodshed. A theological justification of revolution is verbal posturing that can only mire the church deeper in the illusion that it can be the church of the poor while continuing to lust after the power of this world. The church should indeed contribute to the political imagination of society but to do so requires disciplined reflection in an effort to understand our political and societal alternatives. The church will accomplish this task only when it can provide the symbols and the experience of a community that points beyond the current assumptions of what constitutes the "political."

The church's great failure in social ethics has not merely been her willingness to support the status quo, but her inability to stand as an alternative to the current forms of the political. The most damaging aspect of our current social and political malaise in America is that we no longer have the language to articulate our profoundest social issues in the political realm. We have no way of articulating Lincoln's "Second Inaugural" because we have allowed our social images and symbols to be blandly degraded in the interest of societal harmony and tolerance. The social ethical task of the church demands nothing less than keeping our grammar pure by calling societal injustice by its proper name—i.e., sin. A society that has degraded the language of sin and judgment is a society that ultimately has no purpose beyond the manipulation of some for the security of others. Such a society will always prefer order and peace to justice.

From this perspective the issue of race is still the primary social ethical issue in America. In "Theology and the New American Culture" I show how the black man possesses a story of tragedy and guilt that we must learn to integrate into America's central stories and images. The self-hate of the American middle class cannot be transformed until we find a way to live into the self-knowledge that the black man carries concerning what it means to be American. Only then can we begin to talk realistically of achieving a good society—when the goodness achieved will not be based on the lies of our assumed righteousness.

The development of men of truthful vision and virtue, however, will not come from wider society. Rather such men will come from the communities that have had the confidence in the truth of their images and symbols to use and embody them seriously and without embarrassment. The great social task of the church is to become a community where symbolic discourse is used and embodied in ritual and practice because of its assurance that God has indeed redeemed the world in Jesus Christ.

I.
Theoretical and
Methodological Issues

Situation Ethics, Moral Notions, and Moral Theology

The situation ethics debate seems to be slowly coming to an end. This may not be due to the fact that the issue has been settled, but as so often happens in intellectual disputes the adversaries simply become bored and begin to turn their interests elsewhere.[1] It may be that the best thing to do is to let the debate end because it would seem that just about all that is valuable has been mined from the issue. However, I wish to reopen some of the problems in the debate. I do so for two reasons. First, even though I agree with most of the criticism of Fletcher's position,[2] I believe that there is something essentially right about the main thrust of his view. It is my feeling however that Fletcher made an error when he identified his position with that of situationalism, because what he was really concerned with was the applicability of our moral notions to various kinds of situations. Fletcher's position finds its moral warrant and persuasiveness in the experience that we all have at times when we wish to say that it is not necessarily always wrong, for example, to tell a lie. The problem with Fletcher was that in his attempt to state his theory of ethical behavior to account for this aspect of moral experience he came very close to destroying any meaningful ethical discourse.[3] In order to bring some coherence to this issue I will try to reconceptualize the problem with which Fletcher was trying to deal so that it does not entail untenable consequences.

---

[1]The debate has occasioned however a good deal of valuable reflection on the nature of the moral life, as witnessed by the high quality of articles in the book, *Norm and Context in Christian Ethics,* edited by Gene Outka and Paul Ramsey (New York: Scribners Sons, 1968). Hereafter referred to as *Norm and Context.*

[2]I will confine myself in this paper to Fletcher's statement of 'situation ethics' in his *Situation Ethics* (Philadelphia: Westminster Press, 1966).

[3]Donald Evans' article, "Love, Situations, and Rules," is perhaps the clearest statement of this. *Norm and Context,* 367-414.

My second reason for reopening the issue is that a restatement of the problem in terms of the nature of moral notions gives an important insight into the proper business of theological ethics. Therefore the argument that I develop here is an attempt not only to say something that I hope will be helpful about the kind of problems envisaged in the situation-ethics debate, but also about the direction that theological ethics should proceed in order to move beyond the somewhat confining interests of the debate itself. I do not mean to suggest that there is only one way to do this for I do not think theological ethics can be limited to one kind of problem. The primary difficulty with Fletcher's position is a tendency to oversimplification about the factors of the moral life. Criticisms of Fletcher have primarily concentrated on his failure to account for the significance and variety of principles and rules for the determination of the moral act. Equally important for our reflection are the issues of the nature of the moral self, the conception of Christian existence, and the nature of moral authority, all of which receive little attention from the point of view of situation ethics.

My basic thesis is that positively Fletcher indicates that our moral notions are not definite enough to take account of the richness of our moral experience. There is more in our moral lives than can be accurately mirrored in our moral language. In effect much of our actual moral life, especially as it is theologically understood, is nothing more than a straining against the confinements of our moral notions. Fletcher, however, failed to make this clear because of his concentration on the "situation" of the moral decision rather than the moral notion. In other words the kind of problem that forms the center of Fletcher's work is more complex, as has often been pointed out, than his simple juxtaposition of situation versus rule allows.

Fletcher's major mistake was the assumption that the idea of decision is the central ethical concept. I am not denying the tremendous importance of the fact that ultimately it is by decision that the ethical life lives; or that without decision and choice it is not possible to speak about a moral act at all. Rather I am arguing that neither the moral life nor our moral philosophy can be based on the concept of decision alone. Prior to decision must come the idea of our moral notions, for without "our moral notions there would be nothing to make decisions about; there would not even be a need to make decisions."[4] To emphasize the importance of moral notions then does not deny the importance of decision, but rather it makes the logical point that when we make decisions they must be made in the framework of our moral notions that are not the result of decision strictly understood. Fletcher fails to see this because he tends to reduce the significance of moral notions to an overly simple idea of rules.

Fletcher's concentration on decision as the primary datum of the moral life reflects a kind of picture of moral experience that is shared by many people today. Those that assume this model of moral experience tend to think of the world primarily as made up of hard facts that are easily recognizable by reason. The moral life is thought to consist primarily of "value judgments" or preferences formed somehow "above" or "beyond" the facts but for which our reason cannot find any grounds to justify. There is not, nor can there be, any relation between the is and the ought. Decision becomes the foundation of morality as it is through decision we create value and thus are committed to what is thought of as relatively arbitrary preferences.[5] The idea that somehow the facts are simply there to be perceived accounts in part for Fletcher's tendency to talk about "situations" as though they are simply given apart from the human beings that make them up.

When this understanding of moral experience is assumed, the main task for moral analysis seems to take the form of metaethical analysis of moral terms. Thus much of contemporary ethics, both philosophical and theological, has concentrated on analysis of the nature of moral judgments made from the point of view of the spectator in an attempt to establish some general grounds for the objectivity of our moral judgments beyond our subjectivistic preferences.[6] This work has helped us understand better the nature of ethical argumentation, but it has tended to

---

[4] Julius Kovesi, *Moral Notions* (New York, Humanities Press, 1967), 111. My debt to Kovesi's general analysis of moral notions will be apparent through this essay.

[5] For a penetrating and provoking critique of this understanding of moral choice and its commensurate view of man see Iris Murdoch, "The Idea of Perfection," *Yale Review*, LIII (March 1964); and "Against Dryness: A Polemical Sketch," *Encounter*, XVI (January 1961).

[6] For a very useful introduction to this form of philosophical ethics see Patrick McGrath, *The Nature of Moral Judgment: A Study in Contemporary Moral Philosophy* (London: Sheed and Ward, 1967).

be extremely abstract. As a result it has ignored the fact[7] that much of our moral experience is a matter, not of judgment, but of how the agent forms himself and his actions from his particular perspective and history. By directing attention to our actual and concrete moral language I am trying to suggest that the moral life is better understood on the analogy of an artist engaged in his work than a critic making a judgment about the finished product.

Many assume that this reassertion of the significance of the subjective is the end of moral analysis. This, however, need not be the case, as the agent does not come to see and form the world devoid of determinative categories. Rather he shapes and is shaped by the notions that he inherits from his social context.[8] If we are to understand this aspect of our moral experience, it is therefore essential that we have a better conception of how our moral language and notions work. For I shall argue that our moral notions are not just arbitrary constructs of our "value judgments," but rather they have much in common with what we think of as our strictly "descriptive categories." In order to show that this is the case I must turn to a more detailed analysis of the nature of moral notions.

The Nature of Moral Notions

Logically it is thought that there is an immense difference between the notion of tables and the notion of lying. We tend to think that the notion of table is clear, distinct, and unambiguous. We assume that we know what tables are because they can be so immediately perceived. In contrast we tend to think that the notion of lying is much more tentative and ambiguous as it does not denote an object that is open to our immediate perception. This contrast, however, fails to appreciate the great difficulty philosophers have traditionally had with such notions as tables. This is not just a matter that one term denotes an object and the other an act, for such a distinction is relatively

---

[7] To be excluded from this judgment is the work of those ethicists who have begun to pay closer attention to moral psychology and the relation of ethics to the philosophy of the mind. I am thinking particularly of Anscombe, Foot, and Hampshire.

[8] For a suggestion about the nature of ethics that is very similar to this see Herbert McCabe, *What Ethics Is All About* (Washington: Corpus Books, 1969).

unimportant in the analysis of the notion itself. Rather philosophers have pointed to the problem that it is impossible to
simply perceive an object that is a table, for what we see are
qualities given to our sense as hardness, smoothness, and the
color of the object. There simply does not seem to be any
reason to say that we construct our notion of table out of
perceptible qualities.

Rather the reason we have our notion of table is the need we
have for tables that is embedded in our social conventions to sit,
to eat on, or to place objects off the floor. Logically the notion
of table cannot be understood apart from these historical contexts. It is therefore our need for tables that determines what
counts for some things to be tables while other objects are
excluded. This is why we cannot define a thing by listing its
constituent parts, as there simply must be something above the
parts that makes them count as the object. That is why, for
example, tables can assume many different shapes and sizes and
still be entitled to be called tables.

Perhaps the point I am trying to make can be made clearer by
introducing a distinction Julius Kovesi makes between form and
matter of a notion.[9] This distinction is often misunderstood, as
the material element is associated with the physical nature of
the object and the formal with its shape. Matter, however, not
only includes the physical nature of the object, but it includes
everything in which an object may vary without ceasing to be
what it is, for example, a table. Thus the shape of an object is
also part of its material element, but because of this we must
necessarily introduce the idea of form. Form is that aspect of
the object that determines it for what it is in contrast to other
such objects. The formal element is that aspect of the object
that allows us to group empirically dissimilar objects together

[9]Kovesi, *Moral Motions*, 3. Though Kovesi says he does not mean to use this
distinction in terms of its traditional metaphysical context, at times he does seem to
associate the formal element with some idea of "essence." Moreover, Kovesi uses this
analysis to try to deny that there is any meaning at all to the philosophical
disjunction between "is" and "ought," evaluative and descriptive. While I think he is
certainly right in denying to the philosopher some of the interpretations and
implications drawn from this disjunction, I do not think Kovesi can avoid the issue
entirely through the form-material distinction. However, the distinction is very useful
as a way of indicating the similarity between our "descriptive" and "moral" notions.
I am grateful to Professor Donald Evans for his penetrating critique of Kovesi's book
in this respect.

because we see that regardless of their material differences they all amount to the same thing. That is they all serve the same function.

For example the reason the notion "error" in tennis can include such different situations as the failure to hit a backhand, missing a net shot, or hitting an overhand into the net is that they all amount to the same thing. In other words, the formal element is the upshot of the situation. Though the various empirical factors are different they are all cases of an error because they all come to the same thing—namely, the failure to make a shot that normally should be made without difficulty. The formal element of our notions is but the recognition that we never simply know facts, but that we know them for some reason.

By stating this distinction Kovesi does not mean to imply that standards are included within the notion itself. A notion, whether it is descriptive or normative, is like a bag by which we group together some of the significant and recurring configuration of relevant facts in our lives.[10]

Therefore the difference between moral and nonmoral notions is not the difference between evaluative and descriptive aspects. A descriptive notion cannot be characterized anymore than an evaluative notion as facts minus the evaluation. Rather the difference between moral and nonmoral notions is the difference between their different formal elements.[11] That is, all notions are ways of grouping an otherwise unspecified group of features. The difference between moral and nonmoral notions is the reason or object of the collecting of these features together. The function of our notions cannot be limited to the need to identify, but includes our need to avoid or promote, to excuse, blame, praise, or to judge and command.

Therefore we can readily agree that virtue and vice do not have the kind of matter-of-fact existence that is observable. Nor is lying a perceivable object or relationship between objects. But this is only to say that they are not objects of our senses in the way colors are. Rather they are objects of our reason, as how we know something cannot be equated with how we perceive it. We do not perceive something called lying, but we know that

---

10*Ibid.,* 83.
11*Ibid.,* 13.

certain acts are acts of lying in the same way that we know certain objects are tables and chairs. Moreover, this kind of knowing is already embodied within our inherited cognitive notions. We do not come to know the world by perceiving it, but we come to know the world as we learn to use our language.[12]

But to say that lying is an object of our reason is to say that in our ability to use moral notions we have the ability to establish reasons why similar sets of factors should be understood as lying. To accept such reasons is the same thing as forming certain rules for the proper use of such notions. Therefore our moral notions are possible in so far as we are rule-following rational beings.[13] This is not to say that rules are some abstract norms written in the sky that are artificially imposed our behavior. But rather the formal element of our moral notions enables us to follow rules to determine significant apsects of our human behavior.[14] The rules are but aspects of the formal element that allow for the meaningfulness of the moral notion from one time to the next. That is, to follow a rule in using a notion is simply to be able to see instances of that notion and to understand why they are such.

To argue in this way makes clear that all behavior that is meaningful is *ipso facto* rule governed, but not necessarily the result of an explicit application of a rule.[15] This is not to deny the distinction that some kinds of activity involve the participant in observance of rules while others do not. For example, the moral anarchist does not live a life that is determined by

---

[12]This kind of point can be argued in a somewhat similar way in terms of the possibilities of describing an action. For an excellent analysis of this see Eric D'Arcy, *Human Acts* (Oxford: Clarendon Press, 1963).

[13]*Ibid.*, 147. Many philosophers are now contending that the basic requirement for a man to be such is his rule governing capacity, for it is this aspect of man's capacity that allows him to govern rather than be governed. For example see Peter Winch, *The Idea of a Social Science* (London: Humanities Press, 1965). This is not a normative argument about what ought to be the place of rules in man's behavior. Rather it is an argument that descriptively tries to make the case that if the idea of behavior is to have any meaning at all it must be rule governed—that is, it must have a normative aspect.

[14]Richard McCormick states this correctly: "The problem of norms or rules of conduct is fundamentally the problem of the significance or meaning of human actions." See his "Human Significance and Christian Significance," in *Norm and Context*, 246.

[15]Winch, 52.

rules in the same way as a monk does. The difference between the two men, however, is not that the one follows rules and the other does not, but is in the kind of rules each follows. The moral anarchist can certainly eschew explicit norms, but that does not mean he can eliminate the idea of rule from the description of his behavior. For so far as he wishes to claim that he has reasons for doing what he does, those very reasons presuppose the notion of rule. Such rules are not dictated from on high, but rather are embodied in the very notions we use.

Therefore just as in using descriptive terms we have to follow interpersonal rules in a public language to talk about aspects or relationships in the world, so in using moral terms we have to follow interpersonal rules in a public language to talk about some aspects or relationships of those beings who are regulated by interpersonal rules.[16] Thus our moral notions are in principle capable of being learned and understood by anyone, as their very meaningfulness is dependent on their "grouping" aspects of our experience that we have in common. This characteristic of our moral language is the basis for the significance of the principle of universality or generalizability for moral judgment and argument.[17]

These issues can be clarified by making explicit an assumption that has been present throughout our discussion of moral notions—that it is only as our notions are needed in a way of life that they acquire meaning. This is an extremely important point because it denies that our notions are primarily for pointing to the material elements of an object or an act. It is often thought, for example, that the way words are learned is by learning "what they stand for," but that this is not the case is illustrated by Kovesi by a simple example.[18] Suppose in my classroom I coin a word "tak" and then draw various shaped figures on the blackboard each of which has a pointed projection. I then point to the projection and say they are "taks." It is assumed that my students from such an exercise will be able to learn what "taks" are for themselves, but there is something

---

[16]Kovesi, *Moral Notions*, 25. This points to the extreme importance of the relationship between language, rules, and community. The way we learn to use a language depends almost totally on the community in which we learn it, for the "gap" between the formal and material elements of our notions is not bridged by logical deduction but by the historical experience of a particular group of people.

[17]*Ibid.*, 55.

[18]*Ibid.*, 39.

odd about the assumption that the students have learned the meaning of "taks" from this exercise. For even if they see a "tak" outside the classroom what are they to do with it? Since I did not tell the students what "taks" are for, they have no way of knowing what the word means—that is, they do not have the rules for the proper use of the word. The meaning and therefore the rule character of the notion "tak" waits for its use, perhaps in a factory where tak-shaped objects are sorted out, or in a game, or in a scientific classification.

Of course this example tends to oversimplify, for most of the notions that we use in our everyday discourse cannot be limited to use in just one way of life.[19] Some of our notions, to be sure, have a very limited and definite use as they are embodied in a closely defined way of life. For example, the notion of an electron has a rather definite formal element because it gets its meaning from the somewhat artificial construction made by the physicist about the atom. However, our notions such as lying or kindness have a formal element that is a good deal harder to make precise because of the extremely rich ways of life in which the notion is used.

However, once this is understood another difference between moral notions and those about objects is apparent.[20] Notions about physical objects are not meant to affect the world they are about. The rules for the proper use of such notions are rules for the proper use of the notion itself, but the rules for the proper use of our moral notions are also rules for what these notions are about—that is human behavior. To know how to use the word "lie" is in effect to know how the word orders that aspect of human behavior which it is about. Thus to learn moral notions is not just to learn about the world, but it is to learn how to order the world. To learn moral notions is in effect to act upon the world, as it trains our vision about the world.

---

[19]"Way of life" is ambiguous, but it is not necessarily referring to a whole life style such as the "Christian way of life." Rather I am using it here to refer to any meaningful pattern of behavior no matter how limited. For example mailing a letter, buying groceries, stopping at a school crossing are examples of a "way of life."

[20]It should be observed that even though meaningful differences can be determined between moral and nonmoral notions, the major thrust of the argument is to broaden the range of what are considered to be moral notions especially in contemporary philosophical ethics. It may be that words such as sadness and joy have far more sigificance for our moral life than the universally agreed words such as right and good.

The moral life is therefore not just the life of decision but the life of vision—that is, it involves how we see the world. Such "seeing" does not come from just perceiving "facts," but rather we must learn how the world is to be properly "seen" or better known. Such learning takes place by learning the language that intends the world and our behavior as it ought to be that the good may be achieved. The moral life is a struggle and training in how to see.

Complete and Open Moral Notions

It is apparent that our moral notions are not the product of abstract reasoning or the creation of moral philosophers. [21] Rather our moral notions are the creation of our common experience of the everyday. Our moral notions arise from the needs and interests and demands embedded in our lives together. Once they are so constituted they then work to form our existence according to their formal element. They therefore at once reflect and form our experience. Because of this the language of moral notions is not that of philosophical definiteness, but that of common sense. Often when a moral notion that has its place in common sense is given philosophical status the result is a onesided or distorted picture of our actual moral existence.

Our moral notions are embodied in our language because they are the means by which we group together some of the most significant and relevant recurring aspects of our experience. So there are of course very great differences between our various moral notions in regard to the functions they play in their different ways of life. Many of our moral notions, such as good, can be used in so many different ways that they seem to be nothing but a formal element. [22] On the other hand some of our moral notions are so exact that they are limited to a number of very definite material situations for which they will count, for example, murder. It may also be the case that there are some complex situations that are simply not grouped to-

---

[21]This does not deny, however, that some of the contributions of seminal thinkers have not found their way into common sense, thereby affecting our inherited moral notions.

[22]Kovesi argues that words such as right and wrong rather than being discriminators are more like reminders for the reasons why we formed more definite moral notions in the first place, p. 109.

gether under one notion, but depend on several moral notions in order to explicate them.

It is impossible to state all the possible variations of these relationships between a moral notion and the relevant facts of a situation, but generally moral notions can be classified either as complete or open. An open moral notion is one where further specifications are needed to enable us to make a judgment on a specific act. A complete moral notion already will embody these further specifications within the notion itself. In other words such notions include all we need to know to judge an act as good or bad in itself. The great majority of our moral notions are of the former type as our everyday experience does not require the rigor of definiteness envisaged in the idea of completeness.

The fact that this is the case helps us to understand our tendency to resort to "it depends" when confronted by a question such as "is it always wrong to tell a lie?"—that is: is it always wrong to say what is not the case with the intention to deceive? The reason that we are hesitant to answer such questions in the affirmative is that we know or can envisage cases which, even though they involve intentional deception, do not properly seem to be included under the notion of lying. For example we feel that something is wrong about describing a case as lying where someone intentionally deceives in order to save the life of another even though the relevant material factors of the situation seem to entail such a judgment. The difficulty that we feel is due to the formal element of our notion of lying not being specific enough to exclude such a judgment.

Suppose, however, that instances of intentionally deceiving someone else to save the life of another were so common in our experience that we had a notion for it, for example, "saving deceit."[23] Moreover, this notion was not even associated with lying but instead had an entirely commendatory connotation. If this were the case then we might be much more willing to say that lying is always wrong because in such a circumstance the formal element of lying would be much more complete.

It is interesting to note in this regard that the more basic a moral notion is in regard to the significance of our lives together the more it tends to be a complete notion. For example murder,

---

[23]*Ibid.*, 107.

even in our commonsense usage, is a rather complete notion. Not all killing counts for murder, but because killing is such a significant human act we have learned by experience how important it is to understand it rightly. Thus we clearly limit murder as a notion by distinguishing self-defense, protection of another from attack, and involuntary killing. That is why as it now stands murder is a relatively complete notion.

Few of our moral notions, however, have this kind of completeness and therefore we constantly find that our experience tests our moral notions in the light of implications or applications that we had not originally envisaged in them. What this reveals is that our moral reasoning, especially in cases of moral doubt, is not deductive but analogical. That is to say, we do not find what we ought to do by having an abstract principle from which can be deduced the "right act." Rather what we do when we engage in moral reasoning is, by comparing cases, to try to find out what is common to the situations. What is common is not empirical similarities, but rather how the formal elements of the moral notions are comparable. That is, we are trying to find out if the upshot of the situations, even though different empirically, is the same. In this sense moral reason is more dependent on imagination than strict logical entailment.

By engaging in such analogical reasoning we find that we occasionally have to limit the range or the applicability of a moral notion. In doing so, however, we are not necessarily invalidating it, but rather we are making more definite its former vagueness. Any analysis of our moral notions done in this way reveals the fact that our moral experience is richer than our inherited conceputal apparatus can take into account. This is not to be construed as a denial of the importance of our inherited moral notions, but only to indicate that they cannot be accepted *prima facie* as complete moral terms. The problem with our moral notions is not necessarily the role they play in our common sense; it arises when we try to make them do more than their formal element was intended to do.

Moral Notions, the Exceptional, and Ethical Reflection

It is now possible to draw a few conclusions from this analysis of moral notions for the situation ethics debate. It now seems clear that the "rightness" of Fletcher's position that I indicated at the start of this essay is the result of the open nature of many of our moral notions. Fletcher's use of the extraordinary situation is a way of locating the indefiniteness that is often involved in the formal element of our moral notions. By calling into question or denying the appropriateness of certain notions to cover unique cases, Fletcher reveals the limits of the notion that perhaps had not been obvious before. Or he reveals that some of our significant moral experiences are simply not covered by one moral notion. Moreover, such an analysis shows that the formal element of a moral notion may not be perfectly reflected in the concrete rule for its use. It is this aspect of our moral notions that I think provides the ground for the idea of *epikeia*—that is, where the strict interpretation of the law is denied because it is inconsistent with the purpose of the law.[24]

This analysis also makes clear, however, that it is one thing to attempt to limit the applicability of certain of our moral notions, but it is another thing entirely to try to say that a moral notion is rendered meaningless in the light of the unique situation. Rather it is apparent that examples of extraordinary situations can be delineated only within the context of moral notions. This is not to say that the way in which the situation is understood necessarily dictates the decision that the agent must make, it still must be his decision. However, the significance of our moral notions is not denied by such situations, for without such notions it is impossible to think of the situation as being extraordinary.

Fletcher fails to appreciate the fact that moral notions are not atomistic ideas separated from actual life, but rather gain their position because they play a part in a whole way of life. To deny their significance in the name of the situation in the way that Fletcher does is not only to question them but to deny there can be such a thing as a moral way of life. Of course this is not to deny that one might want to question a particular way of life, but if one does so then one must be aware that that is what one is doing. It is not just a matter of denying a rule, but it is to question the significance of that form of life entirely. It may be that in the light of a new experience we

---

[24]For a fuller discussion of the notion of *epikeia* see Bernard Häering, "Dynamism and Continuity in a Personalistic Approach to Natural Law," in *Norm and Context*, 210.

reach the conclusion that a certain moral notion is wrongly applied in a way of life. Or it may be that certain of our moral notions are associated with social conventions in such a way that we might want to argue that such a convention is wrong. In the light of this Fletcher's work can be appreciated as an attempt to make us conscious of some of the limits and inappropriateness of some of our moral notions. In so far as it does this it performs a valuable service for our moral reflection.

Fletcher's own analysis, however, labors under the misapprehension that our moral notions are always abstractions from our actual moral experience. He ingores the fact that our moral notions do not just inform us about what is going on, but actually arrange what is going on by selecting the variables to be understood in a particular way. Thus our moral notions are not abstractions derived from a heaven of moral absolutes, but they are rather concepts that help us to define areas of significance for our lives together. As such they are not blinkers that prevent us from seeing the situation but rather they are implicit in any meaningful behavior in so far as it is one thing and not another. The question therefore of various moral notions and rules is primarily the question of the significance of particular kinds of human action. As such the question is not adhering to rules or to the situation, but what the situation is and how it should be correctly understood.

More importantly, however, this analysis of moral notions provides an indication of what ought to be the nature and direction of ethical reflection in both its philosophical and theological modes. It shows clearly that the moral philosopher and theologian cannot and do not start their thinking in an ethical vacuum. Rather they begin with the richness of human experience that is embodied in our everyday moral notions. That is why our philosophical and theological ethics can often be called in question because they fail to give an account of what we know otherwise to be good. Because of this we should take seriously our vague feelings that something is wrong with an ethical position even though we are not sure what it is. For it is obvious that our philosophical and theological attempts to give an account of moral good have often resulted in an intellectual bewitchment that blinds us to the actual richness of the good.

Even though this has often been the case, it does not mean that the moral philosopher or theologian is limited to simply restating our everyday notions. To be sure, the importance of trying to understand our everyday moral notions cannot be underestimated, but the object of moral reflection is more than this. We must begin with and take seriously the everyday, but we cannot remain there if we are to do our job effectively. We cannot stop there, for the same reasons that men cannot assume in their regular behavior that common sense moral notions are normative. The ethicist contributes to the moral task of everyman by proceeding as far as possible with rigorous and consistent rational reflection about the nature of various moral notions. In so doing he does not alleviate the moral problems we all face, for thinking as clearly as possible is not all that is necessary for the moral life. It can at times even inhibit us from doing the good.

But we must engage in the task if for no other reason than that our moral notions embodied in common sense often have their meaning (formal element) changed, forgotten, or transformed by our changing social and historical context. Thus the moral theologian cannot assume that he simply "knows" the meaning of a moral notion simply because he uses it himself in everyday speech. Rather he must investigate its use and therefore its significance in his own social situation. The importance of this basically descriptive task cannot be underestimated, for too often moral notions have been used to justify and warrant moral evil that was not originally associated with them. This is especially pernicious as the notion itself may still carry with it the authority of its past association. Thus the moral theologian cannot cease from trying to detail with some exactness the proper use of our moral notions.

This is complicated by the fact that the formal element, and therefore the material aspects relevant to it, are usually indefinite, often ambiguous. It is probably true that the moral theologian simply by the process of reflection cannot remove such indefiniteness or ambiguity, though in certain instances he may be successful. What he can do, however, is make clear that the use or non-use of a moral notion in relation to a situation is odd or unusual. For example, morally an abortion is not simply described as a "termination of pregnancy" nor do we usually feel it right to say, "That abortion was a morally good act." To point out the oddness of these ways of talking does not necessarily carry a negative judgment. Rather it calls for the speaker to give reasons why we should accept his unprecedented usage.

The importance of this for the moral life is not to be under-estimated, as it is just by such challenges that we are forced to make clear why certain notions are applicable to our situation or act. By having to formulate our reasons we contribute to the enrichment of our moral notions and visions.

A further reason why the moral theologian cannot be content with common sense may not be in every case completely distinct from the above, but it is a sufficiently special case to deserve its own treatment. We find that we are constantly confronted in our moral experience by situations that do not have one moral notion applicable to them. The extraordinary situations that the existentialist and moral situationalist discuss are often of this type. When confronted by such situations, especially if they are fairly frequent or especially significant, we try to contrast and compare this experience with others that we have had in the past so we may be informed as to how it is best to be understood. This is not just a matter of comparing empirical similarities, but it is an attempt to find the formal element appropriate to it.

This kind of reflection is engaged in by all men in their lives and the moral theologian has no monopoly on it. As a matter of fact, it may well be that on the whole the moral theologian follows other men in their ability to understand and apply the appropriate moral understanding to a new and difficult situation. This is often done by men who might be called moral virtuosos or geniuses who make the application or form the situation more by intuitive insight than logical rigor. That this is the case does not mean that the task of the moral theologian is unimportant, for if the insight of the moral genius is not ultimately backed by good reasons, it stands the change of being perverted or lost in the stress of life.

Moreover, the moral theologian may be able to expand our moral consciousness by the slow work of conceptual analysis, by painstakingly arguing why a notion should be applicable to wider or narrower materially relevant factors. An example of this is the application of the notion of nonviolence and defense of the other to war.[25] The traditional discussion of the just war doctrine is a conceptual expansion of the significance of the

---

[25] An example of the kind of analysis I have in mind here can be found in Ralph Potter, *War and Moral Discourse* (Richmond: John Knox Press, 1969).

prohibition of murder to one of man's most doubtful institutions. One may disagree with the just war doctrine and still see that here moral reflection is operating to expand our moral vision to include the reality of war in a significant way. That is to say that here moral reflection is engaged in increasing our capacity for moral discernment.[26]

But the process can work in a negative manner, since what at one time was thought to be clear may be questioned in the light of new factors. For example, abortion has traditionally been treated under the category of murder. The question that is now being asked with new force is whether there are not meaningful differences between certain cases where the fetus is prematurely removed and murder, differences that would cause the removal of a fetus before birth to be seen in a different way. It may be that moral reflection cannot determine the ultimate decision that one must make on such issues, but at least it helps make clear what the issue is. The kind of analysis I envisage here does not necessarily remove the complexity of moral decisions or judgments, but rather it tries to throw light on just why such decisions are complex or ambiguous. In so far as traditional casuistry accomplished this task it was engaged in a valid and necessary enterprise of ethical reflection.

Finally the moral theologian cannot be satisfied with received moral notions, because we inherit them not as a coherent whole but as scattered and limited pieces of our experience. The complete ones are so definite that they are not sufficient for all our moral experience, or if we try to make them such we run the danger of excluding other aspects of our moral life. This difficulty is often not felt existentially because we inherit from our culture and institutions an ordering of our various moral notions that implies a kind of coherent hierarchy among them. However, we often find in the face of societal changes or concrete situations that the nature of such a hierarchy is neither definite enough nor normatively sufficient. The upshot of this is that we cannot depend on our received moral notions to provide us with a consistent form of life even if they are valid in themselves.

---

[26]For an excellent analysis of the idea of discernment that has affinities with some of the points that I am arguing here, see James Gustafson, "Moral Discernment in the Christian Life," in *Norm and Context*, 17-36.

It is necessary, therefore, if we are to try to assume an overall pattern of life, to try to determine the interrelationship between our various moral notions. We do this by positioning one notion in reference to another in order to qualify the extent of one with the other. By so doing we establish a hierarchy that enables us to form a consistent pattern so that we will not always be undoing what we have just done. For example, most of us do this for our everyday behavior by assuming certain fundamental options, such as that the purpose of life is to achieve happiness. It is also done by philosophers, who tend to be much more rigorous in their analysis of the moral good. Existentially it is probably not possible or necessary that such a pattern be rigidly consistent, as one must finally admit that our moral experience is too rich to be forced into one model. There are things that we simply do because we think them right, even though we are not sure how they "fit." This, however, does not relieve us of the need for engaging in such reflection.

It is perhaps in relation to this kind of problem that the concern of the theological ethicists is most immediately apparent. For it is his business to try to suggest the form or arrangement of our moral notions as people who adhere to very definite ideas about the world, man, and God. He criticizes and uses other such arrangements of moral notions constructed from other possible points of view. In doing so, however, he does not begin with "unique" moral notions, but with the moral notions we all share as humans. In this context Barth's claim that the ethical good is determined solely from ,the command of God is simply fantastic. Ethics is fundamentally reflection on our received human experience as to what is good and bad, right and wrong. It cannot escape from that experience to a realm where the good or right can be known with more exactness.

However, the moral theologian does not just accept the formal element of these notions as given, as his own special commitments may limit or expand the meaning of such concepts. This is not a process peculiar to theological ethics but is the same kind of business that the philosophical ethicist is engaged in from the point of view of other commitments. Theology is at least the conceptual arrangement of religious notions in such a way that they inform, qualify, and limit one another. Theological ethics is the juxtaposing of such notions in relation to our moral notions to show their ethical significance. That is why theological ethicists often try to suggest central metaphors around which our other moral notions can be explicated and analyzed.[27] For example, joy is an inherited moral notion, but it may be that its formal element is expanded or limited within its theological context.[28]

Often this kind of analysis is done in order to show how our religious notions enlighten or reveal aspects of our existence that otherwise we might fail to appreciate or wrongly understand. For example, the idea of sin has often been used by theological ethicists to inform men of the nature of human existence. Such an analysis does not change the way things are but only reveals an essential character of our existence. Reinhold Niebuhr represents this kind of theological reflection, as he analyzes the nature of man and his institutions from his understanding of the Christian doctrine of sin.

But religious notions do not only inform about the nature of existence, they also imply how our behavior ought to be shaped. That is to say, they have a formal element that is definite enough to indicate what counts for certain aspects of our lives. Therefore theologically the notion of love not only informs us about an aspect of human experience, but also includes what ought to count for love in human behavior.

In conclusion I would like to suggest that this analysis indicates that contemporary theological ethics has perhaps been too preoccupied with relatively peripheral issues. It should again turn to an investigation of basic religious notions such as repentance, forgiveness, guilt, in order to reemphasize their relationship to the moral life. For the Christian moral life, like any other moral life, is not solely the life of decision. It is also the life of vision—a vision that is determined by the religious and moral notions that constitute it. To be a Christian in effect is learning to see the world in a certain way and thus become as we see. The task of contemporary theological ethics is to state the language of faith in terms of the Christian responsibility to be formed in the likeness of Christ.

---

[27] For a moral argument that works this way in a nontheological context see Iris Murdoch *The Sovereignty of Good over Other Concepts* (Cambridge: Cambridge University Press, 1967).

[28] An example of such an analysis is Barth's discussion of joy in *Church Dogmatics* III/4 (Edinburgh: T. and T. Clark, 1961), 371-85.

2.

The Significance of Vision:
Toward an Aesthetic Ethic

Christian ethics has succumbed to modern man's one-sided understanding of himself as actor and self-creator.[1] Through a critical analysis of the philosophical ethics of Iris Murdoch, I will show that this image of man has been fundamentally wrong in ignoring the significance of vision for the moral life.[2] Defining man as maker has not only made it impossible to account for fundamental affirmations at the heart of Christian existence; it has also made contemporary ethics unable to come to terms with the human condition in its modern dress. The metaphor "vision of the good" provides an important corrective to this dominant image of "man the maker," for ethics has more to learn from art than from the more "willful" aspects of our being. Of course I am not trying to deny the importance of action for our moral behavior, but actions must be based on our vision of what is most real and valuable.

The ethicist's primary task is to help discover the essential metaphors through which men can best see and understand

---

[1] For example James Sellars coins the honorific phrase "ageric man" for this phenomenon in his *Theological Ethics* (New York: Macmillan Co., 1969), but the general idea can be found in almost all contemporary Christian ethics especially as it is dominated by the notion of responsibility. For one of the most perceptive accounts of this view of man in a nontheological context see Hannah Arendt *The Human Condition* (Garden City: Anchor, 1959).

[2] Miss Murdoch is best known for her novels even though she has written extensively in philosophical ethics. This is partly because her philosophical essays have appeared over a long time span as scattered articles in various journals. In this article I shall concentrate on her explicit philosophical essays partly because Miss Murdoch, for reasons that will become clear below, denies that her novels are philosophical or didactic. For those interested in her novels the best critical studies of them are: A. S. Byatt, *Degrees of Freedom* (London: Chatto and Windus, 1965): Peter Wolfe, *The Disciplined Heart* (Columbia, Mo: University of Missouri Press, 1966); and Rubin Rabinovitz, *Iris Murdoch* (New York: Columbia University Press, 1968). As far as I have been able to determine there exists no comparable treatment of her ethics.

their condition. Contemporary ethics, the ethics of ageric man, has merely mirrored men's illusion of power and grandeur. It has failed to emphasize the categories that could give men an appreciation for their condition as finite, limited, and sinful beings; thus it has failed in its moral task. By making man's will the source of all value we have turned away from the classical insight of Christian and philosopher alike that the measure of moral goodness ultimately lies outside ourselves.

The image of man the maker has therefore had a detrimental effect on Christian theology and ethics. God has been driven into the universe of the "wholly other," leaving the world to whatever fate man's absolute freedom determines for it; even if he is present or is the God of history, he does little more than confirm the irrepressible march of human creativity. On such a view, any life-directing attraction toward God's creative and redemptive being becomes unintelligible.[3] Christian ethics in such a context inevitably tends to be Pelagian; the aim of the Christian life becomes right action rather than the vision of God. The special nature of the Christian moral life is understood as a matter of one's inner disposition; in public the Christian behaves like the non-Christian man of good will. By contrasting Miss Murdoch's understanding of man with the prevailing "man the maker" image I hope to broaden our understanding of the ethical in a way that will provide a richer account of the Christian moral life.

Man as the Creator and Creature of Illusion: The Difficulty of "Seeing"

Man, for Miss Murdoch, is defined by his inability to bear reality. Modern man's understanding of himself is far too grand. He optimistically combines a naive faith in science with the assumption that we all have the possibility of being completely rational and free. Contemporary philosophical ethics, in both its existential and analytical forms, tends only to confirm this self-understanding. Under the guise of neutrality the moral life is reduced to matters of choice. But no ethic which ignores sin

---

[3]For a very suggestive position contrary to this see Roland Delattre, *Beauty and Sensibility in the Thought of Jonathan Edwards* (New Haven: Yale University Press, 1968); and his "Beauty and Politics: Toward a Theological Anthropology," *Union Seminary Quarterly Review* 25 (Summer 1970) 401-19.

can provide an authentic account of man,[4] for ultimately we
are not "isolated free choosers, monarchs of all we survey, but
benighted creatures sunk in a reality whose nature we are
constantly and overwhelmingly tempted to deform by fantasy."[5] Thus our very attempt to avoid the reality of sin is a
symptom of our sinfulness.

Because our freedom of choice is actually very limited, we
are constantly tempted to engage in fantastic reverie in order to
protect ourselves from the unpleasant realities of our existence.[6] Confronted by the fact that our lives are bounded by
chance and death, we anxious and self-preoccupied people construct a veil to conceal the essential pointlessness of our existence. To be human is to create illusion. Philosophers manifest
this human sickness in their quest to pierce through the phe-
nomenal world to some perfect and necessary form and order.[7]
Most of us, less pretentious than philosophers, are content to
console ourselves with stories that impose a pattern upon a
reality which would otherwise seem intolerably chancy and
incomplete.[8]

Man's capacity for illusion is only complicated by his ability
to catch glimpses of the truth. We cannot long look directly at
reality, so we use past formulations of the truth as a defense
against the constant struggle to pierce through the veil. Miss
Murdoch often explores this phenomenon in her novels. She
will put her own philosophy into the mouth of a character in
such a way that it becomes untruth in the particular context of

---

[4]Iris Murdoch, "On God and Good," in *The Sovereignty of Good* (New York:
Schocken Books, 1971), p. 47. This recent book also includes two of Miss Murdoch's
previously published essays: "The Idea of Perfection," *Yale Review,* 53 (March 1964)
342-80; and *The Sovereignty of Good over Other Concepts* (Cambridge: Cambridge
University Press, 1967). In citing these latter essays I will first give the page in the
original and in parenthesis the citation in the new collection. Hereafter cited as
'Perfection' and 'Sovereignty.'

[5]Iris Murdoch, "Against Dryness: A Polemical Sketch," *Encounter* 16 (January
1961) 20; hereafter cited as "Dryness."

[6]"Sovereignty," 3 (78-9)

[7]Iris Murdoch, "The Sublime and the Good," *Chicago Review* 13 (Autumn 1959)
42; hereafter cited as "Sublime." Miss Murdoch has Kant primarily in mind here as
she thinks he is the paradigm instance of the attempt to make moral judgment as
instantiating of a timeless form of rational activity in order to avoid the messiness of
history. Kant's respect for the other is but the respect of universal reason in his
breast, not the contingently real historical person.

[8]"Sovereignty," 14 (84)

the novel.[9] Truth (or beauty) cannot be possessed, for in seeking its consolation by possession we remove the otherness which gives it value or truth.

The most compelling example of this is human love. Most of our loving is more an assertion of self than a recognition of the other. We seldom love the other as he is; rather we love the other by imposing upon him our own preconceived image of who he is. For we cannot stand to love the other, in his particularity, as a contingent being destined for death. To love such an object is sure to bring pain, since we are destined to lose it. We therefore love the other only as we make him an aspect of our plan; we assume this assures his eternity (and ours). We do not fall in love with a real person, but with the person we have created through our fantasy. Such love is a way of loving ourselves. One of the most persistent themes of Miss Murdoch's novels is the presentation of people who are so captured by pictures of another that they fail entirely to see the other as a distinct reality.

Not only has modern philosophical ethics failed to speak to man's actual condition, but through its assumption that man is free and able to do the good it has only added to man's illusions. It has accepted the scientific account of the world as consisting of fact and value, but value is no longer given reality apart from man's willing of it. Man is thus conceived to be as free as he chooses, creating his values in relation to an empirical world he can easily comprehend. Because modern ethics wants to create the impression that we can change our moral self through choices, it has failed to note that moral change and achievement are slow. We are not so free that we can suddenly alter ourselves, for what we can see and thus desire compels

---

[9]This practice should be sufficient to indicate how careful one must be in using Miss Murdoch's novels to illustrate her philosophy. Her philosophy is the attempt to find the right context to say the obvious, but it is inherently abstract. Only in art and in particular the novel can the complexity of the intermingling of truth and falsity in our lives be realistically pictured. Philosophical ethics can be only a pointer to the good, not its embodiment.

Miss Murdoch has published fourteen novels (all by Chatto and Windus). They are *Under the Net* (1954), *The Flight From the Enchanter* (1956), *The Sandcastle* (1957), *The Bell* (1958), *A Severed Head* (1961), *An Unofficial Rose* (1962), *The Unicorn* (1963), *The Italian Girl* (1964), *The Red and the Green* (1965), *The Time of the Angels* (1966), *The Nice and the Good* (1968), *Bruno's Dream* (1969), *A Fairly Honorable Defeat* (1970), and most recently, *An Accidental Man* (1972).

us.[10] Our moral goodness does not develop by a backward movement into the rulings of an impersonal public language concerned with external action. It is, instead, a movement of understanding onward into increasing privacy.[11]

Rather than attempting to free each man from his paralyzing preoccupation with himself, modern moral philosophy has only increased and legitimatized this excessive self-concern. For our self-centerdness it only prescribes further self-reflection, since it has thought that our main moral errors result from adherence to illogical and confused moral reasons or arguments. This the primary responsibility for determining the reality of events still rests on the individual person. Both analytic and existentialist ethics share "a terror of anything which encloses the agent or threatens his supremacy as a center of significance. In this sense both philosophies tend toward solipism"—i.e., just the condition that is the main cause of man's moral failure.[12] "Self-knowledge, the minute understanding of one's own machinery, does not free the self; it only mires us deeper in our illusion of individual significance. When we achieve clear vision the self becomes a correspondingly smaller and less interesting object."[13]

Modern moral philosophers have failed to understand that moral behavior is an affair not primarily of choice but of vision. They see all moral agents as inhabiting the same world of facts; thus they discriminate between the different types of morality only in terms of acts and choices. But differences of moral vision or perspective may also exist.[14] When we assess other people, we do not consider just their solutions to particular problems; we feel something much more elusive which may be called their total vision of life, "as shown in their mode of speech or silence, their choices of words, their assessments of others, their conceptions of their own lives, what they think attractive or praiseworthy . . . in short, the configurations of

---

[10]"Perfection," 375 (39)

[11]*Ibid,* 366 (28)

[12]Rabinovitz, *Iris Murdoch,* 7

[13]"On God and Good," 67-8. As might be expected, Miss Murdoch thinks psychoanalysis is an attempt to cure the disease with the medicine of the sickness. In *A Severed Head* (New York: Avon, 1966) she draws a rather unflattering portrait of such a psychoanalyst.

[14]Iris Murdoch, "Metaphysics and Ethics" in *The Nature of Metaphysics,* ed D.T. Pears (London: Macmillan, 1957) p. 116; hereafter cited as "Metaphysics"

their thought which show continually in their reactions and conversations."[15] Our morality is more than adherence to universalizable rules; it also encompasses our experiences, fables, beliefs, images, concepts, and inner monologues.

Modern moral philosophy has ignored the significance of vision because it is still tempted, in a Kantian fashion, to reduce morality to a single formula.[16] Once we appreciate the importance of vision for our moral existence, we must realize that a new moral concept cannot necessarily be achieved by the specification of factual criteria open to any observer.[17] Men differ not just because they select different objects or facts from the common world but because they see different worlds; their perspectives have been formed from highly individual experiences. Also if we admit that a man's morality is made up not only of his choices but of his vision, it becomes clear why this morality may not be open to argument and alteration. Ethics cannot be reduced to the study of rational argument. Our moral existence can be taken seriously only when the vision developed out of an individual's experience and vision is comprehended.

Modern moral philosophy has taken Wittgenstein's famous argument against the idea of an "inner object," "private ostensive definition," or private language as decisive grounds for discounting this kind of "internal" vision. Miss Murdoch agrees that Wittgenstein argues decisively against the assumption that such words as "red" can be thought of as meaning something private. She denies, however, that this argument can be made to apply to the kind of "internal" vision she considers essential to

---

[15]Iris Murdoch, 'Vision and Choice in Morality' in *Christian Ethics and Contemporary Philosophy*, ed Ian Ramsey (New York: Macmillan Co., 1966) p. 202; hereafter cited as "Vision."

[16]"Metaphysics," 120-1. "Philosophers have been misled, not only by a rationalistic desire for unity, but also by certain simplified and generalized moral attitudes current in our society, into seeking a single philosophical definition of morality. If, however, we go back again to the data we see that there are fundamentally different moral pictures which different individuals use or which the same individual may use at different times. Why should philosophy be less various, where the differences in what it attempts to analyze are so important"; "Vision," 217. Miss Murdoch thinks that analytical ethics cannot do otherwise if it is really to investigate moral language. Not to do so only shows that it is still under the influence of past metaphysical theories of ethics. She does not deny that it may be possible to specify certain minimal conditions necessary for the moral life such as that attempted by R.M. Hare, but the ethicists's primary task is to suggest the highest morality not the minimal.

[17]"Vision," 203

our moral existence.[18] There is a difference between the notion of inner or private psychological phenomena, open only to introspection, and the notion of personal vision which may find expression overtly as well as inwardly.[19] This vision is no more private and inaccessible than our use of language. We learn our language in public context, but after so doing we may well give it a special meaning in terms of the uniqueness of our biographical development.[20]

The moral life, then, is more than thinking clearly and making rational choices. It is a way of seeing the world. Moral philosophy cannot abstain from recommending the best way of seeing the world; since it cannot help but commend an ideal, it should at least endeavor to commend a worth ideal.[21] Miss Murdoch does not shrink from such a task, and it is to this aspect of her moral philosophy that we must now turn.

Reality as Contingent: The Good, Love, and Attention

Miss Murdoch's stress on vision in ethics does not imply that she regards seeing as an end in itself. Rather it is one way in which she makes clear that the moral life cannot be divorced from the substance of the world. The ethics of vision is therefore the ethics of realism.

Moral virtue in its most general sense is the self's correspondence to reality, but we do not see reality by just opening our eyes. To know the real rather than being in a state of illusion and fantasy is a difficult task. Nor is realism a self-evident good, for we resist knowing the world in its contingency. The world does not come with a general coherence or unity which can give meaning to our lives. "We are what we seem to be, transient mortal creatures subject to necessity and chance. This is to say that there is, in my view, no God in the

---

18"Perfection," 349-60 (9-22)

19"Vision," 200

20In her article, "Thinking and Language," Miss Murdoch argues that language and thought are not necessarily coextensive, as we often use language to recover and fix our unique mental past. The only reason that behaviorists think they can avoid the private nature of much of our thinking is because they ignore the complexity of the mental process in the hope of achieving a scientific simplicity. It is bad philosophy because rather than being philosophy it attempts to be a *pseudo*-science. *Proceedings of the Aristotelian Society, Supplementary Volume xxv* (1951) 25-34.

21"Sovereignty," 2 (78)

traditional sense of that term; and the traditional sense is perhaps the only sense . . . Our destiny can be examined but it cannot be justified or totally explained. We are simply here."[22]
To recognize the contingency of our existence is to affirm and embrace the fact we are faced with real death which denies final significance of our lives.

Most modern philosophers think that the contingent character of the world necessarily implies the impossibility of transcendence. But Miss Murdoch is extremely critical of those philosophers who assume that man's only alternative in such a universe is to become the creator of his own self and values. She believes that transcendence becomes possible precisely as we gaze and affirm the contingent character of our lives. The metaphor that best embodies this possibility of transcendence is the (Platonic) idea of the Good.[23] The Good is what "God was (or is) a single perfect transcendent nonrepresentable and necessary real object of attention."[24] The Good may never be exemplified in the world we know, but its existence is sure, for without it the moral life is impossible. It is only as our vision is centered on the Good that our subjectivity can be overcome and the objectivity of the other in its particularity affirmed.

Good as transcendent reality "means that virtue is the attempt to pierce the veil of selfish consciousness and join the world as it really is."[25] The Good is the central metaphor because we do not naturally or easily come to understand the nature of the world; the strenuous moral task is to come to see the world as it is. Because the Good is undefinable this task can never be finished; the world is inexhaustibly random and particular.

The moral life is thus better understood on the analogy of the aesthetic mode of seeing and beholding than in terms of action and decision. For the right answer is mainly a matter of really *looking* while avoiding the constant temptation to return

---

[22]*Ibid*, 4 (79). Exactly in what sense Miss Murdoch denies the reality of God is not clear, for we shall see that she associates the idea of the Good very closely with the traditional conception of God.

[23]*Ibid*, 21-2 (92-3)

[24]"On God and Good," 55

[25]"Sovereignty," 23 (93)

to the self with the deceitful consolation of self-pity, resentment, fantasy, and despair.

As the category of goodness comes into use in the market place, it combines a brief intuition of unity with an increasing perception of complexity and detail. When we seek for what is best in any sphere of life, we receive this double revelation of both random detail and intuited unity. This is seen clearly in art and intellectual work; the artist reveals the unity through excellent appreciation of detail.[26] One becomes good by learning to live with the idea that the Good is not given or unified but comes, rather, from facing reality in its variety. Only then can any vague intuition of the unity underlying the variety be genuine. The Good is mysterious and undefinable because it cannot be contained in a formula. To try to encapsulate the Good is to ignore the inexhaustible randomness and unsystematic variety of the world.[27]

The ethical problem is how to be joined to the Good without illusion or fantasy, for right action and freedom are possible only on the basis of our prior attention to the Good. Only love can effect such a union with the good.[28] In its most basic sense, love is simply the discovery of reality,[29] the extremely difficult realization that something other than ourselves is real. Love is the recognition that our ultimate destiny does not lie in the attempt to discover a realm beyond sensible reality; it lies in the acceptance of the world's unrepeatable particularity. Love is

---

[26]The problem of the relation between unity and particularity is one of the central problems of Miss Murdoch's philosophy and artistic enterprise. For how do you teach and demonstrate the significance that each human being is precious and unique without doing so in terms of an ideology or abstraction? Miss Murdoch in her novels thus attempts to find a way between naturalism and symbolism, and her moral philosophy is the endeavor to explicate the concrete universal. "Perfection," 367 (29)

[27]In *The Unicorn,* one of Miss Murdoch's most explicit philosophical novels, Max Lejour says in response to the suggestion that Good is a matter of choosing or acting, "That is the vulgar doctrine . . . What we can see determines what we choose. Good is the distant source of light, it is the unimaginable object of our desire. Our fallen nature knows only its name and its perception. That is the idea that is vulgarized by existentialists and linguistic philosophers when they make Good into a mere matter of personal choice. It cannot be defined, not because it is a function of our freedom, but because we do not know it." (New York: Viking Press, 1963) pp. 108-9.

[28]"Sovereignty," 36 (102)

[29]"Sublime," 51

nothing less than "the nonviolent apprehension of differences."[30]

Love, so understood, cannot be limited to the relation between people even though interpersonal love is love in its most
intense, profound, and difficult form. Love is any relationship
through which we are called from our own self-involvement to
appreciate the self-reality that transcends us. That is why it may
be a profound moral experience to take self-forgetful pleasure
in the sheer alien pointless independent existence of animals,
birds, stones, and trees.[31] The profound relationship between
beauty, good, and the truth is the fact that each of them
provides the occasion for such "unselfings." The beginning of
the moral life may be nothing more dramatic than the recognition of an inanimate object in all its particularity and detail;
even such a recognition forces us to turn our vision outward at
least for awhile. This helps explain why Miss Murdoch's novels
are so full of realistic descriptions of places and nature, for our
ability to notice and recognize the particularity and beauty of
the everyday things that surround us is a significant aspect of
our moral experience.

This understanding of love also explains the close connection
between art and morals. For good art, unlike bad art or random
occurrences, exists over against us in such a way that we must
surrender to its authority. Both love and great art show us our
world with a clarity which startles us because we are not used to
looking at the real world at all. Art, whether representational or
not, reveals to us aspects of our world that we are usually too
dependent on conventionality and fantasy to be able to see.[32]

---

[30]*Ibid*, 54. Like so many of Miss Murdoch's themes this understanding of love is
drived from Simone Weil. Forexample Miss Weil says in *La pesanteur et la grace*
(Paris: Plon, 1948), 'La croyance à l'existence d'autres êtres humains comme tels est
amour,' 73. The significance of the idea of "nonviolence" should not be overlooked
here, for Miss Murdoch thinks most of our love, since it is self-regarding, necessarily
does violence and causes suffering to the other. In her novels she explores this
phenomenon at length displaying how rare selfless love is.

[31]"Sovereignty," 11 (85)

[32]"Sovereignty," 15-16 (85-6). Art is the best clue to the nature of the good for
"we can see beauty itself in a way in which we cannot see goodness itself. I can
experience the transcendence of the beautiful, but (I think) not the transcendence of
the good. Beautiful things contain beauty in a way in which good acts do not exactly
contain good, because beauty is partly a matter of the senses. So if we speak of good
as transcendent we are speaking of something rather more complicated and which
cannot be experienced, even when we see the unselfish man in the concentration
camp." "On God and Good," 60

Art shows us how difficult it is to be objective by showing us how different the world can look. Art can thus enlarge the consciousness and enliven the imagination of the consumer, calling him from his obsessive self-concern.

The novelist must constantly test his vision by giving persons other than himself the right to exist and to have a separate mode of being. The artist at work is thus the paradigm of the moral man, the lover who being nothing himself, lets others exist through him.[33] The mark of the great novelist is the acceptance of his own characters as having life and independence separate from his creation of them.

In the creation of a work of art the artist is going through the exercise of attending to something quite particular other than himself. The intensity of this exercise itself gives to the work of art its special independence. That is, it is an independence and uniqueness which is essentially the same as that conferred upon, or rather discovered in, another human being whom we love.[34]

The concept of love is closely linked with the correct understanding of freedom. The capacity to love is the condition necessary for freedom. For freedom is not the sudden leap the isolated will makes from one impersonal logical complex to another; it "is a function of the progressive attempt to see a particular object clearly."[35] Such freedom is thus not the ability to have our way or to assert our will in an efficacious way. Rather, it is the disciplined overcoming of the self that allows for the clarification of our vision; to be free is to exist sanely without fear, to perceive what is real.[36] The virtue most necessary for freedom is humility. For humility is not a phony

---

[33]Iris Murdoch, "The Sublime and the Beautiful Revisited," *Yale Review* 49 (December 1959) 269-70. On this criterion Miss Murdoch regards the novelists of the eighteenth century and Shakespeare as the artistic norm. Hereafter cited as "Revisted." In this connection the comment by John Fowles in *The French Lieutenant's Woman* (New York: Signet, 1970) to explain why novelists write is interesting. He says the one reason shared by all novelists is "*we wish to create worlds as real as, but other than the world that is. Or was. That is why we cannot plan. We know that a genuinely created world must be independent of its creator; a planned world is a dead world*" (81).

[34]"Sublime," 54-5

[35]"Perfection," 361 (23)

[36]Iris Murdoch, "The Darkness of Practical Reason," *Encounter* 28 (July 1966)

attempt at constant self-effacement, but the selfless respect for reality. So understood, freedom is very much the same as virtue:

It is concerned with really apprehending that other people exist. This too is what freedom really is . . . Freedom is not choosing; that is merely the move that we make when all is already lost. Freedom is knowing and understanding and respecting things quite other than ourselves. Virtue is in this sense to be construed as knowledge and connects us so with reality.[37]

Freedom is therefore not an absolute condition to be assumed, but a matter of degree. We each have it to the extent that we learn respect for reality.

If we look at ourselves realistically we see how inappropriate it is to associate freedom with will as a principle of pure movement. For example, when we are in love or feel strong resentment, it is of little use to try to choose to stop being in love or to stop feeling resentment. What we need is not will but a reorientation of the vision to a more compelling object.[38] In the absence of an object capable of creating a new situation, our efforts of will are ineffective. Contrary to Sartre, freedom is not in the self but in the other. Without love, without recognition and respect for the other, freedom is but an illusion of our neurotic self-preoccupation.[39]

The concept that ties these various themes together is that of attention. The category of attention is one which Miss Murdoch quite consciously borrows from Simone Weil to express the idea of a just and loving gaze directed upon an individual reality.[40] The moral life is more a matter of attention than it is of will; one becomes good by training attention to recognize the loved object with equality and fairness. For the lover is constantly tempted to see himself as being either above or below the object of his love, and this can only result in a master-slave relationship.

Attention is that aspect of our moral life which enables us to love the other as an equal through the accurate apprehension of

---

[37]"Revisited," 269-70

[38]"On God and Good," 55-6

[39]"Sublime," 52

[40]"Perfection," 371 (34). Gibson Winter in *Being Free* (New York: Macmillan Co. 1970) uses a very similar notion to analyze black power, 62-3.

his reality. Since we can only define choices within the world we can see, the proper development of attention is crucial; clear vision is the result of moral imagination and moral effort.[41] Moral goodness is not automatically open to all but is an esoteric achievement that requires discipline and training. In the context of attention and vision the moral life is something that goes on continually rather than something that surges with explicit moral choices. Our freedom as such cannot be just a matter of having clear intentions (contra Hampshire), but rather a concomitant of the justice of our attending to the world.[42] Moral progress is won through meditation, and morality is more a matter of purity of heart than of external choices. To take up the cry "we have to choose," as English philosophy, popular existentialism, and contemporary Christian ethics do, is only to avoid the real issues of the moral life and to compound our moral perplexities.

Opposed to attention, as slavery and violence are opposed to love, is fantasy, the attempt to impose our preconceived image on the object of our love. The two great enemies of loving attention are social convention and neurosis, which are the forms of fantasy. We may fail to see the individual because

we are ourselves sunk in a social whole which we allow uncritically to determine our reactions, or because we see each other exclusively as so determined. Or we may fail to see the individual because we are completely enclosed in a fantasy world of our own into which we try to draw

---

[41]*Ibid,* 373 (37). I think Miss Murdoch's suggestion here has some affinities with certain ideas about moral language developed by students of J.L. Austin (a philosopher for whom she has great respect). I am thinking particularly of Donald Evans' exposition of the idea of an 'onlook' in his book, *The Logic of Self-Involvement* (London: SCM, 1963).

[42]Miss Murdoch may be understanding Hampshire's category of "intention" in a too limited sense. Hampshire uses the idea of "intention" primarily as a way of indicating the difference between action and purposive behavior, for an action is intentional in the sense that its intelligibility is dependent on the agent. Thus 'intention' includes everything that was once associated with consciousness. It may be true, however, that he has tried to make the idea of "intention" carry more weight than it is capable of, and the result is a too narrow understanding of the "internal." See his *Thought and Action* (New York: Viking Press, 1960) and *Freedom of the Individual* (New York: Harper and Row, 1965). Miss Murdoch's most extended critiques of Hampshire are to be found in "The Idea of Perfection" and "The Darkness of Practical Reason." Even though she singles out Hampshire for attack there are some profound similarities between them; for example, see Hampshire's early essay "Fallacies in Moral Philosophy" *Mind* 68 (1949) 452-69. Miss Murdoch dedicated *The Sovereignty of Good* to Mr Hampshire.

things from outside, not grasping their reality and independence, making them into dream objects of our own. Fantasy, the enemy of art, is the enemy of true imagination: Love, an exercise of the imagination.[43]

Attention is thus the effort to overcome the many illusions in which we become ensnared by accepting the opinions of others, conforming to social niceties, or spinning our own private reveries. Only as we refuse to be bound by these illusions can our reliance on convention pass over into goodness that rests on love.

One of the themes Miss Murdoch develops especially in her novels is the difficulty in handling the inevitable guilt and suffering that accompany our love of others. When we try to use our suffering as a means of purification, we only increase our self-fascination.[44] Although suffering always appears on the surface to be the giving of the self for the other, it is seldom ennobling. Most victims of suffering either sink into spiritual lethargy or become afflicted with self-hatred and participate in their own degradation.[45] As sufferers we cannot bear to contain our suffering within ourselves, and we must seek a new victim in order to pass on our suffering. More likely than not, the sufferer strikes first at those who attempt to reduce his suffering. The chain of suffering and violence in which we are all caught continues to grow in length and magnitude until it encounters a truly good person, who suffers quietly without attempting to pass the evil on. This is the paradigm case of the good man for Miss Murdoch—i.e., it is the Christian saint without God.

Miss Murdoch knows that our moral existence is ambiguous: we are creatures who are seldom completely good or completely

---

[43]"Sublime" 52. The way Miss Murdoch understands the relation between imagination and truth is extremely rich and suggestive. By imagination she means "a type of reflection on people, events, etc., which builds detail, adds color, conjures up possibilities in ways which go beyond what could be said to be strictly factual. "The Darkness of Practical Reason," 48.

[44]Miss Murdoch's novels often concern people who try to will suffering as a means of self-renunciation. Tallis in *A Fairly Honorable Defeat* and Lisa in *Bruno's Dream* in very different ways are involved in such an attempt. However Miss Murdoch's most sustained and brilliant treatment of this theme is through her portrayal of Hannah Crean-Smith's imposed self-exile in *The Unicorn.* Hannah withdraws literally into her room in an isolated house in order to do penance for her unfaithfulness to her husband. Yet her renunciation of power is only apparent, for her suffering provides the basis for her hold on the rest of the characters of the novel.

[45]Iris Murdoch, "Knowing the Void," *Spectator,* 197 (2 November 1956) 613

bad. Each of us has aspects of his life that are determined by true love and attention, but for most of us much of our lives is spent in the blindness of our own self-enclosures. A good scholar is not thereby assured that he will be a good father; the self-centered artist may be a loving husband.

Moreover, we are beset with the relativity of our limited "vision." A way of seeing that may have been truthful in one situation may be untruthful when imposed on another. Contingency constantly challenges our most assured notions of what is good. For example, even though it is clearly a good to renounce the self, at times this act may itself become a retreat into fantasy, a refusal to accept our own reality.

Miss Murdoch is not overly optimistic about the possibilities of achieving the good in this life, but she is sure that if it does happen, it does so only by the hard and painful effort of the transformation of our vision. In the last analysis, it is not so much by our effort that we are able to love as it is by the fact that reality itself lures us from our self-centeredness. She is extremely sceptical of the romantic's attempt to force himself to enjoy the other. Rather, it is the other that forces us to attend to him as the other. The time simply comes when all we have left is to face the truth. If there is any grace in our lives at all, it is just this aspect of our existence.

This is obviously not an ethic that conceives of the moral life as a simple or unitary aspect of our existence for the sake of gaining a kind of completeness or neatness. This does not mean that she is recommending we live without reflection or self-examination, but reflection must direct us to reality, not away from it. Miss Murdoch does not attempt to see the moral life in any other way than it is, complex and various. The moralist cannot somehow change the ambiguity of our ethical existence. All he can do is analyze its infinite richness and multiplicity, and perhaps suggest metaphors through which individual moral vision can be enriched and deepened.[46] The moral life does not consist just in making one right decision after another; it is the progressive attempt to widen and clarify our vision of reality.

A corollary of this understanding of the moral life and ethics is a renewed appreciation of the opacity of men. We are not simple beings who act from clear motives and intentions. One of

---

46"Dryness," 19

the things we constantly discover is how unsure we ourselves are of even the "real" reason for our actions. We are so captivated by our illusions that even in acts in which we think we are most self-forgetful, we are actually concerned with ourselves. There is no worse form of self-involvement than that which becomes fascinated with self-destruction.

What finally must be respected is man's inherent contingency. For contingency is the very essence of personality.[47] We do not gain our reality from the eternal; we become real only as we embrace reality as it is—contingent and purposeless. It is only when we do this—when we accept our death—that the virtue of humility is created. For only the humble man, because he sees himself as nothing, can see other things and men as they are.

He sees the pointlessness of virtue and its unique value and the endless extent of its demand. Simone Weil tells us that the exposure of the soul to God condemns the selfish part of it not to suffering but to death. The humble man perceives the distance between suffering and death. And although he is not by definition the good man perhaps he is the kind of man who is most likely of all to become good.[48]

Vision, Christian Ethics, and Christian Moral Behavior

There are many possible ways of construing the significance of Miss Murdoch's thought for Christian ethical reflection. In this concluding section I will concentrate on her understanding of vision; I think this provides the context for a reintroduction of some of the concerns of the Christian moral life which recent discussion has ignored. Because contemporary Christian ethicists have assumed that "the ethical" primarily concerns action and decision, they have found little moral significance in basic affirmations about God, Christ, grace, and sanctification. Even if they have discussed such theological categories, this has had little effect on their understanding of the nature of Christian ethics or the form of the Christian moral life.

However, once the question of "the ethical" is broadened to include vision, we can comprehend that being a Christian involves more than just making certain decisions; it is a way of

---

47"Sublime," 271
48"Sovereignty," 37 (104)

attending to the world. It is learning "to see" the world under the mode of the divine. Thus, it is not a matter of indifference how the nature of God and his relationship to the world is conceived. Christian ethical behavior cannot be simply to assume a "loving" attitude; it must adhere to and locate the self in respect to basic affirmations about God and man. A Christian does not simply "believe" certain propositions about God; he learns to attend to reality through them. This learning requires training of our attention by constantly juxtaposing our experience with our vision.

This means that there is an unmistakably pragmatic aspect to the Christian life, not in the sense that "it is true because it works," but because it is always being tested by our encounter with reality. We adhere to a reality whose depth we do not know, for we cannot comprehend its manifold richness. Such comprehension comes only as we grow in our understanding of God and his relation to the world.

The significance of the Christian's vision may not be immediately apparent. His faith does not relieve him of the problems and anxieties other men face in determining their concrete behavior. He must still face the fact that he will suffer and die. To be a Christian means to face these realities for what they are, without deception or illusion. To perceive them in this way may mean, however, that the Christian is freed to act in a way that would not otherwise be possible.

In the light of this understanding of the significance of vision recent attempts to translate the Christian language into secular concepts seem to be misguided. For our attending cannot be separated from the language or metaphors which form it. If these metaphors do not help us "see" the world as it is, then no amount of translation will remove their essential untruth. They should be given up. But the claim of the Christian is that his language actually envisages the world as it is. It is not a matter of transforming the language to fit the world in the name of relevancy; but it is a matter of transforming the self to fit the language. The problem is to become as we see.

The Christian life is a constant struggle to wrestle the truth out of the everyday. Recent Christian ethics has concentrated its attention on the crisis situation or the "big event." The Christian life is defined in relation not to the humdrum but to revolution and conflict; the everyday is morally uninteresting.

But when the Christian life is understood as the life of attention, the emphasis is placed squarely on the everyday. For the moral significance of our lives is not constituted by moving from one significant social problem to another; rather, it depends on our willingness to work at being human through the manifold particularity of our lives. It is a matter not of finding the ultimate truth but of finding what the truth is in the small questions that confront us every day. It is a matter of what we do with our time, whether we are willing to work to make our marriages worthwhile, how well we perform our everyday tasks. The main problem of the moral life is not to come to monumental decisions but to live through the contingencies of our lives.

The Christian has no assurance he will be any better than any other man at this task. He must honestly admit that he simply does not understand what difference "being a Christian" makes in every aspect of his existence. At the least, however, to be a Christian must mean that one is determined to see life as it is, since we are assured that we have no reason to fear the truth.

Miss Murdoch might object that this is far too optimistic, since the truth is never found in an easy or painless way. We come to the truth only through suffering and anguish, so that in order to recognize the truth we must be drawn from our comfortable and self-contained worlds of illusion. She seems to think that men are capable of standing such a process without being destroyed—that there is a kind of salvific content in recognizing the purposelessness and nothingness of our own lives. Christians have also maintained that the gospel reveals the truth of our existence; but, contrary to Miss Murdoch, they have felt that such a truth would be destructive if it were not that we are sustained by a being beyond ourself. That is just the good news of the gospel: we are told the truth about ourselves in such a way that the destructiveness heals rather than obliterates. Christian ethics must honestly face the difference implied between these two views.[49] For it is a question not just of the nature of Christian existence, of who is right and who is wrong, but of the significance of human life itself.

---

[49]The best treatment of this theme by a theologian is to be found in Julian Hartt's *A Christian Critiquie of American Culture* (New York: Harper and Row, 1967).

3.

Toward an Ethics of Character

No ethic is formulated in isolation from the social conditions of its time. The contemporary emphasis in Christian ethics on the dynamic and self-creating nature of man is a reflection of the kind of society in which we live. Perhaps our ancestors were born to preestablished roles in a world where faithfulness to those roles guaranteed the fulfillment of moral duty. But we are born into a social world that forces us to be free, to be autonomous; for now the moral imperative is to actually fashion our lives by choosing among the numerous alternatives our social world presents to us.

In such a world it is not surprising that current moral discourse employs the language of freedom and responsibility to focus on man as self-creator.[1] The moral life is not constituted by correspondence to an objective moral order; rather it is to be constantly readjusted to the nuances and ambiguities of our ethical choices and experiences. Modern ethicists recognize that there is often more to our moral situation than our principles and rules contain; so much of our significant moral experience and life simply does not fall within the areas marked off by clearly defined roles or principles. "Responsibility" names the fact that often we are simply forced to fall back on ourselves in order to make decisions that have no relationship to objective standards of right and wrong.

In a social situation that seems to force the individual to be on his own, it is no surprise that the subject matter of ethics is centered around "problems," i.e., situations in which it is difficult to know what one should do.[2] Ethical discussion then

---

[1] For a much fuller account of the idea of responsibility and its use in contemporary theological ethics, see Albert Jonsen, *Responsibility in Modern Religious Ethics* (Washington: Corpus, 1968).

[2] For an extraordinarily perceptive article that makes this point in a philosophical context, see E. Pincoffs, "Quandary Ethics," *Mind* 80 (1971) 552-71.

focuses on the best way to respond to such "problems": Should an ethical decision be determined primarily in relation to principles and rules, or by a loving response to the peculiarities of the immediate situation? Those who argue for "principles" suggest that only their approach assures objectivity in morals, or that love is sentimentalized if it is not "imprincipled." Contextualists maintain that adherence to principles results in a false security that makes one insensitive to the complexity of modern moral issues.

Ethicists on both sides of the "context versus principle" debate have made the same error: in focusing on "the problem," both have tended to ignore the ethics of character. "Problems" or "situations" are not abstract entities that exist apart from our character; they become such abstractions to the extent that we refuse to be other than we are. Perhaps the ethics of character has won a distasteful reputation because "having character" is associated with being set in one's ways, inflexible, or unbending.[3] But unless the positive significance of character is appreciated, freedom and responsibility cannot be understood in their proper moral context; for we are more than just the sum total of our responses to particular situations, whether the moral significance of such responses is determined by the situation itself or by its lawfulness.

To emphasize the idea of character is to recognize that our actions are also acts of self-determination; in them we not only reaffirm what we have been but also determine what we will be in the future. By our actions we not only shape a particular situation, we also form ourselves to meet future situations in a particular way. Thus the concept of character implies that moral goodness is primarily a prediction of persons and not acts, and that this goodness of persons is not automatic but must be acquired and cultivated.[4]

In this essay I will try to make clear the meaning of character, its nature in relation to the self, and its moral significance. Such an analysis will be primarily philosophical. This should not, however, obscure the fact that there are also basic theological issues at stake. For example, contemporary theological

---

[3]For an extended discussion of character viewed primarily as an "armor" or limiting aspect of our human freedom, see Wilhelm Reich, *Character Analysis* (New York: Noonday, 1949).

[4]Robert Johann, "A Matter of Character," *America* 116 (Jan. 21, 1967) 95.

ethics offers many recommendations about the nature and shape of the Christian life: "Christians are to do the most loving thing"; "Christians are followers of God's will"; "Christians conform to the shape of grace." But it is not at all clear how such recommendations are to be taken. What does it mean for men to embody a particular way of life (imperative) as that which gives form to "what they really are" (indicative)? Not only do such recommendations seem too abstract to bear on actual living of our lives; even on their own terms, it is not clear what kind of proposal is being made about our actual moral formation.

These recommendations seem to summarize particular life styles, ways of living out what the individual proponents think it means to be a Christian in the circumstances of our times. Yet this does not add much clarification; as James Gustafson has pointed out, there are many ambiguities in the phrase "styles of life."[5] Not only do too many styles seem applicable to Christians, but the referent of the word "style" is by no means clear. Is a "style" meant to be a descriptive generalization that allows one to predict what the behavior of Christians will be, or is it an evaluative judgment of what Christians ought to be like? Both elements seem to be intended, but the relation between them remains very much a mystery. Furthermore, does "style" primarily denote deeds that are characteristic of the Christian, or does it refer more to dispositions, attitudes, and intentions? This raises an even more perplexing problem: Exactly how is the relationship between a person and his acts to be understood? Is there a difference between what the person is and what he does? Do a person's actions follow from the kind of person he is, or does his character depend on the kind of action he engages in? Beyond even these questions is the problem of what it means to act at all.

These are extremely hard questions, but their difficulty does not excuse the failure of contemporary moralists to consider them. In the Protestant context, this failure may reflect the traditional concern to deny that the actual shape of a man's life has any efficacy in the attainment of his righteousness. Protes-

---

[5]James Gustafson, "Christian Style of Life: Problematics of a Good Idea," *Una sancta* 24 (1967) 6-14; reprinted in his *Christian Ethics and the Community* (Philadelphia: Pilgrim 1971) pp. 177-85.

tant ethics has taken seriously its mission to guard against "the temptation to confuse the shaping of life in accord with one's belief with the attainment of grace and God's righteousness."[6] In order to do this, Protestants have tended to emphasize the dual nature of the self: the "internal" justified self is divorced from the "external" sinful self, the passive self from the active. This has been more than just a theological description; there are enormous practical consequences if what a man does and how he acts have relatively little to do with his real "internal" justified self,[7] if man's "external" acts are only the ambiguous manifestations of his "true internal" self. Because of this emphasis, Protestant ethics has paid relatively little attention to how men's disposition, intentions, and actions actually embody whatever is considered to be the normative "style" of the Christian life.

Roman Catholic moral theology has continued to be more open to the language of character and virtue, as these concerns have played so important a role in the Catholic tradition as it has been shaped by Aristotle and Thomas. Moreover, recent Catholic moralists have emphasized the "whole person" rather than judgments of particular acts divorced from the total development of the moral agent.[8] Yet even in the Catholic context it

---

[6]Gustafson, p. 14

[7]This kind of problem can already be found in Luther, especially in *The Freedom of the Christian*. See *Three Treatises*, tr. W. A. Lambert (Philadelphia: Muhlenberg, 1957) p. 297.

[8]See, e.g., Charles Curran, *A New Look at Christian Morality* (Notre Dame: Fides, 1968) pp. 204-7; and John Milhaven, *Toward a New Catholic Morality* (New York: Doubleday, 1970) pp. 22, 87, 107. Milhaven, in a recent article "Objective Moral Evaluation of Consequences," *Theological Studies* 32 (1971) 407-30, emphasizes Thomas' understanding of the relation between virtue and moral knowledge, but he thinks psychological analysis is now more appropriate for such issues. While this may be the case, it certainly is a matter that must be demonstrated rather than assumed. It is not clear how completely Milhaven integrates the emphasis on the significance of the agent into his general position; he continues to defend a form of consequentialism in which the impersonal moral judgment of the spectator makes irrelevant the agent's own understanding of what he was doing. One cannot help but get the feeling that many of the so-called "new-liberal Catholic moralists" still continue to accept the "old morality" presupposition that ethics is primarily concerned with judgments about particular problems. If this is the case, the difference between the new and old moral theology is not primarily in method but in style and specific conclusion. Put in historical terms, this means that the new Catholic ethics, like the old, has not provided an adequate account of the relation between the virtues and the more "objective" and problem-oriented ethics traditionally associated with the confessional.

is hard to find sustained analysis of the nature of the idea of character that its ethical significance would seem to demand. I am sure any explanation for this would be extremely complex, since it would have to combine sociological insight with a history of moral theology. Even if I were competent to supply such an account, it would direct me too far away from the main purpose of this essay. Rather I want to try to begin the kind of analysis of the nature of the idea of character and its moral significance that is required if we are to adequately account for this aspect of the Christian moral life. I do not pretend to say anything that Aristotle and Thomas did not say as well or better.[9] But perhaps this essay will at least provide the impetus to read their work with fresh eyes.

Meaning of Character

It is no accident that the concept of character is most appropriately used in contexts suggesting individuality; for, etymologically, the word "trait," which is often closely associated with it, is connected with making a distinguishing mark.[10] In this sense a character may be a distinctive figure in arithmetic or it may be used to point out a particular feature of an inanimate object. Therefore it is not surprising that character is also used to mark off the distinctive in a human being.

However, character takes on an added meaning when it is applied to persons. It denotes not only what is distinctive but what is in some measure deliberate, what a man can decide to be as opposed to what he is naturally. Because a man chooses to have a kind of character, we can assume that by knowing his character we have some indication about what he is likely to do. For example, we think of a man as naturally and incurably slow, but we feel that one can choose to be more or less honest or selfish. A man's

inclinations and desires, which are part of his "nature," may suggest goals; but such inclinations and desires only enter into what we call a man's "character" in so far as he chooses to satisfy them in a certain manner, in

---

[9]For an analysis of Aristotle and Thomas on virtue and character, see my *Character and the Christian Life* (San Antonio: Trinity University, 1974).

[10]R. S. Peters, "Moral Education and the Psychology of Character," *Philosophy* 37 (1962) 38.

accordance with the rules of efficiency like persistently, carefully, dog-
gedly, painstakingly, or in accordance with rules of social appropriateness
like honestly, fairly, considerately, and ruthlessly.[11]

Probably because the notion of character seems to have this
fundamental connection with personal effort, it is often
thought of an implying effort done for moral praise or blame.
Nowell-Smith expresses this by saying: "Pleasure and pain,
reward and punishment, are the rudders by which moral character is molded; and 'moral character' is just that set of dispositions that can be molded by these means."[12] Supporting this
argument is the fact that so many individual character words
imply a moral judgment. Yet, as R. S. Peters points out, the
relationship between the descriptive and evaluative aspects of
character language is actually much more complex than this. An
indication of this is the fact that we may be quite hazy about
the spheres in which praise and blame apply and yet talk with
some assurance about a person's character.[13]

This kind of ambiguity is clarified if we distinguish between
"character traits" and "having character." A "character trait"
usually refers to a distinctive manner of carrying out certain
activities. Thus we can describe a person as being a perfectionist
in his work without implying that he exhibits this trait in all his
activity. Sometimes we use certain trait words to characterize
the way a person carries out all the various activities of his life.
We sometimes use such trait words to imply a negative evaluation of a person whose adherence to one particular style of
behavior causes him to act inappropriately in certain situations.

The notion of "having character" is clearly set apart from the
idea of a "character trait." To speak of a man "having character" is not to attribute to him any specific traits; rather the
point is that, whatever activity he takes part in or trait he
exhibits, there "will be some sort of control and consistency in
the manner in which he exhibits them."[14] We often speak of
integrity of character, thereby closely identifying integrity and
consistency with the meaning of having character. We talk of

---

[11]*Ibid.*, p. 38.
[12]P. H. Nowell-Smith, *Ethics* (Harmondsworth: Penguin, 1961) p. 304.
[13]Peters, p. 39.
[14]*Ibid.*, p. 43.

strength or weakness of character as a way of indicating whether a man may be relied upon and trusted even under duress.
Character in this sense is what Hartmann calls moral strength,
which is the capacity of "the person to speak for himself, to
determine beforehand his future conduct not yet under his
control, therefore to guarantee for himself beyond the present
moment."[15]

Character understood in this way implies that man is more
than that which simply happens to him; for he has the capacity
to determine himself beyond momentary excitations in the
acts.[16] This is not just a matter of being able to will one's
present decision as determinative in and for the future; as
Hartmann argues, this volitional possibility ultimately depends
on the identity of the person himself.

One who promises identifies himself as he now is with what he will be
later. . . . The breaking of a promise would be a renunciation of himself, its
fulfillment a holding fast to himself. On this personal identity depends a
man's moral continuity in contrast to all natural and empirical instability;
on it, therefore, depends at the same time the ethical substance of the
person.[17]

Thus it is character that gives a warrant for our expectation of a
link between what the individual is and the sequence of his
actions and attitudes.[18]

Once the distinction between "character traits" and "having
character" has been made clear, we can better appreciate the
complexity of the evaluative and descriptive aspects of character language. When we think of a person's character, a distinguishing trait such as honesty or kindness is usually what we
have in mind; but when we speak of a man as "having charac-

---

[15]Nicolai Hartmann, *Ethics* 2 (tr. Stanton Coit; London: Allen and Unwin, 1963)
287.

[16]In the light of this understanding of the idea of character the problem with
situation ethics is that, in spite of its claim to provide men with autonomy, it is
working with a very passive model of the self. The self is always lost amid the
contingencies of the particular situation. For men to have autonomy in any meaningful sense, they must be able to meet "the situation" on grounds other than those
which the situation itself provides. Such grounds must be based on their character.
Situation ethics seem but a secular restatement of the passive view of man associated
with the traditional Protestant insistence on the centrality of justification by faith.

[17]Hartmann, p. 288.

[18]Martin Buber, *Between Man and Man* (Boston: Beacon, 1955) pp. 104-17.

ter," we are more apt to be thinking of something like integrity, incorruptibility, or consistency. The former denotes more the common meaning of "virtues," while the latter indicates a more inclusive and unitary concept. Both usages denote the distinctive, and both require effort on the part of the agent. They not only differ in level of generality, but having character also denotes a more basic moral determination of the self.

The use of "character" (mainly implied in specific character words such as "honesty") in the sense of denoting specifiable traits usually suggests an immediate moral evaluation, whereas to say a man "has character" is much more ambiguous; for even though normally to say that a man has character is to praise him, we do not think it odd to say that a man has character and yet deplore a large part of his conduct. For example, we might well say that a thief has character (he can be trusted to be a thief, and perhaps one who is clever or courteous), but we would not wish to imply by this that he is thereby a good man. This simply makes the point that, though most of us would give positive valuation to the consistency, integrity, and reliability that "having character" implies, yet these alone do not completely specify either the nature or the moral value of the traits which are part of such character.

Character As Qualification Of Our Self-Agency

We have already indicated in several different contexts that man's capacity for self-determination is crucial if he is to "have character." At the very least, this capacity implies that a man is more than that which happens to him. Though the importance of physiological and environmental factors is not to be underestimated, a man is not simply formed by the interaction of these forces. Rather man is in his essence self-determining; through his heredity and environment he acts to give his life its particular form. A man's present choices and actions control his own future by shaping the kind of man he is. Man is at the mercy of external forces only if he allows himself to be, for man is not just acted upon but agent. To be a man is to be an autonomous center of activity and the source of one's own determinations; all he knows, all he wills, all he does issues from that very act by which he is what he is.

This strong sense of agency, however, does not deny the aspects of man's life that can be thought of as his destiny. We do not have unlimited possibilities, we are "destined" to a certain range of choices by our culture, society, and our particular biographical and psychological situation. It is our destiny to be born at a particular time in a certain society rather than another. In this sense we do undergo much, and much happens to us in our lives. However, we recognize that a man can gain character by responding in significant ways to events beyond his control. In so responding, he is not just being a passive agent, but he is actively forming himself to endure what he is undergoing in a particular way. Though it is undeniably true that we are destined men, we are also agents who have the capacity to give that destiny a form appropriate to our character. Though character may grow out of what we suffer, its main presupposition and condition must remain the agency of man.

It is impossible in this essay to adequately explicate or defend this understanding of self-agency, even though a complete exposition of the idea of character would require it. Suffice it to say that this idea of self-determination has much in common with recent developments in the philosophy of action where the self is understood primarily in terms of man's ability to act.[19] Metaphysically, this notion of the self rests on the irreducible difference between what happens to a man and what he does (though for certain purposes or disciplines the language of action might be translated into the language of passion). In this context the self is neither understood as a mysterious entity that somehow exists behind our actions nor reduced to the external conditions of the act. Rather the self is not different from our agency, for we have the power of efficient causation through our capacity to intentionally form our action.

The last point is crucial, for there is a vast difference between calling human action purposive and calling it intentional. The concept of intention is confined in its application to language-using, reflective creatures who are able to characterize their own

[19]For an introduction to the philosophy of action, see *Readings in the Theory of Action*, ed. N. S. Care and Charles Landesman (Bloomington: Indiana Univ., 1968). A few of the important books in this area are: Austin Farrer, *The Freedom of the Will* (New York: Scribner's, 1958); Stuart Hampshire, *Thought and Action* (New York: Viking, 1960); A. I. Melden, *Free Action* (New York: Humanities Press, 1964); Charles Taylor, *The Explanation of Behavior* (New York: Humanities Press, 1964); G. E. M. Anscombe, *Intention* (Oxford: Blackwell, 1958); Richard Taylor, *Action and Purpose* (Englewood Cliffs: Prentice-Hall, 1966); D. G. Brown, *Action* (Toronto: Univ. of Toronto, 1968).

conduct, whereas the concept of purpose is not so limited.[20] Only men can be characterized as intending what they do, whereas animals may be said to have purposes. Thus to argue that action is basically intentional is to point to the fact that action can only ultimately be described and understood by reference to the intention of the agent. Only the agent can supply the correct description of an action, whereas purpose can be characterized from the observer's point of view.

Action is not called intentional in this sense as a way of indicating some "extra" feature that exists when it is performed, but as a way of denoting what makes it human action at all. To say action is intentional is to clearly differentiate intention from the kind of cause that is known by observation, for intentions represent a class of knowledge that can be known without observation;[21] Hampshire calls this nonpropositional knowledge.[22] To characterize our knowledge of our actions in this way may be a bit misleading, because it makes our intentions appear to be some strange kind of private knowledge accessible only in a mysterious way. But these philosophers characterize our knowledge of our actions in this way in order to suggest that such knowledge does not conform to the validating conditions ordinarily prescribed for empirical knowledge. The idea behind nonobservational knowledge is that the agent knows what he does, not because he observes himself doing what he does, but simply by doing it. Melden puts the matter correctly when he suggests that knowledge of our own actions is noninferential. The agent knows what he is doing directly, by no process other than translating his intention into action.[23] I do not intend to write this sentence by observing what I do. I know what I intend immediately because that is what I intend and thus do. In other words, the knowledge I have of my intentions and my doings is not something I acquire, it is something I have simply because it is I who am acting. I cannot be an agent and fail to have such knowledge, for the condition of my agency is that I have a reason for what I do. Our actions

[20]Stuart Hampshire, "Reply to Walsh on *Thought and Action,*" *Journal of Philosophy* 9 (1963) 413.

[21]Anscombe, *Intention,* pp. 13-15.

[22]Hampshire, *Thought and Action,* p. 103.

[23]Melden, *Free Action,* p. 139.

cannot therefore be considered apart from our agency; they are intelligible only on the basis of that agency.

Man's capacity for self-determination is dependent on his ability to envision and fix his attention on certain descriptions and to form his actions (and thus his self) in accordance with them. A man's character is largely the result of such sustained attention. His reasons for his action, his motives and intentions are really explanatory because they are the essential aspect in the formation of the act and consequently in his own formation. His reasons do not "cause" him to act, but by embodying them he as the agent effects the corresponding action.[24] Man's agency may not be determined by any external cause, but it is only effective when it is determined in one direction rather than another, i.e., when a man chooses to live his life by certain beliefs and intentions rather than others, and embodies this fundamental choice in his concrete choices. Man chooses within an indeterminate range of possibilities by ordering them in accordance with his intentions. To be free is to set a course

---

[24]"Cause" here appears in inverted commas to indicate an issue of controversy. Philosophers such as Melden, Anscombe, and Richard Taylor argue that since actions are only intelligible in terms of reasons or motives, they are not open to an account in terms of Humean causality (Melden, p. 53; Taylor, pp. 9-98). They argue that since Humean causality presupposes a contingent relation between cause and effect, the relation of logical necessity between the agent and his act precludes causal explanation; for the intention of the agent is necessarily connected with the external act simply because the intention to do a certain thing cannot be described without making reference to its object. But even if this argument is sound, it need not preclude that "reasons"—insofar as they are wants and desires—are still properly thought of as the "cause" of our action. For two excellent discussions that argue this way, see Alvin Goldman, *A Theory of Human Action* (Englewood Cliffs: Prentice-Hall, 1970) pp. 76-85, and Georg Henrik von Wright, *Explanation and Understanding* (Ithaca: Cornell Univ., 1971) pp. 95-131. For the purpose of this essay it is not necessary to make a decision about this issue; however, it is obviously of great significance for any full theory of agency and especially for basic methodological questions concerning the nature of the social and behavioral sciences and their relation to ethics; for at the least the agency theory of human behavior makes clear that the social sciences cannot model their explanatory patterns after the natural sciences. See, e.g., Charles Taylor, *The Explanation of Behavior;* Peter Winch, *The Idea of a Social Science* (New York: Humanities Press, 1958); *Readings in the Philosophy of Social Science,* ed. May Brodbeck (New York: Macmillan, 1968), and Alasdair MacIntyre, *Against the Self-Images of the Age* (New York: Schocken, 1971) pp. 211-279. In the context of these methodological questions the kindest thing that can be said of Milhaven's statement that "the use of the behavioral sciences *is* morality" is that it displays a rather shocking naïvete and innocence (*Toward a New Catholic Morality,* p. 125). The important relation between ethics and the social sciences is not well served by the ethicist's accepting at face value the procedure and conclusion of the social scientist on the grounds they are "empirical."

through the multitude of possibilities that confront us and so to impose order on the world and one's self.

Character is thus the qualification of our self-agency, formed by our having certain intentions (and beliefs) rather than others. Character is not a mere public appearance that leaves a more fundamental self hidden; it is the very reality of who we are as self-determining agents. Our character is not determined by our particular society, environment, or psychological traits; these become part of our character, to be sure, but only as they are received and interpreted in the descriptions which we embody in our intentional action. Our character is our deliberate disposition to use a certain range of reasons for our actions rather than others (such a range is usually what is meant by moral vision), for it is by having reasons and forming our actions accordingly that our character is at once revealed and molded.

The idea of character, therefore, involves the complex question of the relation between our "reasons" and the "corresponding action." Aristotle was fond of saying that "virtues develop from corresponding activities," which implies that it is possible to establish a rather direct relationship between the virtue and a certain set of actions that have a publicly agreed-on description (*Nicomachean Ethics* 1103a21). But Aristotle's understanding of this relationship is far too simple; it rests on the assumption that the standards of morality of the current Greek society are normative. No doubt, even in the context of our extraordinarily pluralistic society such as assumption can account for a great deal of our moral behavior, but it is not sufficient. It fails to explain why at times our description of an action ceases to be in conformity with its established public description. Nor does it allow for the possibility that my individual reasons for an action may be far different from the public understanding of such an action; for example, a courageous man may have to perform an act that is publicly associated with cowardice. Perhaps the creative moral life can be understood as the constant struggle to enliven and enlarge the relationship between the established description of an action and its moral basis.

Put another way, this kind of problem indicates that our character has both a public and a private dimension. Our character is always secret to some extent; no matter what our public actions may look like to the observer, only our own avowal can finally be taken as the description of what we were doing. To be sure, moral or legal considerations force us to judge certain kinds of acts from the observer's understanding of what "has happened."[25] Such judgments do not strike us as coercive, since the descriptions according to which our intentions form our character are already socially determined (and thus observer-determined).[26] Yet character, even though it must be at least potentially public, is also irreducibly private; we alone form our character by choosing among the descriptions society offers and deciding how to combine and order them. This is but a way of restating the assertion that our character is the qualification of *our agency;* thus it is and can only be ours in a way no one else can duplicate or share.

In emphasizing the agent's perspective, I am not recommending ethical solipsism. Thinking something right or wrong does not make it so. Kurt Baier has rightly suggested that the minimal condition for being a morally serious person is willingness to judge our action from the point of view of anyone—i.e., we are willing to defend our action on grounds that are open to public debate.[27] Only as we are willing to subject our reasons (descriptions) for our actions to something like the universaliza-

---

[25] This involves the very complex question of the relationship between responsibility and action. We are often held responsible for an action we did not do strictly speaking, but for which we are responsible because we failed to employ knowledge of skills that one would expect normal persons under similar circumstances to employ. Implied by this is a denial that the moral life can be interpreted primarily as a choice between the subjectivity of the agent or the objectivity of the observer. The important ethical question is not whether moral options are subjective or objective, but whether they are true or false.

[26] This has extremely important implications for ethical reflection, for it makes clear the correctness of Plato and Aristotle's assumption that ethics is a branch of politics. The work that has influenced my reflection in this respect is G. H. Mead's conception of the social self, even though it is obvious that I reject some of his strong behaviorist assumptions. See, e.g., *The Social Psychology of G. H. Mead,* ed. Anselm Strauss (Chicago: Univ. of Chicago, 1956). Alfred Schutz's *Collected Papers* (The Hague: Nijhoff, 1962) is also very suggestive for an understanding of the social dimensions of the self. Dewey's thought, of course, also has tremendous importance for understanding the relations of the self to society.—The implications of this idea of the self for the social sciences are numerous. Very generally, however, I suggest that the social sciences investigate the core of descriptions generally accepted by the participants in a society; in this way social scientists could analyze the limits within which action can take place in one society. The rate of change in a modern society is a function of the pluralism of its basic descriptions.

[27] Kurt Baier, *The Moral Point of View* (New York: Random House, 1966) pp. 100-109.

bility principle is ethical judgment and argument possible at all.[28] This emphasis on the agent's point of view, then, does not undercut the importance of moral argument, judgment, and practical reasoning; it does indicate that the moral life involves more than these issues. Willingness to examine our actions from a moral point of view is certainly a condition of morality; but such investigation makes no sense unless we are willing to first engage in certain actions or ways of life. A man is good not only because his acts are justifiable, but because he is willing to face hard decisions entailed by his embodiment of commitments that go beyond the minimal conditions for moral argument.[29]

To understand character as the qualification of our agency is not to affirm that we can and should become whatever we wish. To strongly emphasize our agency is not to deny the significance of the passive aspects of our existence. Much that we are is that which "happens to us." Our intentions embody the "given" aspects of our existence as elements in the envisaged project. Through such an embodiment we conform our lives to what we think to be "reality," in its descriptive as well as its normative mode. The point I have tried to make, however, is that part of what constitutes "reality" for men is what we are able to contribute through the active ordering of reality by our intentional action.

These last two points can be brought together, since our society and its stock of public descriptions form large parts of

[28]My affinities with the Kantian tradition are obvious. However, for the exposition of the generalization principle closest to my own, see Marcus Singer, *Generalization in Ethics* (New York: Knopf, 1961).

[29]As Richard Price observed, most men whose behavior is in the main decent and regular "are perhaps what they appear to be, more on account of the peculiar favorableness of their natural temper and circumstances; or, because they have never happened to be much in the way of being otherwise; than from any genuine and sound principles of virtue established within them and governing their hearts. The bulk of mankind is not composed of the grossly wicked, or of the eminently good; for, perhaps, both these are almost equally scarce; but of those who are as far from being truly good, as they are from being very bad; of the indolent and unthinking; ... the wearers of the form without the reality of piety; of those, in short, who may be blame-worthy and guilty, not so much on account of what they do, as what they do not do" (*A Review of the Principle Questions In Morals,* ed. D. Daiches Raphael [Oxford: Clarendon, 1948] pp. 230-31). The ethics of character is an attempt to indicate that "what men do not do" is important for the kind of men they are; and "what men do not do" is not just their failure to judge their own individual actions from a "moral point of view," but their failure to take a stance out of which all their action develops.

the passive aspects of our existence. Yet no man can simply be passively formed by his society. He may find it easier to simply acquiesce in the expectations and demands of his society. But such a conformity is not completely passive, for it must still become a qualification of his agency. His resulting character is still uniquely his, as much as the character of other members of the society who have interacted more creatively with that society and are more visibly different from the society's normal expectations. It is certainly true that much of our life consists in assuming societal roles or patterns of behavior, which may be good or bad. Yet it must still be our agency that embodies and enacts these roles.

It is not possible to establish abstract criteria that can accurately indicate how much our character is determined and how much we determine ourselves. These obviously vary from society to society, from one position in society to another, from individual to individual. Our original genetic temperament and social position largely determine the range of descriptions which will be possible for us. My point is the more general one that, regardless of the way our character is actually formed in its concrete specification, it must be nonetheless *our* character if, as I have argued, men are fundamentally self-agents.

Character As Moral Orientation Of The Self

Character is tremendously important for our moral behavior; for what we do morally is not in itself determined by the rules we adhere to or how we respond to one particular situation, but by what we have become through our past history, by our character. Experiences like facing death and falling in love are very important for what we are and do; yet they are often ignored in the analysis of moral experience simply because they are not in propositional form. It is our character that gives orientation and direction to life. The clarity and singleness of men's characters vary greatly in their concrete manifestations. Perhaps the clearest example of character is one in which a life is dominated by one all-consuming purpose or direction. The moral value of such a character depends on the substance of the purpose to which it is dedicated. Most of our characters do not exemplify such an all-consuming aim; rather each of us has a set of intentions and descriptions integrated in some hierarchy of priority which provides a general orientation.

If character is understood as the orientation of our self-agency, it cannot be finished once and for all; it is impossible to perceive beforehand all that is implied in the descriptions which we have made our own. We often find that the patterns we use to form our actions have more to them than we originally suspected. To have character is necessarily to engage in discovery: by our continuing action we discover unanticipated new aspects and implications of our descriptions. For example, we may find that we have embodied two different descriptions which we originally felt to be in harmony, but which prove to be contradictory as they are further specified in concrete actions. We discover the conditions for the success of the other. Thus we may find that we cannot wish to gain as much money as we can and at the same time treat all men fairly. At some point, in relation to a particular situation, we discover that though our agency can be determined by either one of these descriptions, they cannot both be harmonized in the same act. We must choose one or the other, and thereby become as we have chosen.

It is possible, of course, that we shall simply be inconsistent, one time acting to gain money and the other time to be fair. Such inconsistency does not mean that we do not have character, it only means that there are inconsistent elements in the character we do have, or that our character is determined primarily in view of expediency, accommodation, etc. We may think that this does not provide a very successful or particularly attractive way to be, but nonetheless it is the way we are. Of course, it is possible that both these ways of being, gaining money and acting fairly, may be harmonized in terms of a further goal, such as ambition. Thus one may find that he can further his ambition by acting in one situation to gain money, in another to leave the impression that he is a fair person. But his criterion for being one or the other is determined by his ambition.

I have thus tried to clarify the idea of orientation that I am associating with character. Character may be a general direction without necessarily being conceived in a highly specific manner or in terms of a definite goal. We may consider such definite formation morally important, but this is not a conceptual necessity. Our character may consist of simply meeting each situation as it comes, not trying to determine the direction of our lives but letting the direction vary from one decision to another. Or we might even approve of the man who at times acts inconsistently with his character.

Such inconsistency may be important in providing a transition from our past to our future, especially when our character is so formed that we are closed to the future and fail to acknowledge the significance of new elements that confront us and challenge our past determinations. We may expressly try to protect ourselves in some narrow way from the vicissitudes of living life in a creative manner. This can be done by simply limiting our actions to a well-laid-out routine which allows a safe boredom and protects us from the ravages of the unknown. But it is equally true that our character can be formed in such a way that it provides the means by which we reach new appreciation of the possibilities of our future. Indeed, if we are to determine our own future, it is precisely upon our character that such an openness depends.

In arguing that character need not inhibit our ability to react responsibly to new circumstances, I do not wish to leave the impression that welcoming novelty is the main problem of the moral life. This would be true only on the assumption that the future brings nothing but good; but it may in fact be good to ignore the new which denies the good of the past. Character is morally significant because, if rightly formed, it provides a proper transition from our past to our future; for the task of this transition is not to accept the future unconditionally, but to respond and remake the future in the right kind of way. Our future is what we determine it to be from the depths of who we are; it can be as rich or as narrow as we make it. It is not enough that we as moral agents take into account all that is in the situation objectively understood, for what is also "in" the situation is the possible change we can make by the fact that we are certain kinds of persons. Our moral life is not limited to passive accommodation to the good; it includes changing the world through intentional activity, rooted in our character. Moreover, the kind of person we are, our character, determines to a large extent the kind of future we will face. Only if we have a morally significant character can we be relied upon to face morally serious questions rather than simply trying to avoid them.

Running through my discussion of the idea of character has been an understanding of freedom I wish to make more explicit at this point. Freedom, or the autonomy of the self, is not a status to be assumed but a task to be undertaken. Put differently, "free will" does not describe a faculty of the self, but the way we decide to engage in actions under certain descriptions rather than others. To be free is the successful embodiment of the descriptions we choose as morally true. Freedom is not the will jumping from one isolated instance to another; the correlate of freedom is not the will at all, but the truth of our intention. Freedom is genuinely a virtue, a determination of the self, that protects us from being at the mercy of the moment. Our freedom, therefore, is not antithetical to our determination through our character; our freedom is possible just to the extent we are so determined.[30]

Especially since character is thus formed in freedom, no one type of character is normative for all men. The actual character of a man is too much the product of the contingencies of his life for such a concrete recommendation to be viable. Men are simply different, and the difference does not necessarily denote degrees of goodness or badness. Individuals have formed themselves differently in relation to their individual circumstances. Such variety of goodness frustrates the philosopher's desire for a simple description of the moral life, but the reality is undeniable.

To accept the variety of the good embodied in our actual lives, however, is not to refuse all recommendations about the kinds of character a man should have. It is simply to recognize that such recommendations do not necessarily determine their concrete specifications. In this essay I have attempted to describe the significance of the idea of character for the moral life, but a descriptive argument is not enough. The question of the kind of character one *ought* to embody cannot be avoided. This normative question involves such complex issues that it is best discussed in another context. However, I would like to make two brief normative suggestions, one moral and one theological.

---

[30]The many issues surrounding this interpretation of freedom are too numerous to consider here. For a good collection of essays concerned with this problem, see *Free Will and Determinism,* ed. Bernard Berofsky (New York: Harper & Row, 1966). For an extended discussion of freedom very similar to the position I am suggesting, see Austin Farrer, *The Freedom of the Will.* I suspect this understanding of character and freedom will provide a fresh way of dealing with the problem of grace and free will, for it makes intelligible the Christian claim that we are most free when we are completely determined by God's will.

The question of how our character is acquired and developed is a morally significant question. The most general statement about the character of morally serious people is that it has not been left to chance. One of the constant themes running through moral philosophy has been that the unexamined life is not worth living. This theme is very much at the heart of the moral significance of character, for it is through consciousness (intentionality) that we shape ourselves and our actions. And what else does consciousness mean but the effort to see and understand our actions in terms of their most significant moral descriptions? For the idea that the moral life is the examined life is but a way of saying that we can choose to determine ourselves in terms of certain kinds of descriptions rather than others. Thus, to live morally we must not only adhere to public and generalizable rules but also see and interpret the nature of the world in a moral way. The moral life is thus as much a matter of vision as it is a matter of doing.[31]

This recommendation that we consciously strive to develop our character does not imply an unwarranted concern for the moral man with his own perfection or righteousness. I wish to give no comfort to the prig or prude. Character as I have analyzed it is not an end in itself but that which gives our lives moral orientation by directing us to certain kinds of activities. The possible moralizing misuses of character in no way detract from the moral value of character properly formed. It is not finally a question of whether we have or do not have character, but rather the kind of character that results from our way of seeing the world. The moral importance of the idea of character is not that good men think a great deal about acquiring and having character; rather it is that the concerns represented by the idea of character play an essential part in their being good men.

On a theological level, the idea of character provides a way of

---

[31]Iris Murdoch has written persuasively on the importance of "vision" for the moral life; see her "Vision and Choice in Morality," in *Christian Ethics and Contemporary Philosophy,* ed. Ian Ramsey (New York: Macmillan, 1966); and "The Idea of Perfection," *Yale Review* 53 (1964) 343-80. A full exposition of Miss Murdoch's thought was given earlier in this book, Chapter 2. "The Significance of Vision: Toward an Esthetic Ethic." Also see my suggestion about the relating of language and ethics, "Situation Ethics, Moral Notions, and Theological Ethics," Chapter 1. For an extremely suggestive article that indicates how some of the implications of this article might be developed, see James McClendon, "Biography As Theology," *Cross Currents* 21 (1971) 415-31.

explicating the normative nature of the Christian life. The Christian life is not simply a matter of assuming a vague loving attitude, but rather it is a concrete determination of our being developed through our history. The Christian is one so formed as he assumes the particular description offered him through the Church. This formation is the determination of our character through God's sanctifying work. Sanctification is thus the formation of the Christian's character that is the result of his intention to see the world as redeemed in Jesus Christ.[32]

The Christian life so understood is not made up of one isolated "loving" act added to another. Rather it ought to be the progressive growth of the self into the fuller reality of God's action in Christ. Such growth in the Christian life is necessitated not only by the new contingencies we face as individuals; it is called forth by the object of the Christian's loyalty. The Christian tradition possesses rich images to characterize such a life. The primacy of one image or set of images is a theological question I cannot settle here. Rather I have developed a position from which such an argument can be meaningfully carried on.

---

[32]For a fuller exposition of the relationship between character and the doctrine of sanctification as it appears in Calvin and Wesley, see my *Character and the Christian Life.* Also see the last chapter of James Gustafson's *Christ and the Moral Life* (New York: Harper & Row, 1969) for some similar suggestions.

4.

The Self as Story:
A Reconsideration of the
Relation of Religion and Morality
from the Agent's Perspective

For purposes of analysis moral philosophy should remain at the level of the differences, taking the moral forms of life as given, and not try to *get behind them* to a single form.

There is perhaps in the end no peace between those who think that morality is complex and various, and those who think it is simple and unitary, or between those who think that other people are usually hard to understand and those who think they are usually easy to understand.[1]

This essay, while informed by theological commitments, is a philosophical exercise to expand the arbitrary limits embodied in the religion-morality discussion. Often implicit in the arguments of those who deny any specificity[2] to Christian moral

---

[1]Iris Murdoch, "Vision and Choice in Morality," in *Christian Ethics and Contemporary Philosophy*, edited by Ian Ramsey. (New York: Macmillan, 1966), pp. 195-218. Hereafter cited as *Ramsey*.

[2]I am using the term "specificity" in order to avoid the connotations of superiority usually associated with the claims about the "uniqueness" of the Christian moral life. My interest in this essay is not to show that the Christian moral behavior is at least ideally better than other ways of life, but that Christian moral behavior does or may involve ways of being that are distinguishable from those not sharing Christian convictions. Of course theological ethicists may try to suggest why the form of moral life embodied by Christians is more appropriate to the nature of human existence than other alternatives, but this paper only tries to provide the basis for that kind of task. Since I will argue, however, that much of our moral behavior can be justified on grounds that make no theological commitments it should be clear I have little sympathy with the semi-sociological claims that the moral ethos and social institutions of a society quickly go to ruin without a religious foundation. On the contrary I assume that Christians have much to learn morally from general human experience and other religious traditions.

The relationship between Christian moral behavior and reflection on that behavior must remain ambiguous in this paper. Generally I assume that the conduct of Christians is prior to and the necessary presupposition for reflection on that conduct. However the assumed specificity of this conduct does not depend on the ability to empirically establish in the contemporary context that Christians act differently from

behavior is the assumption that there is one form of the moral life, that underneath the variety of human activity there is one moral way of life, one form of moral justification that is the same for all men. It is my contention that it is possible to appreciate the variety of the moral without falling into the vicious relativism that those who take the unitary view so fear. It should be clear that the significance of this argument is not limited to Christian ethics. I assume that Jewish, Muslim, Hindu or other religious ethicists will also wish to claim some specificity for their own position.

The task of this essay is to expand the phenomenology of moral experience in a way that makes conceptual sense of the kind of "religious" intentions that form Christian behavior and the corresponding explanation of that behavior. Those who take a more unitary view of morality tend to limit ethical reflection to those aspects of our moral behavior that can be logically displayed. Thus the moral life tends to be restricted to arguments concerning specific problems.[3] But moral behavior involves more than simply the decisions and choices men make about specific problems; it also includes the kind of men they are (their character and virtues), the kind of beliefs they hold, and the way that they integrate and organize their resources and energies to form a coherent life plan. The moral life is not simply a matter of decision governed by publicly defensible principles and rules; we can only act in the world we see, a seeing partially determined by the kind of beings we have become through the stories we have learned and embodied in our life plan.

It is necessary to maintain the specificity of Christian moral behavior in order to do justice to the theological claim Christians make that their moral life is intimately connected with their religious convictions. Christians believe their moral values are an inseparable part of the meaning of the faith they confess. When religious men are confronted with the religion-morality issue—especially set in terms of Hume's contention that an

other men. Rather such a claim depends on an analysis of the basic affirmations found in Christian tradition whether Christians correspond to them or not. Rather it means that if theological ethics is to objectively, critically, and fairly analyze the nature of the Christian moral life it cannot separate the form of that life from the particularity of the affirmations that make such a life intelligible. In other words the specificity of theological ethics is not its methodology but its content.

[3]E. Pincoffs, "Quandary Ethics," *Mind* (October, 1971), pp. 552-571.

"ought" is not deducible from an "is,"[4]—they cannot provide an answer that does not do violence to their theological beliefs. For example, it makes no sense for them to say that their belief in God is merely factual; their belief in His existence and nature is part and parcel of a whole way of being.

That religious affirmations have this character helps explain the temptation that theologians and other men sympathetic to religion have had when challenged about the meaningfulness of religious affirmations to abstract the "moral" as the kernel of truth from the "religious." Thus faith is interpreted to be primarily the affirmation of a moral commitment rather than a matter of belief in God, Christ, or other more strictly "religious" matters. Though there have been some highly creative attempts at this abstraction, it is self-defeating as it succeeds in saving a function for "religion" at the loss of its substance. It separates the theologically inseparable at a loss to religion and ethics.

---

[4]For example see Kai Nielsen, "Some Remarks on the Independence of Morality from Religion," in *Ramsey*, pp. 140-151.

It would take me too far afield to try to unravel the various interpretations of the "supernaturalistic fallacy" and how it does or does not relate to Hume's claim that "ought" may never or may only be sometimes derived from "is." Generally it has not been sufficiently noticed that the naturalistic fallacy argument actually involves two different points. The first is concerned about the meaning of ethical terms and contends that moral words cannot be without remainder translated into non-ethical terms. The second argument is more of a logical point as it denies that no proposition containing an ethical term can be deduced from a purely "factual" proposition. The former argument I am in some sympathy with though I think it is often stated and used in an infelicitous way.

The latter form of the argument I find deficient as it presents a misleading picture of moral argument and psychology. It fails to take account of the many kinds of "institutional facts" that sustain our moral appeals and arguments that are clearly descriptive and yet involve moral obligation. For example such statements as "You ought to help him for he is your brother" help us to see that much of our language is normative and descriptive in ways that are not easily separable. For an application of this point to theological ethics see D. Z. Phillips, "God and Ought," in *Ramsey*, pp. 133-139. W. D. Hudson offers a critical discussion of the "institutional fact" argument in his article "Fact and Moral Value," *Religious Studies*, 5 (1968). Pp. 130-144. Secondly this alleged separation of "facts" and "values" drives an artificial wedge between our beliefs and our actions, for there is an intimate connection between what a man believes and what he finds intelligible to approve or disapprove morally. Phillippa Foot has suggested a man cannot logically feel pride unless there is an internal relation between his beliefs and their object. From this perspective it is simply false to assume that what we believe ("facts") are separable from what we ought to do. See her "Moral Beliefs," in *Ethics*, edited by Thomson and Dworkin. (New York: Harper and Row, 1968). Pp. 239-260. Hereafter cited as *Ethics*.

Vision, Stories, and Character

Contemporary ethics has paid little attention to character, vision, stories, and metaphors as part of our moral experience. Yet these aspects of our moral life provide the basis for our claim about the particularity of the Christian moral life. We neither are nor should we be formed primarily by the publicly defensible rules we hold, but by the stories and metaphors through which we learn to intend the variety of our existence.[5] Metaphors and stories suggest how we should see and describe the world—that is how we should "look-on" our selves, others, and the world—in ways that rules taken in themselves do not.[6] Stories and metaphors do this by providing the narrative accounts that give our lives coherence.[7]

Contrary to the assumption of many, principles are not the moral essence of stories as if they might be abstracted from the

---

[5]In what follows I am purposefully leaving vague the meaning of story and metaphor. Any attempt to provide a conceptually responsible definition of either in the bounds of this paper would be insufficient to account for the variety of the different kinds and uses of stories. Any attempt to develop this position beyond the methodological point I am concerned with would necessarily entail a more critical use and analysis of these aspects of our moral experience.

[6]For this sense of "look-on" and for many other things I am dependent on Donald Evans, *The Logic of Self-Involvement.* (London: S.C.M. Press, 1963.)

[7]For example James Olney says metaphors "are something known and of our making, or at least of our choosing, that we put to stand for, and so to help us understand something unknown and not of our making. The focus through which an intensity of self-awareness becomes a coherent vision of all reality, the point through which the individual succeeds in making the universe take on his own order, is metaphor: the formal conjunction of single subject and various objects. Our sense that there is a meaning in something—in a poem, in experience—comes only when the elements that go to make up that thing take on a relation to one another; in other words, the meaning emerges with our perception of a pattern, and there can obviously be no pattern in chronologically or geographically discrete items and elements. We must connect one thing with another and finally assume the whole design of which the element is only a part. Metaphor supplies such a connection, relating this to that in such and such a relevant way. The reader, like the poet, extends the possibilities of meaning-pattern in himself: he extends, that is, the pattern, or the adequacy of the pattern, which in turn may be taken, as it were, for a metaphor of his self. Metaphor is essentially a way of knowing. To a wholly new sensational or emotional experience, one can give sufficient organization only by relating it to the already known, only by perceiving a relation between this experience and another experience already placed, ordered, and incorporated. A metaphor allows us to connect the known of ourselves to the unknown of the world, and, making available new relational patterns it simultaneously organizes the self into a new and richer entity; so that the old known self is joined to and transformed into the new, the heretofore unknown self." *Metaphors of Self: The Meaning of Autobiography* (Princeton: Princeton University Press, 1972), pp. 30-31.

story and still convey the same meaning. Rather, our principles and rules are but shorthand reminders necessary for moral education and explanation; their moral significance is contained in stories. Though policy statements or principles—such as "I have decided to live an agapeistic life"—appear to be story-neutral, they are nothing of the sort. For our principles "are intelligible at all only if their implicit 'stories' are explicated. The need for stories then lies precisely in the fact that policy-statements are about intentions to act in certain ways, and action is inconceivable apart from stories. . . . The precise meaning of and hence the differences between Confucian policy-statements and Christian policy-statements are entirely a function of their differing stories."[8]

A commonplace example can illustrate the irreducibility and significance of metaphors and stories for learning to see the world in which we must act.[9] Suppose a woman is trying on a hat she thinks she likes but remains somewhat doubtful that it is right for her. A friend observing her indecision observes, "My dear, it's the Taj Mahal," and suddenly her indecision is resolved. It is of course possible to say that the friend has simply employed a colorful way to suggest that the hat is too ostentatious, but such a suggestion fails to convey the sense of the metaphor. One can no more translate the metaphor into "literal" language than poetry can be translated into prose, for in a certain correct and straightforward way the hat is the Taj Mahal. Poetry and literature do not just bolster our moral intentions; they affect how we perceive the world and hence what the moral life is about. For poetry does not just describe the known; it reveals dimensions of the unknown that make the known seem unfamiliar.

Perhaps an ethical example would make this point more persuasively. A man may exemplify in his every action what we consider to be the application of the rule to treat others fairly.

---

[8]William Poteat, "Myths, Stories, History, Eschatology, and Action: Some Polanyian Meditations," in *Intellect and Hope*, edited by Langford and Poteat. (Durham: Duke University Press, 1968), pp. 216-217.

[9]I borrow this example from James McClendon as he borrowed from Wisdom. See McClendon, "Biography as Theology," *Cross Currents*, 21, 4 (Fall), pp. 415-431. For an excellent article on the issue of the irreducibility of religious metaphors see Andrew Burgess, "Irreducible Religious Metaphors," *Religious Studies*, 8 (December, 1972), pp. 355-366.

He not only always treats others justly, but he even goes out of his way to serve their needs. In other words, he seems to be the perfect example of one who actually lives and orders his behavior so as to love others as he loves himself. He might claim that his behavior is not determined by any such maxim of fairness, for he is but "loving and treating others as if they are his brothers in Christ." While it is undeniable that this man's behavior embodies basic moral rules, his understanding of "all men as brothers in Christ" can no more be translated into rules of fairness than the Taj Mahal can be understood simply as a synonym for "ostentatious." For him, men are not just to be treated fairly, they are literally brothers in Christ. This will at times entail concrete behavior that is not envisaged in the rule to treat all men fairly and benevolently. It is this irreducible aspect of their religious beliefs and commitments that makes religious people so uncomfortable with any attempt to abstract a "moral core" from their religious convictions.

It would be unfortunate if this formal claim were limited to religious or metaphorical language. Rather these are but paradigm instances that make clear an essential aspect of all language used ethically.[10] For our moral language does not just describe what is; it describes how we ought to see and intend the world. The truth that is at least partly captured in the naturalistic fallacy is that moral language necessarily must presuppose a world that is not but should be. Our metaphors and stories entice us to find a way to bring into existence the reality that at once should be but will not be except as we act as if it is. Morally the world is always wanting to be created in correspondence to what it is but is not yet.

This does not mean we morally intend the world "as if" our basic commitments were true or that we can transform our existence to make them true even though they are fiction. Our religious stories and metaphors give expression to the normative commitments we need to make if we desire to live our lives in a morally appropriate way. The association of religious morality with fundamental metaphors and stories does not mean it is

---

[10]I put the matter in this way since I do not think there is any one "ethical" or "religious" language that one can discover the "logic" or "oddness" of. Ethical men and religious men use language and some forms of language and vocabulary may become more or less standard for them, but this does not mean there is a special language that can be identified apart from its use by such men.

logically different from other moral language; or that it can be dismissed as dealing with the "irrational" aspects of our moral existence.

Because ethicists have concentrated on moral justification of principles associated with specific actions and practices, they have tended to overlook the importance of stories for the moral life. The prevalent model of the moral life has tended to support the assumption that there is only one way to be moral.[11] To be sure in specific situations there may be no specifiable difference discernible between the man who embodies the ethics of fairness and the man who acts toward others as his brothers in Christ. Rules and principles appear to be sufficient because they are typically associated with rather common moral problems and situations.

But our moral lives are not simply made up of the addition of our separate responses to particular situations. Rather we exhibit an orientation that gives our life a theme through which the variety of what we do and do not do can be scored. To be agents at all requires a directionality that involves the development of character and virtue. Our character is the result of our sustained attention to the world that gives a coherence to our intentionality. Such attention is formed and given content by the stories through which we have learned to form the story of our lives. To be moral persons is to allow stories to be told through us so that our manifold activities gain a coherence that allows us to claim them for our own. The significance of stories is the significance of character for the moral life as our experience itself, if it is to be coherent, is but an incipient story.[12]

Our character is constituted by the rules, metaphors, and stories that are combined to give a design or unity to the variety of things we must and must not do in our lives. If our lives are to be reflective and coherent our vision must be ordered around dominant metaphors or stories. Therefore it is crucial to our moral life to allow the metaphors that make up our vision to

---

[11]For example see Iris Murdoch's devastating characterization of the liberal and optimistic view of the self and moral choice she thinks is assumed by contemporary philosophical ethicists in *Ramsey*, pp. 197-198.

[12]Steven Crites, "The Narrative Quality of Experience," *Journal of the American Academy of Religion*, XXXIX, 3 (September, 1971), pp. 291-311. For some very useful suggestions about how autobiographies can be more or less true see Roy Pascal, *Design and Truth in Autobiography* (Cambridge: Harvard U. Press, 1960).

check and balance each other in terms of their appropriateness for the various demands of our life and the overall life plan that we live.[13] From this perspective, it makes sense to suggest that the man who serves others as brothers in Christ may engage in activities the man who acts fairly simply does not perceive as obligatory.

The metaphors and stories we use to organize our life plan are inherited from our culture and our particular biographical situation. Christianity can be understood as but one set of coherent metaphors and stories that constitute an understanding of the nature of the world and a possible life plan.[14] Christianity involves a claim about how our lives must be centered to correspond to the truth of human existence. It is certainly not my intention to argue that Christianity is the only religion to provide men with such accounts of the moral life. But I do defend the position that Christian ethics must not be reduced to a conception of the moral life that does not share its stories and metaphors. It cannot be assumed that moral behavior for Christians is the same as for other persons, though there may be great areas of agreement. Indeed I will suggest below that there are good reasons to affirm a kind of "overlap" in the morality of Christian and non-Christian men of good will. But such an "overlap" does not provide evidence against my thesis for the specificity of the Christian claims about the nature of the religious-moral life.

In summary, I have suggested that a claim for the specificity

---

13For an analysis of the idea of "life plan" see Charles Fried, *An Anatomy of Values* (Cambridge: Harvard University Press, 1970), pp. 97-101. Fried uses this phrase to indicate "that persons must and do exhibit some order, some consistency in their ensemble of ends, that their ends as a whole comprise a system." As such our life plan should be formed rationally which Fried identifies with Rawls' two criteria of justice. One of the most important tasks before contemporary ethics is to develop the kind of position Fried represents in relation to the actual language of metaphor and stories we use to score the variety of events that make up our lives. For it is through such an analysis that we would understand better how issues or distributive justice should form our life plan; or how an ethic of obligation is to be related to an ethic of virtue.

14Austin Farrer has done the most disciplined reflection on how images and metaphors work and their relation to history. For the images and stories at the heart of the Christian life are formed and informed by the person of Jesus. The significance of this for how Christian ethics is to be understood is crucial for in a certain sense it is probably incorrect to think of Christ as a story. Austin Farrer, *The Glass of Vision* (London: Dacre Press, 1958).

of theological ethics is defensible once we realize that to be "moral" involves learning to see the world in a way that our lives have coherence and unity. I have argued that this aspect of our moral existence is better associated with certain stories and metaphors than with explicit moral principles, no matter how general.

In order to expand and clarify these brief and insufficiently developed suggestions, I will show how this position qualifies the two most prominent ways of understanding the relation of religion to morality—i.e. (1) religion as the motivation for moral action, and (2) religion as the higher or heroic ethic to basic or necessary social morality. By taking up these alternatives I plan to counter two possible objections to this position. The first objection is that I have not shown how Christian stories make a difference for actual moral behavior. Stories and character, a critic might say, are primarily "internal" or motivational aspects of moral action and have no external manifestations. The second objection is that I have made my case by rendering moral argument and judgment problematic, since I have provided no way for transmoral appeals between stories. These are obviously substantive objections that must be countered if my position is to be defensible.

Stories, Motivation, and the Agent's Perspective

An account of Christian moral behavior that on the surface appears quite similar to my position is found in Braithwaite's essay "An Empiricist's View of the Nature of Religious Belief."[15] Braithwaite suggests that Christian behavior is distinguished from others because the Christian entertains certain stories that encourage him to follow an agapeistic way of life. However, Braithwaite assumes that the good (what agape demands) can be known and done independent of any commitment to the truth of the stories, as the stories simply give Christians added support for their attempt to act agapeistically. This is a position taken by many philosophers in the interest of maintaining the autonomy of morality.[16] For example, Bernard

---

[15]R. B. Braithwaite, "An Empiricist's View of the Nature of Religious Belief," in *Ramsey*, pp. 53-73.

[16]The idea of autonomy of morality is extremely ambiguous as sometimes it refers to the autonomy of the self and at other times to the sufficiency of moral

Gert suggests that "providing men with the motives for being morally good men" is one of the main tasks of religion. He indicates, however, that when morality is thus supported by religion we encounter a danger that some people may fail to "realize that it is not religion which determines what is moral."[17]

Much of contemporary theological literature has often seemed to accept this motivational account of the specificity of Christian behavior and theological ethics. The act of the Christian is not overtly different from that of the non-religious man of good will. If the Christian differs at all it is in terms of what motivates his action and behavior. The religious man and the secular man join arms in the struggle against war, racism, and injustice—the difference if any concerns "why" they are personally there, not the "what" they are actually doing. Thus "love" becomes the preemptory norm of Christian ethics as it denotes a dispositional characteristic rather than a criterion of action.[18]

It is interesting that those who accept this account of the relation of religion and morality nevertheless in other contexts criticize the "privatization" of religion, for in theory their own theoretical account of Christian ethics implies that the "religious" aspect of moral action is limited to personal motives.

The predominance in the theological context of the motivational account of the relation between the religious and the moral is best explained in sociological terms. However, the philosophical position involves issues that cannot be avoided if I am to make good my claim to the specificity of theological ethics. For the philosopher's relegation of vision, story, and metaphor to the private or motivational part of our moral behavior stems from the attempt to raise moral argument from the morass of subjectivistic preferences. Thus the philosophical ethicist's assertion that the "private" can have only non or

terms, arguments, and justification as needing no extra moral support. I have not attempted in this essay to deal with the former issue. For a good treatment of it see Richard Mouw, "Commands for Grown-Ups," *Worldview*, 15, 7 (July), pp. 38-42; and Donald Evans, "Does Religious Faith Conflict With Moral Freedom," in *Morality and Religion* edited by Outka and Reeder (New York: Doubleday, 1973), pp. 348-392.

[17]Bernard Gert, *The Moral Rules* (New York: Harper and Row, 1966), pp. 231-232.

[18]For an excellent analysis of the concept of Agape, see Gene Outka, *Agape: An Ethical Analysis* (New Haven: Yale University, 1972).

pre-moral status is a correlate of their attempt to transform the arbitrary into the non-arbitrary. The reason for the extremely formal nature of much contemporary philosophical ethics stems from a commitment to find a logic of moral discourse that will permit agreement on significant moral issues regardless of the actual content of people's beliefs and desires. While I have great sympathy with this effort, the result has been a distortion of the nature of moral commitment and a systematic ignoring of crucial social and cultural aspects of moral experience.

The relegation of our beliefs, convictions, and stories to the private or motivational aspects of our moral experience is often supported by the argument that no imperative can be deduced from a factual proposition—i.e., my beliefs cannot logically inform what I ought to do. But this logical point leads to a distorted caricature of the relation between thought and action, for it isolates my intention from my beliefs about the world. [19] In an attempt to maintain the independence of moral judgment from "factual" considerations it forces my actual intentions for *my* moral behavior to be translated into simple imperatives divorced from an understanding of my social and cultural location. It posits for moral decisions a timelessness that frees agents from the complexities and limitations that are always present in their lived biographies.

Our cognitive capacities as moral agents are dependent on our being timeful beings who are able to form our intentions in efficacious ways. But the very efficacy of our intentions is dependent on the content of our beliefs about ourselves, others, and our environment. In other words, our beliefs, desires, and intentions cannot be isolated as the "motives" of our moral action where motive is understood to be independent of the description of the action as a moral action. The motive certainly cannot be thus isolated if the agent's intention is taken seriously as part of his moral activity since intentionality cannot be reduced to psychological-causal accounts of motivations.

The model of moral behavior that relegates religion to motivation assumes that the content of the motivation—that is the

---

[19]Alasdair MacIntyre, *Against the Self-Images of the Age* (New York: Schocken, 1971), pp. 130-135; see also Stuart Hampshire, *Thought and Action* (New York: Viking Press, 1959).

[20]Braithwaite, p. 70.

agent's description—is irrelevant to "what was actually being done." Thus Braithwaite explicitly states that holding a proposition may produce a state of mind that makes it easier to carry out a particular course of action, "but the connection is causal: there is no intrinsic ʌconnection between the thought and the action."[20] But that is clearly wrong; it is wrong because it assumes that moral judgments and decisions are observer determined—i.e., that the observer is the ideal judge whose description of an action defeats all other accounts.[21] This mistake is often found in moral philosophers who write about virtues or moral character. For example, Gert claims that our judgments of intentions, motives, character traits, even of the person as a whole "depend ultimately on our moral judgments about actions."[22]

It is obvious why Braithwaite and Gert are anxious to make this move, for otherwise the actual content of the agent's understanding of his action would be given moral status. Moreover this position seems to embody the moral wisdom that we must finally judge men by their fruits. Yet it is equally clear that this position is descriptively and normatively wrong. For when we do make judgments about men, we judge not only their acts, "their solutions to specifiable practical problems, we consider something more elusive which may be called their total vision of life, as shown in their mode of speech or silence, their choice of words, their assessments of others, their conception of their own lives, what they think attractive or praiseworthy, what they think funny: in short, the configuration of their thought which shows continually in their reaction and conversation."[23]

We rightly consider such matters significant because as agents we know that we do not always understand our actions according to the public rule-determined accounts an ethicist might use to describe them. This is not to say that the agent's account is necessarily inconsistent with the observer's description, but only that insofar as it is the agent's action it cannot be reduced to the latter. The intentions from which we act are not just

---

[21] For what remains one of the best contrasts between the observer's and agent's point of view see Stuart Hampshire, "Fallacies in Moral Philosophy," *Mind,* 68 (1949). Pp. 466-482.

[22] Gert, p. 17.

[23] Murdoch, p. 202.

further support for what we know to be right on other grounds, though they may at times be that. Rather the intentions that we embody as agents include the description of in fact what we are doing, providing what we do is rightly understood to be our act.

Contrary to Braithwaite's contention, my position is that the relation between thought and action is not causal but necessary. The literature surrounding this issue in recent philosophy has been immense, but for our purposes the primary point can be stated in a simple and largely non-controversial way. Our reasons for our actions are not the "cause" of our behavior; "causation" in this sense implies a contingent relation between the cause and effect as separable events.[24] From the agent's perspective, what I have done is not separable from the intention of my action including the motive. If I am asked what I am doing at this moment, I will respond that I am writing an essay and such description will not nor cannot be contingently related to my reason for acting since it is logically dependent on an accurate description of what I am doing. Put differently, the very condition of my being an agent is that the knowledge (reasons for) that I have of what I am doing is in fact what I am doing. My "reasons" do not "cause" me to act, but by embodying them I act to form the corresponding action.

This argument should not be construed as a warrant for solipsism or a vicious subjectivism. Nothing that has been said entails the impossibility of testing the appropriateness of the agent's description of what he claims to be doing.[25] Moreover the question of the precise relation between the "intention" and the "corresponding action" remains one of the most diffi-

---

[24]For an analysis of the ambiguous meaning of "cause" when used to describe the relation of reason to action see Alvin Goldman, *A Theory of Action* (New Jersey: Prentice-Hall, 1970), pp. 76-85; and Richard Bernstein, *Praxis and Action* (Philadelphia: U. of Pennsylvania Press, 1971).

[25]For example Hepburn suggests the adequacy of "fables" can be tested by their coherence, comprehensiveness, vividness and whether they back up what we know to be good. Nor would I deny that our highly personal stories can be universalized but it is not clear how helpful this is, for it seems to be true that the more specific (or higher) a maxim is the more the attempt to universalize it tends to make the principle trivial. Put another way the more the maxim tends to be the story appropriate to my particular biography that is distinguishable from basic moral presuppositions I share or should share with all men the less helpful the principle of universalizability becomes as a criterion of moral judgment. R. N. Hepburn, "Vision and Choice in Morality," in *Ramsey*, pp. 181-195.

cult problems that any ethics must face.[26] But at least this argument makes clear why no ultimate distinction can be made between an ethic of intention and an ethics of consequence; as Dewey correctly maintained, "the key to a correct theory of morality is recognition of the *essential unity of the self and its acts,* if the latter have any moral significance, while errors in theory arise as soon as the self and acts (and their consequences) are separated from each other, and moral worth is attributed to one more than to the other."[27]

Therefore there is no reason to claim with Braithwaite and Gert that intentions are only tangentially related to moral activity. An agent's description of his behavior in terms of his religious commitments cannot be isolated into the realm of motive without falsifying the nature of our intentionality. In other words I have argued that some philosophers, by bracketing the moral import of an action other than the one from the observer's standpoint that is universalizable, have been led by this methodology to falsify the relation of thought to action. The agent's description of the action is thus pushed into a realm of motivation only contingently related to what ethically he has done. This forces a wedge between thought and action that distorts the nature of moral behavior, especially as it relates to the conditions necessary for us to be moral agents.

The objection that the stories that inform our motives make no moral difference is therefore easily denied once we properly appreciate the intrinsic relation of the agent to his acts. For individual acts, it may of course be possible for the observer to subsume actions by different men under the same description. There may even be good moral reasons for doing this, since

---

[26]Of course involved in this statement hangs a good deal of the ambiguity of moral behavior in our time. For morality depends on being able to keep united the possible disjunction between our action (consequences) and our intention. But a highly differentiated society tends to drive a wedge between act and intention that makes the attribution of responsibility an extremely difficult matter. In one sense the importance of the principle of universalizability in current ethics is an attempt to provide a basis for a theory of obligation because we are no longer members of a morally coherent community that unites intention and circumstance in one description of the moral act.

[27]John Dewey, *Theory of the Moral Life* (New York: Holt, Rinehart, and Winston, 1967), pp. 150-151. Put in more traditional language the argument above concerning the relation of thought and action is the basis for Thomas' refusal to separate or give independence to the cardinal (natural) virtues is but to say that the virtues are the qualification of a single agent.

societies depend on a common stock of moral descriptions. But this does not conclusively establish the identity of acts within the ongoing character orientation of these men. For while the differences in their immediate descriptions of that action qua action may be irrelevant in the immediate context, it is not indifferent for the form of life they embody and the kind of actions they may be led to do or not do in the future.

However, this argument is not sufficient to sustain the point I am trying to make. For the philosopher may respond that he is not concerned with the reasons or description agents do give of their actions, but the description they should give as moral agents. Moreover there would seem to be sound reasons for this kind of response. It would be morally disastrous to warrant the idea that an agent is free to describe his action in any way he desires relative to the contingencies of his biography. The ethicist therefore claims that our actions should in-principle be open to description in accordance with a rule that is publicly defensible to other rational men. Our ethicist need not deny that men in fact embody metaphors and stories that they think inform them about what they are doing; he need only assert that these metaphors and stories are only ethically interesting insofar as they can be translated into universalizable rules. The ethicist may further recommend that it would be better if men determined their lives and action explicitly in terms of such rules rather than depending on these more fanciful aspects of their experience. In other words, this normative theory proposes that we should—even if we do not now—relegate the metaphors and stories we imaginatively entertain to the "motives" of our actions.

I have tried to suggest above why moral principles are not sufficient divorced from their incipient stories. However, the challenge at this point is how my stress on the agent's perspective can avoid ethical relativism. This is not a problem I can even begin to treat adequately; however, I will make some suggestions about it by analyzing the idea that religion is to morality as higher ethics or ideals are to basic morality.

Stories, Morality, and the Principle of Universalizability

In his essay "Social Morality and Individual Ideal," Strawson makes an important distinction between the realm of the ethical and the moral.[28] He associates the former with those aspects of our lives we identify with higher morality. The ethical includes ideal pictures of the good such as self-sacrifice, asceticism, human solidarity and cooperation. Such ideals often take the form of general descriptions about man and the world. These "visions of the ideal" may captivate our imagination even though they do not find expression in our life. Through our lifetime we may adhere to several such ideals even though they may be mutually incompatible, which is why the region of the ethical is characterized as where there are truths but no truth.

A widely accepted understanding of the region of the moral associates it with the idea of rules or principles governing human behavior, rules with universal application within a community or society. This idea of the moral is related to the ethical insofar as any ideal image, no matter what its form or content, demands for its realization the existence of some form of social organization. Thus the sphere of morality could be identified as the existence of some set of rules which command near universal acceptance if society is to exist. Strawson objects to this as an extremely minimal conception of morality; he maintains that a rule is not moral unless it is regarded as applying to all human beings, not just those in one society. "Moral behavior is what is demanded of men as such." [29] However, Strawson points out that the minimal understanding has the virtue of making clear that morality is essentially a function of social grouping; within such concrete contexts notions as conscientiousness, duty, and obligation are not abstractions but essential to our everyday behavior.[30]

The distinction between the realms of the ethical and the moral seems to provide a natural way to specify the relation between religion and morality, since theological ethics can be interpreted as dealing with the ethical while morality itself rests

---

[28]P. F. Strawson, "Social Morality and Individual Ideal," in *Ramsey,* pp. 280-298.

[29]Strawson, p. 285.

[30]He is of course directing this at Miss Anscombe's suggestion that our notion of duty and obligation no longer makes sense because they are intelligible only on the assumption of God's rule of the world. Strawson is hesitant to attribute quite the significance to the principle of universalizability that I do below, as he sees no reason why a system of moral demands characteristic of one social system should or could ever be found in every other. However he (291) also says that "certain human interests are so fundamental and so general that they must be universally acknowledged in some form and to some degree in any conceivable moral community."

on a basis open to all men irrespective of their theological convictions. Morality can be explicated by the principle of universalizability, since it involves the basic principles necessary for men to maintain their social existence. Higher morality, whether it has religious content or not, would concern those aspects of our moral behavior that have to do with our ideals, visions, and understanding of the nature and meaning of existence. Put another way, morality involves that behavior which is obligatory, religion that which is good (for Strawson).[31]

Gert's analysis of morality supports this understanding of the relation between morality and religion; he suggests that moral rules do not tell us to promote the good, but to avoid causing evil. For rational men can differ over what the good is, but reason demands that we avoid evil. Thus morality is concerned with the minimization of evil. Moral philosophy prevents people from doing what is morally wrong because they misunderstand morality.[32]   Religion, on the other hand, is concerned with those aspects of our existence where there is no moral obligation or morally right answer to a problem. "Religion seems to be to provide a positive guide to moral action in those cases where morality does not provide a clear answer."[33] There can properly be a Christian ethic or a Moslem ethic only for those matters where there is no morally right course of action. Thus there is a much better possibility of mounting persuasive arguments in the realm of morality than in the realm of the ethical.

There is an obvious natural relationship between the realm of the moral and the principle of universalizability. The heart of the universalizability argument is the attempt to exclude first-person or "singular exceptions" justifications of our failure to meet our moral obligations. Singer is quite right to identify the generalization principle—i.e., "What is right (or wrong) for one person must be right (or wrong) for any similar person in similar circumstances"—with traditional conceptions of fairness and

---

[31] For articles dealing generally with supererogation see J. O. Urmson, "Saints and Heroes," in Essays in Moral Philosophy, edited by A. I. Melden (Seattle: University of Washington Press, 1958), pp. 198-216; Joel Feinberg, "Supererogation and Ruler," in Ethics, pp. 291-411; and Roderick Chisholm, "Supererogation and Offense: A Conceptual Scheme for Ethics," in Ethics, pp. 412-429. Some of the criticisms I make below of the "higher-lower" scheme of relating religion and morality obviously owe much to their articles.

[32] Gert, pp. 29, 47, 142.

[33] Gert, p. 231.

justice.[34] Thus the principle of universalizability is a criterion of moral principles that everyone must acknowledge regardless of his status, peculiar biographical history, or the commitments and beliefs he holds.

Of course many have argued that the principle is not sufficient to this task because of its highly formal and procedural nature. For example, some of its forms seem to allow the universalization of rather monstrous maxims which are clearly contrary to our moral sensibilities.[35] Moreover, the principle seems to be able to justify mutually inconsistent maxims for one situation; this raises serious questions about its usefulness as a guide for moral behavior.

I suspect many theological ethicists have taken far too much comfort in such criticism, which seem to make the status of philosophical ethics as tenuous as its theological counterpart. While not denying the justice of many of the criticisms directed against the principle of universalizability, I think it is a serious mistake to rule it out on either philosophical or theological grounds. For what such criticisms often overlook is that the universalizability principle embodies this commitment: for basic aspects of our lives together, men should be considered as morally deserving just treatment regardless of their particular merits, culture, or station. In other words, the universalizability principle expresses the fundamental commitment to regard all men as constituting a basic moral community.[36] This should not be understood as an ideal that is to be achieved in some far off future; rather, it is a condition without which moral argument and judgment are not possible.

In this respect, the work of Rawls and Gert provide impressive counters to the suggestion that the universalizability principle, if true, is morally trivial.[37] For their analysis of the basis of moral behavior shows the deleterious implications of refusing to

---

[34]Markus Singer, *Generalization in Ethics* (New York: Knopf, 1961), p. 5.

[35]For example see C. C. N. Taylor's criticism of Hare in his "Critical Notice of R. M. Hare's *Freedom and Reason* in *The Definition of Morality,* edited by Wallace and Walker (London: Methuen, 1970), pp. 280-298.

[36]Charles Reynolds, "A Proposal for Understanding the Place of Reason in Christian Ethics," *Journal of Religion* (April, 1970), pp. 155-168.

[37]John Rawls, *A Theory of Justice* (Cambridge: Harvard U. Press, 1971). I do not mean to leave the impression that there are no significant differences between Gert's and Rawls' ethical theory. Moreover each has his own peculiar understanding of what I have called the principle of universalizability. For example Gert argues that the justification of a moral rule depends on its being "publicly advocated—i.e., when and

submit our moral arguments and judgments to the universalizability criterion. Moreover, Gert—through a deduction of
minimal moral rules—and Rawls—through an analysis of
justice—unpack certain implications for moral theory of the
principle of universalizability. So interpreted, the principle is
sufficient to establish the independence of morality from religion. It is a philosophical warrant to the trustworthiness of our
empirical knowledge that there are many good men who have
no religious convictions. Moreover, this does not present a
theological problem, as few theologians have tried to argue that
the good and just cannot be determined apart from God willing
it.[38] The whole natural law tradition is a sufficient indication
that theologically it has always been supposed that rational man
can know and do good on grounds independent of his knowledge of God.[39]

---

only when one regards all rational men as potential listeners and believers that they
all could accept the attitude being advocated." (p. 89) For an excellent review of *A
Theory of Justice* see Stuart Hampshire, A New Philosophy of the Just Society,"
New York Review of Books (February, 1972), pp. 26-33. Hampshire's brief criticism
of Rawls tends to suggest the line of thought I am developing. He says, "Rawls'
suggestion that rational choice of an unbiased social order, where individual differences are unknown and discounted, is the foundation for ordinary moral judgments is
a persuasive and powerful suggestion, and the fact that this reviewer cannot accept
his foundation for his moral judgments, because another possibility—the 'perfectionism' that Rawls discards—better fits his intuitions, reflects the fact that moral
opinion may differ; for the philosophical differences probably follow a difference of
emphasis in moral attitudes (39)." By "perfectionism" Hampshire means a picture of
the kind of character men should have that is admirable. Put in terms of political
philosophy Hampshire seems to be suggesting that Rawls' social contract theory is
mistaken to assume that right conduct is prior to and independent of the goodness of
persons. Hampshire has recently provided a more systematic presentation of this
point in his "Morality and Pessimism," *The New York Review of Books* (January,
1973), pp. 26-33.

[38]John Reeder in response to Patterson Brown's argument that the religious
believer commits himself to God's will as the standard of all moral judgments points
out that for Thomas' or Calvin's view, "God's will *is* the criterion of morality but
only in the sense that God, in his own mode of being, perfectly embodies (and
perhaps also exceeds) human standards of morality—not in the sense that God's will
stands over against all human criteria of morality or that for the believer something is
right simply because the divine being commands it." One of the disturbing aspects of
the discussion of the "supernaturalistic fallacy" is the simplistic view accepted by the
philosophers of the nature of religious morality. For example it is very rare to find
religious people appealing to God's will as a justification for their action. Rather they
make appeals to the kind of God He is, the attributes of His nature, or what He has
done that they consider appropriate to justify a whole way of life. "Patterson Brown
on God's Will as the Criterion of Morality," *Religious Studies*, 5: (pp. 235-242).

[39]Though it may not be immediately apparent it is my conviction that the
interpretation of the principle of universalizability I have offered is very similar to

It might be objected that I have now given up my claim for the specificity of theological ethics. I think this is not the case. First the principle of universalizability as I have interpreted it is a necessary condition of morality, not a sufficient condition. This means that any religious ethic that contradicted the principle would be suspect, but a theological ethic is not limited to what can be said morally using the principle as a criterion. But this also means that much of the work a theological ethicist does in many cultural contexts is not distinguishable from that of non-theological ethicists.

Secondly, though I have admitted that there is a realm of morality accessible to all men, it is not clear that this "realm" has a univocal content. It is a peculiar philosophical temption to think that if morality is objective it must be one thing, or at least have a single and simple basis.[40] However, although I have argued there is a sense in which morality is in some respects *sui generis,* i.e., irreducible to anything else, this does not exclude the possibility that morality "is an organic whole within which a number of originally independent tendencies may have contributed."[41] I am suggesting that crucial to the issue of the specificity of theological ethics is what kind of experience and aspects of our behavior are allowed to count as moral.

The content of morality is not exhausted by those principles and rules that are necessary for societal existence, for these must be and are embodied in beliefs and social practices. In their universalized and abstract form they provide an essential aspect of any morality, philosophical or theological. However as these moral rules and principles are embodied in story and actualized in moral behavior, they involve forms of life that are limited and limiting. For example, a rule against lying might be

---

some aspect of the classic understanding of natural law associated with Thomas. Natural law is one way of making clear the essential connection between man's rational and social nature. The relation between the principle of universalizability and natural law was obscured because of Kant's association of the principle with his extreme individualistic understanding of the autonomy of the self. Once it is understood that this view of the self is not a necessary correlate of the principle of universalizability the relation to natural law is more apparent. For an extremely suggestive article in this respect see David Little "Calvin and the Prospects of a Christian Theory of Natural Law," in *Norm and Context in Christian Ethics* (New York: Scribner's Sons, 1968), pp. 175-197.

[40]W. B. Gallie, *Philosophy and Historical Understanding* (New York: Schocken Books, 1964), pp. 192-211.

[41]Gallie, p. 195.

institutionalized in a society to include all behavior except that involving exchange of goods. The rule might be perfectly universalizable carrying the content of its particular social setting but yet in terms of the characterization of the practice of truth telling there would be no thought of its application to the economic sphere. In other words, in such a society the story associated with the rule not to lie is limited to specified personal relations between men. The example suggests that a higher morality may influence the form basic morality takes in a given social context by denoting areas where basic moral rules apply that are unspecified in the rule itself. If that is the case, then clearly the basic morality is not independent from the higher for either its form or its substance. One could change the story and thereby change the rule.

Though it might be thought that such an example is absurd, I suspect that our moral experience involves more limitations of this kind than we care to admit. Perhaps one reason a philosophical ethicist fails to recognize this involves his commitment to developing what might be called an "ideal basic morality," but such a morality does not exist. Moreover, it is by no means clear that how or what "rules necessary for societal existence" can be determined, for the description of such rules is relative to what is understood to count for social existence. I suspect that the development of an "ideal basic morality" is only possible by taking as normative one society at one historical point in time in order to determine what it requires for "bare" existence.

This is an extremely difficult and complex point to make without leading to confusion and error. Put another way however, I am trying to suggest that even if one allows a description of morality in terms of universalizability it still is not sufficient to account for the rules necessary for the existence of society. For a rule such as "Do not lie" does not in itself determine what kind of behavior counts as lying. Rules can illuminate the commitments we make, but they are not sufficient to determine our moral practices. It is at least not absurd to suggest that religion plays an important part in helping determine what kind of acts count as "lying," "killing," and other prohibitions and duties we consider to be basic for the existence of a good society.

If this point is correct, it would suggest that the understanding of religion and morality in terms of the separation between higher and lower morality is deficient, for religion can and does influence the form and substance of basic morality. However, it is equally true that the basic morality might also have forms independent of religion. In Strawson's categories these would be identified with the ethical. Contrary to Gert, no morality is sufficient for societal life that merely aims at preventing evil. For every society must necessarily try to provide ways of encouraging men to do the good, to create institutions of basic trust, if that society is to survive. For example we are not just obligated by our society not to lie; we are held accountable to tell the truth. Though it would be tempting for the theological ethicist to empty as much substance as possible from the idea of basic morality in order to substantiate the importance of the higher morality, this would be a mistake. For every society's basic morality (rather than minimal, for these are not the same thing) involves much that in principle must be considered essential to and part of the realm of the ethical.

It should now be clear that my concentration on the importance of stories and metaphors for the moral life avoids any implication of a vicious relativism. A "higher" ethic may be different from a basic morality, but it cannot contradict it and be viable. Put differently, even though moral principles are not sufficient in themselves for our moral existence, neither are stories sufficient if they do not generate principles that are morally significant. Principles without stories are subject to perverse interpretation (i.e., they can be used in immoral stories), but stories without principles will have no way of concretely specifying the actions and practices consistent with the general orientation expressed by the story.

II.
The New Morality
and Normative Ethics

5.

Aslan and the New Morality

I

A scene from *The Silver Chair*,[1] the fourth book of C. S.
Lewis' classic children's stories of the land of Narnia, is suggestive for assessing some themes that have become associated with
the "renewal of moral theology." The scene takes place far
underground in the kingdom ruled by the wicked Witch, the
Queen of Underland. The mighty lion Aslan, creator and protec-
tor of Narnia, has called to Narnia two children of our world,
Jill and Scrubb; their task is to find Prince Rilian, who has been
kidnapped by the Witch. This is an extremely important mission, for Prince Rilian's father is near death, and unless the
Prince is returned, Narnia will soon be without a king.

During their perilous search for the prince the children are
joined by Puddleglum, a Marsh-wiggle. Marsh-wiggles have long
arms and legs, bodies as small as dwarves, and webbed hands
and feet. Although Puddleglum is an extreme pessimist, this
does not stop him from doing what he thinks duty demands. As
our scene opens, Jill, Scrubb, and Puddleglum have found their
way to Prince Rilian, whom the evil queen has held captive and
placed under a spell so that he no longer remembers that he
comes from Narnia in the Overworld. Rather, he thinks he is
king of the Underworld in the service of a beautiful and kind
queen whose armies he will soon lead against the people of
Narnia. However, each day the Prince has a "fit" during which
he assumes his true identity as a Narnian; Jill, Scrubb, and
Puddleglum free him from the witch's spell by cutting the
bonds that bind him to the Silver Chair in which she restrains
him during these "fits."

Just as this feat has been accomplished, the Queen herself
enters and Prince Rilian announces his intention to return to

---

[1]C. S. Lewis, *The Silver Chair* (London: Bles 1964), pp. 155-167.

the Overworld as heir to the throne of Narnia. Rather than trying to overpower him and his three new friends by force, the Witch puts some green powder on the fire, begins to play a musical instrument, and engages them in conversation. She begins by politely asking where Narnia is. To their dismay, the children have a difficult time answering; "up" turns out to be a very indefinite "place" indeed. The children are almost convinced that Narnia must exist only in dreams; suddenly Puddleglum, who is sure he will never see Narnia again, insists it is there because he remembers having seen the sun. But the Queen asks what the word "sun" means, and the best the children can do is compare it to a large lamp hanging from the roof. When the queen asks from what the sun hangs, she again creates enough doubt for the children to think that the sun too may only exist in a dream. As the Queen says, "Your *sun* is a dream; and there is nothing in that dream that was not copied from the lamp. The lamp is the real thing; the *sun* is but a tale, a children's story."

Jill, however, with one last effort asserts, "There's Aslan."

"Aslan?" said the Witch, quickening ever so slightly the pace of her thrumming. "What a pretty name! What does it mean?"

"He is the great Lion who called us out of our own world," said Scrubb, "and sent us into this to find Prince Rilian."

"What is a *lion*?" asked the Witch.

"Oh hang it all!" said Scrubb. "Don't you know? How can we describe it to her? Have you ever seen a cat?"

"Surely," said the Queen. "I love cats."

"Well a lion is a little bit—only a little bit, mind you—like a huge cat—with a mane. At least, it's not like a horse's mane, you know, it's more like a judge's wig. And it's yellow. And terrifically strong."

The Witch shook her head. "I see," she said, "that we should do no better with your *lion*, as you call it, than we did with your *sun*. You have seen lamps, and so you imagined a bigger and better lamp and called it the *sun*. You have seen cats, and now you want a bigger and better cat, and it's to be called a *lion*. Well, 'tis a pretty make-believe, though, to say the truth, it would suit you all better if you were younger. And look how you can put nothing into your make-believe without copying it from the real world, this world of mine, which is the only world. But even you children are too old for such play. As for you, my lord Prince, thou art a man full grown, fie upon you! Are you not ashamed of such toys? Come all of you. Put away these childish tricks. I have work for you all in the real world.

There is no Narnia, no Overworld, no sky, no sun, no Aslan. And now, to bed all. And let us begin a wiser life tomorrow. But first, to bed; to sleep; deep sleep, soft pillows, sleep without foolish dreams."

The Prince and the two children were standing with their heads hung down, their cheeks flushed, their eyes half closed; the strength all gone from them; the enchantment almost complete. But Puddleglum, desperately gathering all his strength walked over to the fire. Then he did a very brave thing. He knew it wouldn't hurt him quite as much as it would hurt a human; for his feet (which were bare) were webbed and hard and cold-blooded like a duck's. But he knew it would hurt him badly enough; and so it did. With his bare foot he stamped on the fire, grinding a large part of it into ashes on the flat hearth. And three things happened at once.

First, the children and the Prince were awakened, since the fire was put out and the smell of burnt Marsh-wiggle is enough to awaken anyone. Secondly, the witch cried out in a voice that was quite different than the sweet tones she had been using up until then. And finally, the pain made Puddleglum's head clear so that he could say exactly what he thought.

"One word, Ma'am," he said, coming back from the fire; limping, because of the pain. "One word. All you've been saying is quite right, I shouldn't wonder. I'm a chap who always likes to know the worst and then put the best face I can on it. So I won't deny any of what you said. But there's one thing more to be said, even so. Suppose we *have* only dreamed, or made up, all those things—trees and grass and sun and moon and stars and Aslan himself. Suppose we have. Then all I can say is that, in that case, the made-up things seem a good deal more important than the real ones. Suppose this black pit of a kingdom of yours *is* the only world. Well it strikes me as a pretty poor one. And that's a funny thing, when you come to think of it. We're just babies playing a game, if you're right. But four babies playing a game can make a play-world which licks your real world hollow. I'm on Aslan's side even if there isn't any Aslan to lead it. I'm going to live as like a Narnian as I can even if there isn't any Narnia. So, thanking you kindly for your supper, if these two gentlemen and the young lady are ready, we're leaving your court at once and setting out in the dark to spend our lives looking for Overland. Not that our lives will be very long, I should think; but that's small loss if the world's as dull a place as you say."

The witch cannot bear the truth; at the end of this speech, she turns into her true form as a snake whose head the Prince manages to cut off after a horrible struggle.

By way of commentary on this scene, I will suggest in this essay that in our enthusiasm for the "new moral theology" we have come very close to assuming that only lamps and cats are real and that the sun and lions are to be forgotten as playthings of a child-like past. For we have forgotten that the self must be transformed if we are to see the world as it is, and that the transformation into loving persons is not accomplished overnight by declaring our good intentions but by submitting patiently to the suffering which makes us real. We have impoverished our ethics by assuming that our lives can easily embody and reflect the good. In our moral behavior, we have tacitly accepted existence in a world where Aslan does not exist; in such a world, witches often appear beautiful and kind. Such a situation is all the more pernicious because we claim to base our self-imposed blindness on love, kindness, justice and even Jesus Christ. The main purpose of this essay is to try to locate some of the problems that have led us to confuse illusion with reality, for only when we understand the nature of our self-deception can we begin to appreciate that we belong to the land of the sun.

The kind of problems I am going to attack are not to be identified with any one or several moral theologians. I am much more interested in a general mood that surrounds current ethical reflection and behavior; at times this attitude is mirrored in or encouraged by the work of professional Christian ethicists. Of course, there is great danger in directing my critique at a mood; moods are notoriously hard to pin down. But a pervasive illusion demands a serious attack, even if the enemy is nebulous and elusive.

I am particularly concerned about three problems: (1) the potential of the new moral theology because of its highly general character to be captured by conceptions of the good alien to the Gospels, (2) the tendency to confuse apologetics with ethics, and (3) the reduction of ethical issues to pastoral-psychological questions. I do not think these problems are endemic to the Roman Catholic context, for they arise from general ethical assumptions which are widely shared today. However, Roman Catholics have tended to be particularly susceptible to these problems because they seem to believe in a popular version of their peculiar moral history.

II

This history begins with an account of a very dark age when every aspect of a Catholic's behavior was dominated by a legalistic and authoritarian moral structure. Such an ethic was inhuman, since its concern was only for the multiplication of laws rather than the development of good men. Besides being legalistic, it was excessively judgmental and encouraged a minimalistic understanding of the duties of the Christian life. Man's nature during this time was understood primarily in static terms, with no appreciation of the relativity of our cultural and historical positions. As a result, ethics and the moral life of Christians were divorced from any relation to Scripture and fundamental theology.

But beginning with Pope John and the Council, continues the legend, a new age has been ushered in, marking a radical discontinuity with the repression of the past. Amid refrains such as "Love is the only absolute" and "Christ is the new law," Roman Catholic moral theology and behavior have turned the corner toward a fuller and more morally worthy Christian ethic. Love, *agape,* is now taken as the center, source, and motivation of all moral activity. Ethics must serve the person, for law and norms are significant only as they contribute to the increased humanity of our individual lives. The ethical man is the dynamic agent, not he who only seeks to do what the law requires. A moral life so conceived and so practiced denotes the return to Scripture and fundamental theology, for faith and ethics are not two independent spheres but two sides of the same coin.

While I am sure this account of Roman Catholic ethical thought and behavior is not wholly incorrect, it does tend to oversimplify the picture. At least it seems advisable to make a distinction between the actual practice of the moral life among Catholics and the theoretical exposition of that life found in the textbooks. For it may well be that the tradition and practice embodied in the Church's liturgy and common life are richer than its explicit moral theology. It seems odd that Catholics who are the inheritors of such a rich liturgical and spiritual tradition still associate theology and ethics exclusively with the explicit intellectual formulations of their theologians. Even within Catholic moral theology, the disastrous textbook caricature is not wholly representative. Certainly any sensitive reading of the scholastic tradition gives one quite a different impression of the vitality of Catholic moral reflection.

But this objection to the above account of the development of Catholic ethics is somewhat beside the point. For the account is now so pervasive that its sheer numerical acceptance seems to confirm its truth. Thus I am concerned with the account not primarily because it distorts history, but rather because its acceptance produces the disastrously vague character of the new moral theology. For now any ethics that attempts to dictate or suggest norms for moral behavior is automatically condemned as reactionary. The modern ethical task seems to consist of suggesting compelling slogans which can encompass all kinds of manners of life. The problem with such platitutdes is not that they are wrong, but that they lull us into thinking we know, when we know nothing.

Thus in contemporary Catholic ethics we find such recommendations as these: Christian behavior is fundamentally conformity to Christ; the Christian ethic is the ethic of love; we as Christians should conform to God's dynamic action in the world; natural law "is a *dynamic existing reality,* an ordering of man towards his self-perfection and his self-realization, through all the concrete situation of his life and in intersubjective dialog with his fellow man and with God."[2] But we are never told what attitudes, dispositions, or motives are appropriate to conformation to Christ; what actions or classes of action are enjoined or prohibited by Christian love; how we are to distinguish God's action in the world from that which is not God's; or, finally, what sense it makes to claim that such an interpretation of natural law is a "law" at all. These questions reveal that with broad theological affirmations one has only begun to do theological ethics, for the behavioral significance or specification of such claims is by no means clear. If such affirmations are ever to be more than homiletical flourishes, their concrete implications must be drawn with greater clarity and detail.

If this is not done, the great danger is that we will fill the void with unexamined and perhaps even perverse content. For ethical reflection may exist in a highly abstract form, but men cannot. We must decide to stay married or celibate, to fight in war or not to fight, to teach our children this rather than that.

---

[2]Louis Monden, *Sin, Liberty, and Law* (New York: Sheed and Ward, 1965), p. 89.

If "love" or "being in Christ" does not inform these decisions, then we will make them on some other basis. Most of us simply take our cues in these matters from the accepted values and practices of our social context. As finite beings we simply do not have the time or moral energy to examine every such decision we must make. While this is unavoidable, it does point to the significance of what society we identify with; unless we are sure that we are living in the Overland rather than the Underland, we cannot assume that our decisions are related in even a tangential way to what the Scripture means by "being in Christ" or manifesting Christian "love." The problem is not that a Christian ethic does not find its center in Christ; modern ethicists are correct in this affirmation. But we cannot lightly assume that this affirmation can easily be associated with our concrete life.

In this respect, the divorce of moral theology from confessional practice may have an unanticipated effect. Despite its tendency toward minimalism and scrupulosity, the moral theology of the confessional had the virtue of being concrete. As the new moral theology has become more concerned with the "whole person" and his "entire life," in great danger of becoming a justification for ways of life that are fundamentally foreign to Christian theology, it has sacrificed any mechanism to test concretely the relation of our explicit theological claims with the ways of life assumed to be warranted by them. Thus these claims may become but an ideological justification for practices that are based on different presuppositions about the nature of the world. That this may already be occurring in moral theology is suggested by the fact that Christians are now entertaining the possibility that killing can be a loving act or that adultery can take on the form of Christ. We need not be surprised at this; Christians have long known that witches may appear beautiful and sin enticing. What is new is our forgetting that underneath the beauty lies a snake.

III

Another indication of the vacuous character of moral theology is what I would call the "politicization of the moral." By this I mean that many Christians seem to think one's primary response to moral questions is to take a "liberal" or "conservative" stance. Thus contraception is no longer discussed in terms of the moral nature of marriage and sexuality; rather, one is offered the opportunity of being either for or against *Humanae Vitae*. Being "for" is associated with the legalism and authoritarianism of the past; being "against" makes one a participant in the love and freedom of the "wave of the future." Both sides assume that it is no longer possible to discuss moral questions in terms of rightness or wrongness since the issue has already been emptied of moral content or context. However, I am arguing that to be a good man demands that one be neither liberal or conservative but willing to do the right.

The problem of the possible ideological perversion of the "new morality" is compounded by the tendency to confuse ethics and apologetics—the temptation in the name of relevance to baptize the secular for the glory of God. The tremendous thirst for relevance among theologians and Christians today is understandable, but that makes it no less destructive of the Christian ethical life and reflection. The new morality is a response to the feeling that the church has misled the world by its stubborn defense of a system of unintelligible symbols and of values eroded beyond recognition. It is naturally assumed that the way to expurge our guilt in this respect is by fondly embracing "modern man's self-understanding." Many reason that if Christ's redemption is universal, then the non-Christian man of good will may even have greater moral insight than the Christian himself. Thus the Christian's job is now to catch up with the more progressive morality of those outside the church.

Thus John Milhaven says that while Christ's love is still the heart of the Christian life,

in keeping with contemporary thinking, "love" means something new. Love is no longer basically a trusting submission that searches out God's universal laws for human behavior and institutions. ... Rather the new trend sees God leaving it completely up to man as to how things turn out. Christian "love," therefore, comes to mean that a man takes from God into his own hands all responsibility for what happens. It is up to him, not God, to figure out what will be good for those concerned and how this good can be realized, just as it is up to him, not God, to act and make the good a reality. In this sense, it can be said that the new Christian love proceeds as it would *etsi deus non daretur,* even if there were no God. Facing his responsibility, the Christian sees himself "having come of age" and now "condemned to freedom."

As theology follows the way of American thinking today, the contemporary vision of Christian responsibility is pragmatic and empirical. Responsibility means responsibility for consequences as they take place in human experience.[3]

While I have some question as to how Milhaven is so sure he has identified "contemporary thinking" or "American thinking today," my primary concern is with the further question: given such a description of the content of the contemporary mind, why does Milhaven assume this should be taken as normative. Can one assume that "modern man" is free of the perversities that have characterized man from the beginning? It is interesting that Milhaven seems to glorify the naive optimistic faith that men can be completely rational and free—just at the time when "modern man" seems to be developing a new appreciation of the limits of his power. Perhaps a theology and ethics that seeks to be relevant as its first order of business always tends to be relevant to that consciousness and society that have just ceased to exist.

However, the more serious objection to this form of moral theology is that it fails in its very intention. Such a moral theology cannot be apologetic, for it has nothing to bring to the dialogue; it announces to the secular world, as though by way of discovery, what the secular world has been announcing to it for a rather long time.[4] What we have here is not apologetics, but capitulation. As such, it betrays only the task of Christian ethics, but also the "modern man" it wishes to address. For such a man exists only in rhetoric. Modern man is not faced with infinite possibilites, but with questions such as whether he should work to sustain his marriage, how to find meaning in his work, and what he should do with his time. We are not "men come of age;" like men of any age, we must learn to see ourselves without the grand illusion that we create ourselves or the good. We need an ethic which will help us learn the language[5] and propose forms of the moral life that help us

---

[3]John Milhaven, "The Behavioral Sciences and Christian Ethics," in *Projectives: Shaping An American Theology for the Future*, edited by O'Meara and Weisser (New York: Doubleday, 1970), p. 138.

[4]For a similar argument see Alasdair MacIntyre, *The Religious Significance of Atheism* (New York: Columbia U. Press, 1969).

[5]For a suggestive analysis of the relation of language and ethics see Herbert McCabe, *What Is Ethics All About* (Washington: Corpus Books, 1969); and my "Situation Ethics, Moral Notions, and Theological Ethics," Chapter 1.

escape our illusions and see ourselves, others, and the world with justice and humility.

The basis and aim of the moral life is to see the truth, for only as we see correctly can we act in accordance with reality. Even though the good can be embodied in our choices, we do not create it through our choices. However, we are not able to "see" the good simply by looking; to be man is to create and love illusion, for few of us can bear long to look at the sun. [6] Our vision must be trained and disciplined in order to free it from our neurotic self-concern and the assumption that conventionality defines the real. Ethics is that modest discipline which uses careful language, distinctions, and stories to break the intellectual bewitchment that would have us call lamps the sun and adultery love. Christian ethics is the systematic investigation of the astounding claim that the world and our self is only rightly seen and intended in the light of what God has done in the person and work of Jesus Christ, for Narnia is real exactly because Aslan has created and sustained it through his sacrificial love.

It is only on such a basis that Christian ethics can provide a basis for a proper apologetics or be relevant in a significant sense. For if it accepts the subtle and enticing temptation to take as normative the current accounts of reality, it only ensnarls men further in the darkness of the Underworld. We cannot start with the question of what modern man will accept as true; we must begin with the nature and content of the true and good, whether such a man will accept it or not. An apologetic that is not first based on truth is but propaganda.

I suspect that Christians are always tempted in this respect because they consider themselves charged with the task of convincing others of the truth. But the modern forms of this essential task are a clear witness to our bad faith, for they often represent the desperate attempt of an unsure minority to substantiate their own doubts by calling unbelief "faith" and sin "righteousness." We must face the possibility that the apologetics of a true and faithful conception of the Christian life may create not more but fewer men who will walk in the way.

---

[6]Iris Murdoch, *The Sovereignty of Good* (New York: Schocken, 1971).

IV

Another confusion similar to the identification of ethics with apologetics is the assumption that an ethical response is the same as pastoral compassion. I think I can best illustrate what I mean through an example. Suppose a man comes to his pastor to confess his intimate involvement with a woman other than his wife. The pastor discovers that this man's marriage has never been happy, his wife has always been frigid, and he has tolerated this situation for some time before his current infidelity. Moreover, he did not actively seek to betray his wife; rather, the affair developed from a friendship with one of the secretaries in his office. Their mutual interests (both Cub fans), their natural rapport, their genuine caring for each other finally led them to share a bed.

A practitioner of the old morality would have little difficulty knowing how to respond to this case. It is clear the man is an adulterer; he should submit to due punishment and break off the affair immediately. However, pastorally this surely seems to be an inhuman and insensitive way of dealing with this person. For, in fact, this indiscretion has changed his whole life by giving him new insight into genuine human interdependence. It is as if he has discovered the world for the first time: colors are brighter, birds really sing, and life is genuinely worth living. Moreover, the same is true for his beloved. Rather than judging this to be a grievous sin, the spiritual counselor must see it as a positive good; surely God wills such human fulfillment. I suspect that many consider this positive response to be the truly moral one; it seems to respect all the human complexities involved in the situation.

Yet I think that there is good reason why this latter response should not be considered ethically sufficient. First, such a "compassionate" response amounts to a denial of the significance of language for our understanding of ethical situations. If every act is open to redescription in terms of being a "loving" or "good" act, then ethically we have come to live in a land where the sun is but a large lamp. Let me be very clear about this. I am not saying that we must at all costs maintain that this is an adulterous act in order to point a judgmental finger at this man. My point is that unless we are clear about what has gone on here, we will not be able to minister to this man at all, at least not to minister to him in the name of Jesus Christ. Ironically, when the ethical is completely identified with pastoral compassion, then there is no basis for pastoral concern.

For example, if we say to this man that he really has not committed adultery but done a "loving" thing, then we sell short his moral capabilities. For to insist on describing his action as adultery is to raise a whole range of questions that might not otherwise be considered. For example, what is his obligation to his wife? How has he contributed over the years to the emptiness that is their marriage? What should the significance of sexual intercourse be for the development of a morally healthy marriage? How has he contributed to his wife's inadequacy in this regard? Finally, if he intends to divorce his wife and marry his current love, how is the nature of such a "marriage" to be understood morally? (Of course remarriage may ultimately be chosen. Ethics does not finally dictate what the decision must be. Rather ethics tries to explicate what must be considered in the decision so that whatever decision he makes will have greater moral substance. For surely if a second marriage is necessary it will be more substantive if it recognizes the cloudy history from which it was born rather than assuming it is based on the happy innocence of love.)

Obviously, these are not questions calculated to increase the pastoral subject's current happiness; nevertheless, they are significant questions that offer him the possibility of deepening his own moral stance. They are pain-causing questions, to be sure, but we humans, like Marsh-wiggles, cannot stomp on the fires of illusion without pain. To face reality is to confront our comfortable assumptions: that the primary moral good is to be happy, that such happiness is attainable, and that this happiness can satisfy our being. These are illusions which ignore the fact that we become good only to the extent we are willing to sacrifice and suffer. It is indeed painful to lose such illusions, but only through such painful enlightenment can we appreciate how wonderful it is that lions are different from cats, and that marriage excludes adultery.

I am well aware that this is at odds with many current assumptions about the ethics of interpersonal relations. The new morality sees the acceptance of the other as the good. It urges us to go out to the other genuinely in an attempt to understand him for the unique being he is. It tells us we are out of order if we judge him by abstract norms irrelevant to the contingencies of his situation; rather, we should help him accept his situation so that he can come to a fuller realization of his humanity. For the aim of the moral life, according to these ethicists, is not the good but adjustment, to be able to accept oneself for what one is. Such an ethic represents the triumph of the therapeutic over the moral. Guilt is not an appropriate response to a bad act, but a puritan inhibition to be expurged because it limits my capacity for being fully human. Suffering is not the condition necessary to clear our vision so we can stand to see the inhumanity we inflict on others, but an evil avoidable if we are uncommitted, nonjudgmental, and open to all.

Such a view of the moral life is extremely compelling. It seems to embody the basic human virtues of compassion, kindness, openness, and sensitivity. But it is actually an ethic of sentimentality as it assumes that persons should be accepted in indifference to what they are or have done. (Of course, to point to wrongdoing is not always the same as blaming the person responsible for it.) Acceptance and personalism in such a context condemn the other to his own self-limitations in discerning and achieving the happy life. "Kindness" so understood is but our unwillingness to make our self and the other uncomfortable because the truth has been spoken. Finally, they destroy the significance of human action, for what a person is and does no longer count for anything. Christians today have developed a morbid fear of guilt; we will go to any lengths to avoid admitting that we ourselves or another is truly evil. But only as we are willing to judge the other can we show a true respect for him as a person. For by judgment we accept him as one capable of growth. By speaking the truth in love, we help him face the fact that in loving one he has hated the other; only through such a painful perception can he recognize depths to life which he had not previously seen. If an ethic of "personalism" does not entail a normative conception of what we can and ought to be, then it is but a claim that what we are is good. This is humanism which should not be disguised with the label of "Christian" ethics.

V

This new emphasis that acceptance of the other is good in itself entails a parallel conception of God. God is viewed as the great understander, the paradigm liberal, who perceives all (he reads all the latest counseling theory) and is committed to nothing. He is the All-forgiving who, in the nature of love, excludes no one from eternal beatitude, no matter how perverse the candidate might be. It is hard to comprehend how such a God of eternal kindness could ever have ended up on a cross; surely the formation of sensitivity groups would have been a more effective strategy. Here we no longer have a God who invites men to participate in a kingdom of righteousness where citizenship requires obedience; the "modern" God can have no kingdom at all, since there can be no possible boundaries to his love. To believe or not to believe in such a God makes little difference, since by definition we live in a universe where the pain that difference necessarily occasions is excluded. Yet such a world is also of little interest; in it we could not appreciate how wonderful it is that we have suns and not just big lamps, suffering and judgment and not just happiness.

We all feel uneasy with a position that might entail judgment of another, for we know how great is our own weaknesses. We all seem caught today in the modern form of self-righteousness of the "I am guiltier than you" form. Moreover we know how easily we can perversely turn right judgment into means of imposing our arbitrary will on others. The safeguard against such perversion, however, is not to refrain from judgment but to base our judgment on ethical grounds that make our bio-graphical limitations irrelevant. For our moral judgments toward others and theirs toward us are good just to the extent that we can give reasons for the judgment beyond our own first-person involvement. It is our ability to articulate our cri-teria of judgment and to clarify their significance for our lives together that raises the judgmental situation above the morals of our subjectivities.

In the name of a more humane ethic, contemporary Christian ethics downgrades principles, rules, criteria and institutions; this move is ironical since it is just such objective realities which enable us to be humane. For inhumanity toward another is the imposition of our will for no reason beyond our possession of power. In such an ethic, all moral relations become variations of a master-slave relation rendered all the more perverse because it is done in the name of love. Only as we can enunciate the basis of our judgments and articulate disciplined moral arguments can our relations with others rise above the shallowness and arbitrariness of our individual interests.

Thus the ethicist seeks and analyzes possible criteria for moral judgments that can receive substantiation beyond our subjective adherence to them. This quest is not aimed at defining in a narrow way the limits of human behavior, the "do's" and "don't's" of human life. Rather, it is an attempt to make us alive to the basis for creative human interaction. For only as we can meet the other on common grounds of a more substantive humanity than either of us embodies can our relations ever be freed from the aggression we perpetrate on each other in the hope of gaining a more secure position. Of course, the objectivity of moral criteria and institutions is always in danger of legalistic perversion, but our salvation from legalism cannot come about by simply raising the status of our own subjectivities.

The objectivity of moral argument is ultimately dependent on the shared commitments and values of a community. There is no heavenly realm of values that exist independent of their embodiment in human agents and institutions. Rather, values are shared by these men in this place in and through their common experience. The ultimate appeal in any argument can therefore only be the appeal to the wisdom of the community's experience as it is found in our inherited language, practices, and institutions. Such shared experience grounds the authority necessary to sustain the community's moral life. For the function of authority is to speak back to the community its basic commitments by enunciating concrete goals and norms for united action. It is only when such a community ceases to exist that the voice of authority takes the form of authoritarianism, and coercion is required to force consent. For true authority calls forth the willing obedience of its subjects; it wills the good that unites the one exercising authority with the subject in common action.

This point is particularly important in relation to the divisive discussion associated with *Humanae Vitae*. For the debate reveals that the church lacks the kind of community of commitment that would make such a discussion edifying rather than destructive. In such a context, what we have is a power struggle rather than genuine ethical argument. This places a specially heavy burden on those who dissent, for they must try to formulate their arguments in a way that will increase the possibility of genuine authority being exercised in the church. We must remember that ultimately the important question is not about the licit use of contraception but about the nature of the Christian community necessary to sustain moral judgment that does not kill but makes alive.

Even though I am on the whole sympathetic with those who dissent from *Humanae Vitae*, I am often troubled by the form their arguments take. For their position is often based on the assumption that the church should respect the right of the individual conscience in moral matters, that it is a betrayal of moral autonomy for the church to impose such demands on the individual. But if the right of the individual conscience is given such authority on a matter like contraception, then on what basis does the church command obedience about how Christians should regard persons of another color? Let us be careful that in our concern to "win" this particular skirmish we do not employ means that will destroy the basis for genuine authority on issues that are at the heart of a people who are called to be Christian.

VI

This issue finally uncovers the problem that is most crucial for contemporary reflection in Christian ethics. Even though I think the issues I have discussed are important, they are only symptoms of a much deeper problem. They do not reach down to the heart of Christian existence or behavior. This does not mean that it is not significant to clarify and analyze the Christian moral life, but philosophical discussion only begins to deal with the problems it confronts.

For theological ethics is not a "creative" discipline; rather, it is parasitical on the form of the moral life that Christian men and women act out in their historical context. Christian ethics cannot create the form of Christian life and existence, it can only analyze and conceptually articulate what Christians have found to be the nature of the good in their actual living. I suspect that contemporary Christian ethics is superficial precisely because it is an all-too-faithful witness to the shallowness of our own individual lives.

Because we consider ourselves modern men, our Christian

ethics has uncritically accepted the presumptuous assumptions of modern humanism and embodies them in a thinly veiled form. In the name of love, the new morality warrants the idea that the moral life is primarily the securing of our own happiness, "Christian ethics" can do this because that is what we each assume. Christian ethics in the interest of "personalism" avoids any judgmental form because none of us wishes to be judged and found wanting. Christian ethics in the name of "ethical sensitivity" pays little attention to the nature of moral argument because few of us wish to take up the demanding task of defending our positions with rigor and clarity; we are content with the noncommital mediocrity of "it seems to me." Christian ethics tends to identify all authority with authoritarianism because we do not wish to lay down our individual wills for the good common to a Christian community.

I know of no solution for such a problem. For theological and anthropological reasons I distrust all suggestions that imply that all we need to do is try harder. Our problems and our weaknesses are of a far too fundamental nature to assume they can be resolved by moral effort for such effort only continues to confirm us in our illusion of self-significance. Change will come only when we are compelled by an object that is so true, beautiful, and good that we forget about our petty efforts and genuinely look at the other. Christians assume such an object exists and has taken the compelling form of Jesus of Nazareth. But such an object no longer compels us because we assume that we no longer need redemption or that such a God can redeem us. For we assume and we form our lives with the assumption that to love the world and the other can be done without pain and guilt.

We may not be able to become a redeemed people, but at least we can try to write our moral theology more honestly. We can stop trying to justify the trivialities of our own existence as warranted by the Gospel. If we do that, we may find that even though we are not yet living Christian lives, we are at least on the road to the beginning of what such a life might look like. Unless we allow ourselves to face the reality of life with its pain, suffering, death, wounds, heroism and cowardice, how are we ever to draw near to the fire that is the cross? One cannot draw near to such an object without picking up some painful splinters, but it is through such pain that we find that, by Aslan's mane, there is a joy possible in this life greater than we ever imagined, there is a reality that finally "licks our 'real' world hollow." To the world, a people possessed of such joy will surely appear mad. They may even be strapped down in silver chairs of understanding in order to cure them of their "reality disorientation." Yet this surely is no great price to pay if this world is in fact as "dark and dull as it appears to be," and Aslan is as real and interesting as we find him in his death and resurrection.

6.

Love's Not All You Need

Perhaps the most striking contrast between the new and the old morality is the latter's concentration on law and rules and the former's stress on love as the essence of morality. The new morality claims that the central core of Christian ethics and the Christian life is not a stubborn adherence to rules, or unthinking obedience to the authoritative teachings of the church, but rather that we as Christians should be loving in a way that neither rules nor teachings can embody. Or to state the contrast more vividly we can employ Fletcher's example from the movie *The Rainmaker:* it seems that the old morality was often so full of what is right, it could not see the good done in love because sometimes the good involved sexual intercourse outside marriage.

Thus by emphasizing love as the center of the Christian moral life the new morality tries to strike a stance that is more open and sensitive to the ambiguity of our moral experience. Put more theoretically the situation ethicists are suggesting: (1) that love is the single norm that determines the right-making characteristics of moral action and judgment; and (2) that love is both a general attitude and criteria of actions that is sufficient as a guide for our actual moral behavior.

Though many of us may have some disagreements with aspects of the "new morality" I suspect that this emphasis on love as the essence of Christian behavior strikes us as correct. This is significant because the "new morality" is not just a systematic statement by theologians, but it is much more a description of what indeed we think the moral life is like. The influence of "situation ethics" has not been due to Joseph Fletcher's publishing a book by that title, but because the book articulates for us what we have found to be true about the moral life before we read the book. That is why the influence of "situation ethics" has been so great even though Fletcher's presentation of it has been intellectually destroyed.[1] For in spite of the arguments against it there is much about his main emphasis that strikes us as being right.

I suspect this is especially true in respect to Fletcher's contention that love is the primary hallmark of the Christian life. We know that we are seldom confronted with a situation that can be determined in accordance with some law or rule. The moral life requires a flexibility that only love can guide, as the object of morality is not, or should not be, the conforming to a law, but meeting the needs of the other person with concern and understanding. We have learned that the following of a rule morality tends to be minimalistic and self-serving, fostering self-righteousness at the expense of charity and compassion. Thus to be good we should not ask what the law demands, but rather what we should do to meet the demands of love in this situation. For to ask the question of love denotes willingness to give of the self—to be open to the other's wishes and wants, to see the other as a genuine person—and surely such giving is the very essence of what it means to be good.

Moreover these insights embodied in the ethics of love seem to do more justice to the nature of the Gospel message itself. For in the New Testament we see no angry God of a small people laying down the law as if they were children, but a loving Father who wills to sacrifice himself for the good of mankind. God's revelation of himself in Christ denotes that he is not some abstract God who ties his destiny up with our destiny even to sacrificing himself for us. Thus it seems entirely appropriate to claim that the very essence of God is love, and that the essence of Christian ethics and life is love's response to this great love.

Yet as persuasive as this emphasis on love appears, it is my intention to argue that there are serious deficiencies with this account of the nature of Christian ethics and Christian moral behavior. I want to make my case both theologically and ethically, for it is my conviction that this emphasis on love is bad theology which results in bad ethics, or it is bad ethics that results in bad theology. This point is important as it indicates that our view of the practical must be constantly tested by our

---

[1]For example see the essays in *Norm and Context in Christian Ethics* edited by Outka and Ramsey (New York: Scribner's, 1968).

theological convictions and vice versa. There is and should be an ethical denial of theological convictions—our ethics is the testing ground for the substance and truth of our religious and theological affirmation. In other words, if "God is love" is assumed to be a sufficient presupposition for the Christian moral life then it can be shown that such a God is preferably "no being" or, if existent, ethically unworthy of our respect or obedience.

This is important because the type of unbelief Christians confront today is not the unbelief that denies God in a highly articulate manner, but it is an unbelief that considers such a denial not worth the effort since the affirmation makes no difference in the first place. Modern atheism is not the clenched fist that dares God to exist in a world of such suffering, but it is the shrug of the shoulders. Christians in their apologetic quest for relevancy have encouraged this attitude by identifying the Christian ethics with reigning cultural pieties about the significance of love and brotherhood. By so doing we make the Christian life, like theological belief itself, immune from any criticism, as neither exclude any affirmation or form of behavior from their purview. As Alasdair MacIntyre points out, the theist-atheist debate in the modern world is of little interest because the theist in full retreat offers the atheist less and less in which to disbelieve.[2] We are so fearful that our religious convictions and behavior cannot stand the test of truthfulness, we have in bad faith translated our theology and ethics into platitudes that no one can disagree with, but which no one is very interested in because they are platitudes.

Therefore, if Christianity is primarily an ethic of love I think that it is clearly wrong and ought to be given up, since our moral experience reveals that such an ethic is not sufficient to give form to our moral behavior. It is not just our theological beliefs that should be open to charges of "falsification," but Christianity as a way of life must be subject to the same tests of truth or falsity as other forms of life.[3]

---

[2]Alasdair MacIntyre, *The Religious Significance of Atheism* (New York: Columbia, 1969), p. 24.

[3]"Falsificaton" is a technical term used by philosophers to argue that religious discourse is empty or meaningless. They allege that religious propositions are vacuous because the conditions under which they might be meaningfully denied cannot be specified. In contrast, I am arguing that religious discourse is open to "falsification" so understood, for at least one of the ways the truths of religious affirmations are

It is important, however, that the relationship between theology and ethics be a genuine dialectic. Ethical experience not only tests our theological convictions, but our theological convictions test and form our ethical behavior. There can be no ultimate separation between our theological convictions and our ethical behavior, because our moral values are not ultimately separable from our religious affirmations. Our belief in God is not some "fact" we merely assent to, but involves a whole way of life that is appropriate to such a belief.[4] Ethics is not just a matter of decisions about specific actions, but a way of seeing the world that inextricably involves the understanding as formed by theological convictions.[5] Thus I must make my case against an ethics of love on both theological and ethical grounds—e.g., I must show that our theological convictions themselves cannot be reduced to an ethic of love.

Theologically it is of course natural and correct in the profoundest theological sense to say God is love. At the heart of any trinitarian conception of God is the claim that his very essence is self-giving—that is, that he does not will to be self-contained. Thus the decisive mark of the Father is that he "gives" all things to the son; charity is the defining mark of God's internal life. My problem with the language of love does not arise in the context of this kind of theological affirmation, but when we think these affirmations warrant the use of the phrase "God is love" as a description of God's essence abstracted from its trinitarian home. When this happens, the nature of God no longer defines the love that is his essence, but a general notion of love tends to define his nature.

While it is true that God in his essence is charity, love cannot be assumed as an end in itself—i.e., that love is the purpose of God's eternal will. God is not the God of love because he wills love but because he is the truth of our existence. God's identity

tested is the kind of moral existence they entail. See *New Essays in Philosophical Theology* (London: S.C.M. Press, 1961), and Richard Allen. *The Reasonableness of Faith* (New York: Corpus Books, 1970).

[4]See James Gustafson's discussion of this complex relationship in his "Religion and Morality from the Perspective of Theology," in *Morality and Religion,* edited by Outka and Reeder (New York: Doubleday, 1973), and his book, *Christian Ethics and the Community* (Philadelphia: Pilgrim Press, 1971).

[5]For more extended discussion of this point see "Situation Ethics, Moral Notions, and Moral Theology. Chapter 1, and Chapter 2, "The Significance of Vision: Toward an Esthetic Ethics."

is prior to his presence and the love we find in his presence is possible only because he stands for goods prior to such presence. God does not exist to make love real, but love is real because God exists. God can come to us in love only because he comes to us as God, the creator, sustainer, and redeemer of our existence. He wills we love him; it is not love directed at *any* being, but the particular God of Israel whose freedom is the power and the weakness, of redemption on the cross.

I am aware that you may find this but a play on words. That it is more than this can be shown by the implications it has for how we read the Gospels. In the Gospels it is of course true that love has a prominent place in Jesus' teaching and preaching— e.g., the great commandment—he does urge men to love one another. But he does not urge such love as though it were an end in itself, as though it could be embodied as a general policy, for the love that he commands is the love of the other as God has loved you. The command to love that the Christian has an interest in cannot be separated from he who commands it. Jesus does not come to us as a preacher whose message is that we ought to love, but that we might know that the righteousness of God's kingdom can be found in his person. Jesus comes not to tell us to love one another, but to establish the condition that makes love possible. Thus, his command to love is not an abstract and general policy that can be separated from the story that this is God working for our redemption.

The Gospel is not about love, but it is about this man, Jesus Christ. The ethic of the Gospel is not a love ethic, but it is an ethic of adherence to this man as he has bound our destiny to his, as he makes the story of our life his story. As an ethic of love the Gospels would be an ethic at our disposal since we could fill in the context of love by our wishes, but as a story we cannot control it for one can tell stories only as the story is allowed to tell itself through us. By letting the story live through us we come to be transformed, to be as the story is. It is interesting in this respect that in Luke (Chapter 10) Jesus accompanies the great commandment with the story of the good Samaritan. Contrary to many assumptions, the principle "love your neighbor as yourself" is not the moral "upshot" of that story, nor is the story but an illustration of the principle, but the story is the moral meaning of the principle. Universal ethical principles become ethically significant only as we learn their meaning in stories. For the universal without the particular (stories) is but a shadow reality, subject to our desires, rather than the truth of the story that is Christ's.[6]

In the same way, when Christ is turned into a preacher of love or the optimum example of what it means to be loving, love becomes a norm that defines his work, rather than his work defining the nature of love. As a preacher of love and understanding one wonders how he could have been so stupid to have ever ended on the cross—for who is going to object to that kind of preaching? He is nailed to a cross because he comes as the revelation of God's righteousness, which brings pain as well as understanding. We enter such a kingdom of righteousness by having our attention and will directed not to love but to the person and work of Christ. When love is turned into an abstraction—something Jesus taught we ought not to do—we can easily assume that love is an easy thing. In the Gospels our ability to love is dependent on the hard business of following this man, for our ability to love after Christ is dependent exactly on what he has done for us.

It is interesting theologically that this new ethic of love which seems so radically opposed to traditional forms of pietism resembles the pietist Christology. For Jesus' primary ethical function is that of a teacher—he comes with the recommendations for the good life—a kind of moralistic Emily Post. This new love ethic, however, has Jesus coming not to teach us specific rules, but rather he comes with the astounding platitude that we ought to love everyone. But Christ comes not preaching love, he comes as the form of truth and love that points not to the reality of love but to himself. If we are to be true to the

---

[6]The influence of Elie Wiesel should be unmistakable for anyone familiar with his essays and novels. For a more formal argument of the same point see William Poteat, "Myths, Stories, History, Eschatology and Action: Some Polonyan Meditations," in *Intellect and Hope* (Durham: Duke U. Press, 1968). For example Poteat, commenting on Braithwaite's "An Empirist View of Religious Belief," says, "Policy-statements of a very general sort—like 'I have decided to live an agapeistic life'—though *story-neutral* in appearance, when viewed and elucidated by a moral philosopher of a verificationist turn of mind, are seen in fact to be nothing of the sort. Such statements, when they are responsibly analyzed macrologically, are intelligibly interpretable at all only if their implicit 'stories' are explicated. The need of stories then lies precisely in the fact that policy-statements are about intentions to act in certain ways, and action is inconceivable apart from stories. It is stories which display how the concepts 'action,' 'person,' 'will,' 'heart,' 'inner,' 'outer' are used. The precise meanings of and hence the differences between Confucian policy-statements and Christian policy-statements are entirely a function of their differing stories." P. 217.

Gospels it seems clear if we are to learn to love, we must first learn to follow him.

Although it is a theological mistake to make love the primary message of Jesus, I suspect the temptation to so interpret the Gospel has its basis in the general desire of men to assume that the moral life and the achievement of the good is an easy thing that requires no discipline or training. Love denotes an immediacy of response; we do not have to work to love, either we are or are not in love—the very idea that love requires training is foreign to us. The result is that we cheapen the nature of the love that is Christ's by making him the bearer of a love that does not require the following of him to be morally good. But as we cheapen the Gospel to fit our own illusion about love we also cheapen the richness of our moral lives. For ethically love is not a sufficiently rich term to take account of the depth and heights of the world we must see to be worthwhile and substantive moral beings. In other words, the trivializing of the Gospel into an ethics of love tends to trivialize our own lives in a way that we are no longer able to hear what the claims of the Gospel are. For example, when the Gospel is translated into an ethics of love, the cross becomes but a symbol of our little sacrifices that we associate with our love for others.

But the cross is at the center of Christian ethics because Christ beckons us to face the reality of the world that is in revolt against itself. As Christians our ethical task is to see the world as it is in the confidence that we can look upon and face the agony of the world without its destroying us. Christianity is denied today because we as Christians no longer believe the truth of such a promise. Instead we become living platitudes that refuse to see the world as it is because we have deluded ourselves that somehow love is the answer to every human dilemma.

A Christian ethic is ultimately an ethic of truth or it is neither Christian nor an ethic substantive enough to deal with the human condition. Love can only be authentic when it faces honestly the conditions under which we must love in this existence. Love cannot be blind, but it must see the world as it is. But "what men commonly call love is usually an affectation which shuns like the plague truth between people. And this situation is not altered by the fact that sacrifice is sometimes both demanded and given. Where there is no will to truth, even

sacrifice turns to flattery."[7] There is no better example of this
than the tragedy of the so-called "successful" marriage that has
succeeded because neither partner wishes to risk destroying the
relationship by facing the truth about themselves or the other.
For we each intuitively feel how fragile our life together is as it
hangs on the history of our false gestures to one another and
consequently we cannot summon the courage to risk destroying
what intimacy we have achieved: our illusions have been made
reality in our love. That is why we are often more honest with
total strangers than with those closest to us, because with
strangers we have nothing to lose by betraying the truth about
ourselves. Thus, we prefer to continue to live with the assumption that love brings happiness and contentment as we nestle
deeper into illusions of our self-giving. Yet, ultimately life
forces us, if we are lucky, to face the Gospel claim that love
without truth is accursed love.

Christian ethics as an ethics of love reinforces our illusions by
retreating into an ethic of interpersonal understanding and
acceptance as if becoming an I to a Thou is the height of human
attainment. But ethically our life involves more than person-to-
person interaction; we exist as social creatures, and as such we
confront social problems that require not love but justice. For
example, the emergence of black power is the result of the
black man's perception that he no longer wanted to be loved by
the white—what he wanted was justice—that is, he wanted
power to protect his own interest in a way that did not
continue to depend on the good will of the whites. For good
will is no less tyrannical than bad will in its continued control
of the other. The black man discovered that there is no greater
enemy to his people than the white liberal's attempt at loving
reconciliation, for such reconciliation comes without destroying
the structural racism of our society. Moreover, the black man
has learned that there is no more destructive love than the white
man's need of the "negro cause" to insure the white man's
moral identity and to assuage his guilt.

Our moral lives are not made up of situations where asking
the question of love always makes ethical sense. As Herbert
McCabe points out, "Every moral problem of the slightest
interest is a problem about who is to get hurt; an injunction to

---

[7]Knud Logstrup, *The Ethical Demand* (Philadelphia: Fortess Press, 1971), p. 22.

love everyone concerned does not help to decide that question."[8] For the question is not "to hurt or not to hurt," but whom to hurt with justice. To appeal to love is but to blur the pain and the glory of living morally in this life. The credibility of Christians is hurt not by their failure of good will, but by their refusal to face the reality that even good will cannot act without hurting. The greatest enemy of the Christian life is not self-interest, but sentimentality.

Some may try to associate this point with the old moral textbooks' understanding of the relation of justice and charity. Even though I have some sympathy with that tradition, my position is somewhat different. I am not saying that justice is only called for in complex social situations and that love is perfectly sufficient for other aspects of our moral lives. Nor am I suggesting that justice is a sufficient criterion for basic morality but that love is a higher virtue. I have no sympathy either with the nature-supernature form of Catholic ethics or with the law-gospel separation of Lutheranism.[9] There can be no split between an ethic of creation dealing with institutions and a Gospel ethic dealing with interpersonal relations. Rather my argument is that love, even in interpersonal relations, that is embodied without justice is sentimental and destructive rather than realistic and upbuilding. For there can be no love without respect, and respect must be built on a perception of the other's right of existence as he is, not as he has worth for me.

I suspect that the assertion of the primacy of love as the center of Christian ethics and the popular forms of situationalism accompanying it are usually satisfied with an analysis of reality that cuts no deeper than Robert Anderson's "Tea and

---

[8]Herbert McCabe, *What Ethics Is All About* (Washington: Corpus, 1969), p. 33.

[9]For a good exposition of the nature-supernature distinction and its effect on Catholic moral theology see J. P. Mackey, *The Grace of God, the Response of Man* (Albany: Magi Books, 1966). Mackey shows, contrary to much of the rhetoric, that past moral theology did presuppose a fundamental theology, but it was a theology that assumed that "nature" is relatively autonomous and sufficient in its own sphere, needing only to be "topped" by grace. However, the distinction was never so crudely drawn in the work of the great classical theologians such as Aquinas. DeLubac and Rahner's work, therefore, should in this respect be seen as a return to the more classical tradition of charity as the form of the virtues.

One of the best discussions of the Lutheran distinction between law and gospel and its ethical implications is to be found in Troeltsch's *The Social Teachings of the Christian Churches* (New York: Macmillan, 1931, pp. 515-575).

Sympathy." In that play and movie, the wife of a headmaster of a prep school has sexual intercourse with a young man in order to provide him with the manly confidence necessary for him to make a success out of his life. (The significance our culture associates with the first act of sexual intercourse is fantastic. The great enemy of healthy sex is not lust but this kind of spiritualization of the sexual act.) The situation is built in such a way that it would seem excessively moralistic of anyone to say she was wrong. But what of the claims of others in that situation? What of her husband, for example. Surely her action did nothing to help draw him from some of his insensitivity, which contributed to the situation. What we wish to make clear is that a loving act is not necessarily defined by the acceptance of the other and his perception of his needs. Love, if it stands for truth, may require us to do what appears unloving if we are to treat the other with respect. Moreover to love one as he ought to be loved means we must refuse to meet the needs of some. The greater our love, the more likely the necessity for our betrayal of others.

It is important at this point to make clear that I am not arguing that the emphasis on love in current Christian ethics is wrong because it involves a misunderstanding of love, though that is certainly part of my case. Rather I am trying to make a more radical point: that even if love is freed from its sentimental perversions, it is still not an adequate principle, policy, or summary metaphor to capture the thrust of the Gospel for the Christian's moral behavior. Love is dependent on our prior perceptions of the truth of reality that can finally be approached only through the richness of the language and stories which form what we know. The Christian is thus better advised to resist the temptation to reduce the Gospel to a single formula or summary image for the moral life. Christian ethics and the Christian moral life are as rich and various as the story we hold and the life we must live to be true to it.

Perhaps I can make my argument more compelling by utilizing a scene from Dorothy Sayers' mystery novel, *Gaudy Night.* In this novel, Lord Peter Wimsey has been called to the campus of the women's college at Oxford to discover the perpetrator of a series of destructive acts against the college. In the course of the investigation it comes out that the acts were directed against one of the dons for having failed a student for nonscholarly

work, when the don was at another university. The man who
had been her student had written what appeared to be a
brilliant dissertation, but in her reading of it she thought she
remembered a letter in a library where she had worked that
would have significantly changed the primary thesis of the
man's work. She discovered that he not only had also discovered the letter late in his research, but he had suppressed it
rather than rewrite. His academic failure had driven him to
drink and finally to suicide, for which his wife had continued to
blame the don. As a way of getting revenge the widow, while
working as a maid at the college, had committed the acts of
violence. After all this had come out in a scene where the
widow had been allowed to say some rather damning things
about everyone involved in the case, the don, Miss de Vine, said
to Wimsey:

"I do blame myself, most bitterly. Not for my original action, which
was unavoidable, but for the sequel. Nothing you can say to me could
make me feel more responsible than I do already."

"I can have nothing to say," said Wimsey, "Like you and every member
of the Common Room, I admit the principle and the consequences must
follow."

"That won't do," said Miss de Vine, bluntly. "One ought to take some
thought for other people. Miss Lydgate [another don at the college]
would have done what I did in the first place; but she would have made it
her business to see what became of that unhappy man and his wife."

"Miss Lydgate is a very great and a very rare person. But she could not
prevent other people from suffering for her principles. That seems to be
what principles are for, somehow. . . . I don't claim, you know," he added,
with something of his familiar diffidence, "to be a Christian or anything of
that kind. But there's one thing in the Bible that seems to me to be a
statement of brutal fact—I mean, about bringing not peace but a sword."

What I am trying to say is very close to what Wimsey
suggests, namely that we must be willing, if we are to live
morally in this life, to let others suffer for our principles. [10]
Appeals to love cannot and should not remove this aspect of
our existence. For we do not exist to be together as an end in

---

[10]It is, of course, with fear and trembling that I make this suggestion, since such a
position has been used in the past to justify blatant and unjust coercion in the name
of religious conviction. However, such injustice cannot be prevented by making
tolerance an end in itself, but by trusting in the power of truth. For those who use
force do so because they doubt the "truth" in whose name they destroy. There is no
greater denial of the Gospel than killing for its advancement.

itself, but we exist together for purposes that provide for human flourishing. This can be seen even in such basic units as the family as no family exists in a healthy manner where it is only held together for the sake of being together. When love, forgiveness, and kindness become an end in themselves it simply indicates people who no longer believe in anything. Being unwilling to make others and ourselves suffer for our principles is but to admit that nothing in this life is worth ourselves or others making a sacrifice for. What becomes crucial once this is admitted is not that we suffer, but that we suffer for the truth. That is, that the principles we hold are not arbitrary, but are prerequisites for any attempt to live a morally worthy life.

Perhaps I can make this point more concrete through an example from education. Currently there is a kind of orthodoxy that says the first job of the teacher is to draw the student out—to help him articulate his basic desires and opinions. That is, the aim of education is to bring the student to self-fulfillment by providing him with the opportunity to express himself freely and openly. The criteria of a good teacher is not what the student learns formally, but the kind of relationship he is able to establish with the student that provides a context for trust and love. The content of the subject is relatively irrelevant, for learning is not a matter of learning about something but coming to a better self-understanding. Teaching thus becomes an extremely ambiguous affair, for we must admit that we learn more from the students than they do from us.

However, I think any teacher that says this sort of thing and means it is simply a bad teacher, for a good teacher gives in terms of his discipline more than he gets. What such a statement and philosophy do in the name of love and understanding is deny the educational task of serving the good of the student. But this does not serve the student, for it cheats him of what education can do for him (which admittedly is not all he needs to be a successful human being). For the aim of the educator must be to let truth stand equally against the student as well as the teacher.

Education calls for a patient standing before that which we know not in order to know. Disinterestedness is the hallmark of education, for it requires unselfing that we might be open to that not present in our interests and assumptions of relevancy. Disinterest is not the precondition of intellectual endeavor necessary because the truth cannot be known, but because it can. One does not need to be committed to a metaphysical realism or assume that truth comes with a capital "T" in order to understand this. For the truth is not less real for its being clothed in the contingencies and ambiguities of our historical existence. To discover and know even the most limited forms of truth entails disinterest, because truth is not something we create; it is the lure that calls us from our self-contained worlds of illusion—which are often all the more tempting because they have the stamp of conventionality. Disinterest, therefore, is quite literally the noninterest in the self that is required by the attractiveness of the otherness of reality. The struggle for truth always comes with suffering, as we are forced to give up our cherished conventions about ourselves and the world. Thus disinterest cannot be understood simply as neutrality, since it involves an interested commitment and respect for the otherness of reality. In this regard disinterest and humor bear a profound relationship, as both are sustained by a fundamental commitment to the existence of a reality beyond the immediate. The death of education is to raise the student's subjectivity, his perception of his problems and interests, to a normative status. Education, as I am conceiving of it here, is a painful business for student and teacher, because truth is a tiring business.

Another thing that bothers me about this educational philosophy is its extreme paternalism toward the student as it assumes he is not capable of bearing the truth about reality. Unless the student is treated as one capable of learning, then we cheat him by giving in to his subjectivity. Kindness is not treating the other as he is, but treating him as if he is capable of a good that he does not now possess but is capable of possessing. A particularly poignant example of this is the kind of demands those skilled in working with the retarded must make if they are not to sell these children out to society's perception of their limitations.[11] Moreover, without this insight punishment makes no sense, for punishment is only morally thinkable when it is done as a means of showing respect for the one being punished.

I suspect that the question that many will raise about the

---

[11]For a more extended discussion of the ethics involved in the care of the retarded, see Chapter 10, "The Christian, Society, and the Weak."

kind of argument I have been making and the kind of examples I have used is that they depend on our ability to know the truth, both moral and intellectual. It is just this assumption that the ethics of love has tried to avoid by making the question "What is truth?" morally irrelevant. For the ethics of love is often but a cover for what is fundamentally an assertion of ethical relativism. It is an attempt to respond to the breakdown of moral consensus by substituting the language of love for the language of good and right as the primary determinate for the moral. For what is often implied by the ethics of love is an attitude that assumes that since we cannot know the good perhaps the best thing to do is to live with a kind of fundamental openness to others. The ethics of love is but the ethics of tolerance that makes kindness the central virtue. In such a context love becomes a justification for our own arbitrary desires and likes. It is an admission that we can reach no higher than our own desires, nor can we expect anyone else to reach higher than theirs.

Such an ethics gives a warrant to assume the important ethical virtue is sensitivity rather than rationality, for it is assumed that moral argument is impossible. It confuses the truth of moral argument with persuasion. What becomes important is that people are sincere rather than right and wrong. Indeed, it is no longer possible to think of men doing wrong, as the moral category is assumed to be dependent on—or more intelligible in—psychological terms. It is no longer possible to be evil, we can only be psychologically sick.

In our cultural context the ethics of love seems to involve an almost irresistible temptation to embody an ethical intuitionism that shortcuts any attempt to develop good ethical arguments. The result of this tends to be disastrous, especially in areas such as bio-medical ethics, where we have no precedents or practices to fall back on. For on the whole, in spite of explicit adherence to an ethic of love, we are sustained by the language and practices we inherit to guide us in our everyday decisions and actions. In other words, our actual moral behavior is better than our explicit ethical theory. I suspect that is the reason that the ethics of love appears reasonable at all, because we continue to presuppose moral forms of life that are inconsistent with or at least not justified by our elevation of love as the supreme moral principle or vitue. However, when we confront issues such as those in medical ethics, our explicit ethical theory of love proves woefully insufficient to settle or guide our behavior. Or if it does guide us it is often because love has been translated into a crude utilitarianism that is ethically destructive.

For example, some are suggesting, concerning the population issue, that we should not aid the poor countries as that is simply food wasted. Food should go only to those countries that have a chance of survival. Or that we should not provide free education for the third child as a way of encouraging people to limit their reproductive habits. The men who make these kinds of suggestions are not cruel men or inhumane—rather they are extremely moral men who think their proposals are loving. The object of their love is not this man or that child, but mankind. Great immoralities are not the result of evil intentions, but a love gone crazy with its attempt to encompass all mankind within its purview.

In another context some are suggesting that the recent genetic insights concerning man's "gene slum"[12] entail that we regulate our breeding for the good of the species. For by keeping many alive who in the past would have died, we have created a situation that becomes impossible, since in the coming generation we will be carrying more and more recessive genes. Unless we act, the world's future is to be a hospital of deformed people cared for by a medical profession made up of idiots. Does this mean that in genetic counseling we should be guided not by what the couple wants but by what is good for the species? Should we abort all Down's Syndrome babies out of love for the human species? Are there some things we should not do even though not to do them places the human species in jeopardy?

It would be a mistake, however, if these kinds of issues are only associated with the bizarre for our everyday medical experimentation raises no less complex problems. Should doctors and researchers be allowed to operate on human subjects for the good of mankind when the experiment has no good end in view for the immediate patient? Or on what basis are we to determine who is to get exotic life-saving procedures such as dialysis

---

[12]The phrase "gene slum" is often used by geneticists to refer to the increasing load of genetic mutations we carry as a species.

machines? Should we employ criteria of social worth to select who shall live and die, or should we simply leave it to chance?

These issues make clear the insufficiency of the slogan "always act to do the most loving thing." For they can only be settled by the hard work of moral reflection and argument in order to enliven us to what is at stake in such matters. If this is not done then we will fail to see how quickly love can become an ideology for our own self-interest and unwillingness to suffer. To be a man is to be a lover of illusion, and nothing creates more resistant illusion than the assumption that we must be right since we act from love. The task of the moral life is to face reality as it is; we will not do this if we assume that love can come without discipline and suffering.

Moreover issues make clear that to appeal to love is relatively meaningless unless one is able to specify whom and under what modality one loves. It is easy to say we ought to love, until we know what it is we are to love and under what conditions the love must take place. For example, what is the loving thing to do for a young man with a new family who is hospitalized with incurable cancer? His family thinks the loving thing is not to tell him he is dying to preserve the happiness that is possible in the time left him. What should you do as a nurse or doctor connected with the case? What this kind of example illustrates is how we can create the worst immorality by trying to spare others pain, for we cheat them of their due respect. There is no greater unkindness than to rob others of their right to suffer in order to relieve our nagging fear that perhaps we also should be prepared to suffer. In this case, we cheat this young man of the agony of learning to die well. I suspect that this is also the basis of the unbelievably inhumane deaths we are perpetrating on others in the name of keeping them alive.

What we must face is that love is not the saving of others from suffering, but the willingness to continue to love them in their suffering, and patiently hold the pain and guilt that such love cannot help but bring. If we are willing to do that, we might begin to understand ethically why it is that Christ came not bringing a message of love but brought himself to die and be raised, that the world and we might live free from the fear of reality.

7.

Abortion and Normative Ethics

The human agony involved in abortion is enough to establish it as a significant human problem, but there are two further reasons for philosophers and theologians to turn their attention to it. Abortion is but the first of a whole range of new socio-medical issues that will soon require social decisions; public discussion needs clarification if they are not to be decided by rhetorical violence. Besides, abortion represents the kind of problem that seems to reveal the conceptual limitations of formal normative theories; no one interested in normative ethics should avoid the challenge it poses.

The three books listed below help inform the public debate by revealing the descriptive and normative oversimplifications characteristic of both pro- and anti-abortionists. Since Callahan and Grisez have developed significant ethical positions that stand in sharp disagreement,[1] we will concentrate on the normative aspects of the problem. By critically contrasting them, I hope to show the limitations of each and suggest that there are aspects of this problem where as yet we have no adequate ethical stance.

Before comparing Callahan and Grisez's arguments in detail, a few general observations about each book are necessary. Each has positive and negative features peculiar to itself. Callahan's book is better organized, contains more information, and is written in a more readable style. Given the complexities of the abortion question, Callahan's openness is more attractive than

---

[1]By concentrating on Callahan and Grisez I do not wish to leave the impression that the essays edited by Noonan are not important. In spite of the high quality of these essays, especially those by Noonan, Ramsey, and Gustafson, they do not provide the kind of sustained argumentation that makes a comparison of Callahan and Grisez so fruitful. The books in question are: Daniel Callahan, *Abortion: Law, Choice, and Morality*. (New York: Macmillan Co., 1970); Germain Grisez, *Abortion, the Myths, the Realities, and the Arguments*. (New York: Corpus Books, 1970); John Noonan, Editor. *The Morality of Abortion: Legal and Historical Perspectives*. (Cambridge: Harvard U. Press, 1970).

Grisez's more self-assured and certain position. Moreover, Grisez's book is encumbered by a magisterial manner; it tends to be repetitious and tedious; and his more substantive arguments often get lost amid his destruction of straw men.

More irritating than these stylistic matters, however, is Grisez's not too subtle *ad hominems* against the pro-abortionist. No doubt he thinks it significant to suggest that the pro-abortionist movement was once supported by many people influenced by the communist abortion experiment in Russia, but such a genetic point hardly does justice to the moral sincerity of many that argue for moral and legal abortion on demand today; even more distracting is his suggestion that there is a subtle connection between the advocacy of contraception and the Nazi eugenic movement. A further example of this kind of oversimplification is his treatment of all Protestant ethical thought on the subject under the general heading of "Situationism," which seems to be based on his assertion that all Protestant ethical positions are not "rationally defensible." This aspect of Grisez's book is especially unfortunate, because these arguments are incidental to his substantive argument. In fact, Grisez provides a valuable check on Callahan, in so far as he has responsibly defended the more "conservative" alternative. His book should not be ignored because of some of its unfortunate features.

Why Is Abortion a Moral Problem?

The great strength of both books is their insistence that abortion is a moral issue. By a moral issue they do not simply mean something that men violently disagree about because of differing opinions. Rather they mean that any proposal concerning the nature of abortion depends on fundamental questions concerning the nature of life, its beginning, and the basic relationship men should have toward the life of another. Both are agreed that no amount of "factual" information is sufficient to answer these kinds of questions; the "factual" aspects of the problem are finally important only in so far as they are given significance by a prior moral and metaphysical framework. Thus, to say that abortion is a moral issue is to claim that it cannot be rationally discussed without certain questions being treated.

Nevertheless, there is a fundamental difference in the way Callahan and Grisez conceive the basic moral problem of abortion. On the surface the books look extremely similar because each analyzes the medical, legal, sociological, and psychological aspects of the problems. But whereas Callahan does so because he assumes that such consideration will make a difference in one's moral stance, Grisez uses such information almost entirely as a means to destroy certain "myths" about the practice or social necessity of abortion, or as an indirect support for his moral position, which he considers valid irrespective of such descriptive aspects of the problem. The importance of this point cannot be underestimated, since it is not always noticed that there are ethical issues involved in the very way abortion is conceived to be a moral problem.

In this respect both Callahan and Grisez fail to defend adequately their primary assumptions. The basic focus of Callahan's book is taken from the contemporary experience of the tragedies involved in the backstreet abortion. As such he is concerned that our society should be able to transcend the hard positions drawn between the Roman Catholic insistence on the preservation of potential life and those who argue that it should be a matter entirely at women's discretion. He therefore tries to develop a consensus position which is "Likely to win as large a hearing as possible, even if people will differ about the conclusions different groups or individuals draw." (15) He intentionally uses the largest number of commonly accepted values and employs the moral language likely to gain the widest hearing.

This way of shaping the issue, however, leaves important questions unanswered. There is a fundamental problem in knowing how to determine what are the actual values that most people share on this kind of issue. But even if this could be known, why should he assume that they have some validity for forming a consensus? No one would underestimate the significance of such a consensus, but surely the first job of the ethicist is to state the position he thinks closer to the truth, regardless of whether men adhere to it or not. Otherwise the right or wrong of any act would be determined simply by common opinion.

I suspect, however, that what Callahan actually has in mind by "consensus" refers more to specific problems than to basic values. Such issues as the social cost of current restrictive laws and such hard cases as rape and life against life, stand in the foreground of this thinking. Because of this, he wishes to avoid any suggestion that abortion is subject to absolute or unbreakable rules regardless of the situation. Fundamental to his position is the "conviction that any discussion of a moral problem must blend theory and experience, principles and practice, goals and likely consequences." (12) The moral problem involved in abortion, for Callahan, is a conflict of competing values, and the form of moral reasoning that best serves such a problem is some version of calculating the personal and social consequences involved. But of course the very presumption that abortion is this kind of problem assumes that there are other kinds of claims that can be balanced against that of the fetus.

Callahan is fond of quoting Gustafson's response to Paul Ramsey's argument that God's lordship of life should mean that the fetus cannot be destroyed. Gustafson says, "Paul Ramsey rests his case ultimately on a theological basis; life is sacred because it is valued by God. Good theological point. But one can ask, what other things does God value in addition to physical life? E.g., qualitative aspects of life, etc." Callahan adds that the Christian community has valued many goods over physical life—"the protection of a free conscience, justice, a just peace, the protection of necessary societal values." (311) While this is certainly true, it is somewhat misleading when applied to abortion. The issue is not simply one of sacrificing oneself for a greater good, but rather one of a human being deciding to destroy an at least potential human life in the name of some greater good. To describe the situation solely in terms of a conflict of values fails to do justice to the question of whether we ever have the right to take the life of another regardless of the reasons.

Callahan's assumption that abortion is primarily a problem of value conflict is not very helpful unless he shows what difference this makes for the normative ethical stance with which one approaches the problem. Callahan tries to avoid a choice between deontological or utilitarian theories by suggesting the idea of "policy"—that is, a general direction of thought and action which provides a basic framework for making specific decisions. (20) A policy is not empty of content for it represents a "cluster of values and goals that will pervade particular choices, but it will also leave open different kinds of responses to changing contingencies and needs." (338) This approach has the virtue of recognizing that abortion decisions admit of no simple solution, that there is often a conflict of values and claims, yet it is a guideline in the sense that it provides the standards of relevancy according to which the prudential decision must finally be made.

The principle of the "sanctity of life," since it represents the fundamental consensus value for all sides of the abortion question, should set the primary moral policy for abortion. Callahan resists any attempt to give an explicit theological basis to this notion because: (1) many men are not Christian or religious, (2) its philosophical basis does not do justice to man's responsibility to create his life, since our decisions cannot be "left to God," and (3) it leaves unclear man's essential dignity. (311-313) Any ultimate justification for such a principle must therefore lie in secular human experience. Whether this kind of open-ended policy will actually result in a greater enhancement of the quality of men's lives than the old Christian ethic of limitation must wait until "we possess good studies of the comparative social results of different kinds of ethical codes." (319) What the criteria of such "results" would be Callahan does not specify, but logically it would seem to be the establishment of the general policy "sanctity of life."

While Callahan specifies the meaning of the sanctity of life in terms of more concrete rules, I think it is possible, without looking at his more detailed position, to suggest that the idea of "policy" involves some very real difficulties. If there are not some basic practices concerning the protection of life that are not subject to consequential reasoning, then what possible meaning does "sanctity of life" have which is not platitudinous or subject to later modification? It is not clear, in other words, that Callahan has actually avoided some form of modified utilitarianism. If this is the case, then his general framework may not be completely consistent with some of his more specific proposals concerning the hesitancy which should properly accompany all abortions, regardless of the conditions or consequences. Callahan tends toward a utilitarian position because he is impressed by how often abortion involves a conflict of positive values. He therefore assumes that any moral position which does not allow for some calculation of the conflict is too rigid and absolute. But the implications of such moral policy

could go beyond the specific kinds of conflict situation Callahan has in mind.

To put the matter in a somewhat different way, is it possible
to use a form of consequential reasoning in relation to the
question of abortion and still avoid some of the implications
often associated with utilitarianism? Grisez, convinced that
utilitarianism is the real enemy of the fetus, details the standard
objections to utilitarianism, such as the ambiguity of the "greatest good," the exclusion of the heroic, and its inability to
account for inherent wrong or right. (287-297) One does not
have to agree with Grisez that utilitarians necessarily must
approve of murder in order to be disturbed that utilitarianism
may not provide an adequate account of moral obligation with
respect to the protection of life. Has any utilitarian yet accounted for the basic liberties and rights of each person in a
way that is not subject to limitation for the good of the whole?

This issue involves more than just the nature and criteria of
ethical judgment; it also is a question of how the nature of man
is to be understood. Callahan affirms what he calls the technological ethos, that is "that man should control his own
destiny, make his own choices and use, rather than be used by
nature." (506) Men must understand that they cannot place the
solution to such problems as abortion in the hands of God, for
it is man who is responsible for man and this includes control
over life and death. "Abortion, euthanasia, medical experimentation and prolongation of human life are all problems which
fall totally within the sphere of human rules and human judgments." (340)

As a rejection of a perverse fatalism, these assertions are
salutary. However, in so far as they may represent the idea that
man is merely a being to be manipulated, totally embodied in
his various functions or uses, they involve a view of man that is
at the heart of the abortion question. For if men are only men
in terms of the contributions they can make toward a more
inclusive whole, then the right of the fetus is already presumed
problematic in so far as it has no achieved status. To be sure,
these are implications Callahan does not wish to be drawn; in
his view, the fetus always has the presumptive right to be born.
But if fetal life is defined as less than human it is not clear
exactly what force the "presumptive right" of the fetus entails.

I wonder if Callahan's criticism of the Roman Catholic position for failing to recognize the value conflicts in the abortion situation is entirely fair. Certainly some Roman Catholic arguments have tended to be one-dimensional in so far as the conceptus was assumed, in practice at least, to be the only real value at stake. Moreover such arguments have been overly legalistic, juridical, and deductive. Nevertheless, the concern of Roman Catholics with the status of the fetus is not necessarily one-dimensional, for it can be argued that the fetus has such importance precisely as it represents a basic test case for a whole network of values involved in our ability to sustain our lives together.

The emphasis of the Catholic argument is possibly a way of making clear that what is at stake in the fetus' existence is a fundamental option about our status as men. Protection of the fetus is an affirmation of life from which all other claims draw their significance—i.e., we must learn to regard another's life as good because it has being, not because it is useful. The fault of the Roman Catholic position has been its failure to make clear that the question of the status of the fetus' humanity also involves the status of our own humanity. As a result its position appears to be an arbitrary insistence on the rights of the fetus to the exclusion of all other claims.

Grisez, contrary to Callahan, is quite clear that he has no wish to submit his account to experience if this means how people understand what happens in abortion. Rather the whole purpose of moral argumentation is to find a basis for our judgments on nonexperiential grounds. He criticizes Gustafson's essay, "A Protestant Ethical Approach" (Noonan, pp. 101-122) for arguing that the individual experiences and conditions of the mother (victim of rape, other children to care for; psychological health) should somehow contribute to the decision to abort or not to abort. But once having made the point that appeals to experience cannot avoid judgmental categories, Grisez agrees that Gustafson is right in pointing out "that the ethical aspect of abortion is not limited to the simple question of whether it is morally right to have or perform an abortion, either in general or in various kinds of cases. The factors which lead to abortion, the real difficulties of women in trouble, the social injustices which make life difficult, the conflicting pressures felt by morally sensitive physicians—all these are factors which deserve ethical examination." (269)

In the paragraph following this statement, however, Grisez argues that such questions are not nearly so theoretically complex or so disputed as the single question: "Is it ever right to have or perform an abortion, and if so, under what conditions? Therefore we shall limit our ethical inquiry to this question." But to do so is to avoid the issue, as the problem becomes centered entirely on whether the conceptus is to be considered human life or not. Grisez defends this limitation of what is ethically at stake in any abortion decision on the grounds that "nothing affirmative can remain unless the ethical boundaries of the inviolability of life are recognized and respected." (269)

But is it not possible that the condition of the mother or the social context might embody just such boundaries and in such a way that the life of the fetus is also qualified? There may be good ethical reasons for granting a preference to the fetus in such situations, but the reasons must be given rather than simply rendered irrelevant by one's view of what morally counts. As we shall see, the narrowness of Grisez's original formulation of the problem forces him to try to expand the meaning of the principle of "double effect" beyond its traditional meaning. In doing so it is not clear that he has avoided the kind of problems in which Callahan is involved through his attempt to formulate a more "flexible" position to account for the conflict of values which often seems involved in abortion situations.

This brief exposition of how Callahan and Grisez present the moral issue involved in abortion decisions helps make clear why arguments for and against abortions so often pass one another as ships in the night. To be sure, the emotional intensity of each side tends to create the condition where they do not listen to each other's arguments as they are actually stated, but the failure to encounter one another is also the result of a basic conceptual problem. For the two sides are often not arguing about the same thing, since each has morally described the issue in such a way that the arguments of the other are simply irrelevant or at best tangential. In this respect Grisez's book is somewhat more satisfying, since the moral issue is conceived with greater conceptual rigor and exactness. By comparison Callahan's argument appears loose and uneven. It may be however, that taking the risk of a more complex form of argumentation Callahan has done more justice to the issue and indicated the direction our thinking must follow. At the very least, Callahan's book represents the best effort to date to treat morally the question of abortion in all of its complexity.

Yet both Grisez and Callahan may mislead in virtue of their shared assumption that the primary question involved in abortion is one of the criteria of judgment. This presupposes that what an abortion is is a relatively clear matter and that the only question is its ethical status. But, as the above discussion indicates, the primary question is really perceptual—that is, exactly what constitutes abortion as a moral problem? How should I see or learn to describe what is in fact going on in an abortion? Do various conditions make a difference to the way an act should be described? The difficulties Callahan and Grisez encounter may be an indication that our ordinary perceptual (and conceptual) framework is not sufficient to account for all we feel should be taken into account in some abortion situations. The issue of abortion may reveal not only the poverty of our moral lives, but also of our language.

When Does Life Begin?

Callahan and Grisez agree that this is one of the overriding questions for any analysis of abortion. It does not have the same significance for both, however, since Callahan assumes that there can be other questions of importance in any abortion situation. His discussion here is much more informative than Grisez's since he does not assume that biological data carry self-evident interpretations. There are no pure "facts" which will demonstrate beyond a doubt that the fetus should be considered human. All "facts" are dependent "upon some evaluative system which enables us to distinguish between a 'fact' and a 'nonfact.' " (353) We could not even begin to consider the question of the status of the fetus as life if we did not have some knowledge of what a human being is.

This kind of point is often overlooked by those who wish to argue that the fetus is a human being. Noonan and Ramsey, as well as Grisez, seem to assume that biological research has somehow removed the question from doubt. Thus Ramsey says,

In a remarkable way, modern genetics seems to teach—with greater precision and assurance than theology could ever muster—that there are 'formal cause,' immanent principles or constitutive elements long before there is any shape or motion of discernible size or subjective consciousness or rationality in a human being—not merely potency for these things that later supervene, but in some sense the present operative actuality of these powers and characteristics. These minute formal elements are already determining the organic life to be not only generally 'human' but also *the* unique *individual* human being it is to be. It is now not unreasonable to assert, for the first time in history of scientific speculation upon this question, that who one is and is ever going to be came about at the moment an ovum was impregnated. (67)

For Ramsey this means that "we are all fellow fetuses" and therefore the destruction of the fetus must be regarded as the destruction of full human life.

Grisez's argument is extremely similar to Ramsey's. He distinguishes between the factual question settled by biology, that is, "In the reproductive process, at what point does the human individual originate?" and the metaphysical or theological question, "Should we treat all living human individuals as persons, or should we accept a concept of person that will exclude some who are in fact human, alive, and individuals, but who do not meet certain additional criteria we incorporate in the idea of person?" (273) Of course, he is certainly correct that these are two separate questions, but to claim that the first is a factual question depends on the assumption that what biologists mean by "individuality" carries all the freight that Grisez means in his use of the term.

Biologists have clearly established that the union of the sperm and the ovum at conception creates a cellular structure that is different from either of its constitutive causes. Yet such a "difference" in itself is not the same thing as an individual, at least not in Grisez's understanding of individuality as "one unified in itself and distinguished from others." (26) To impute this kind of "inner unity" to the fetus clearly assumes a substantive notion of individuality that the biological definition does not necessarily carry.

One can appreciate Grisez's concern to reveal the rather startling biological ignorance of many pro-abortionists who argue that the fetus is but a piece of flesh like the appendix. However, what cannot be finally avoided is that the imputation of human life to the fetus is just that—a stipulation, not an empirical deduction. The fact that such a stipulation cannot command absolute certainty does not mean that it is completely arbitrary or devoid of factual basis. But the potential arbitrariness of such a decision suggests that we must be clear about what we mean by describing the fetus as "human" or "person" lest we deny to the fetus essential aspects of "humanity" contained in our broader conception of a fully developed person.

In this respect Callahan is much more careful for he argues that whatever meaning the concept of "human life" is to have must be subject to the findings of a number of disciplines. Not only should genetic information be considered, but also zoological, anthropological, and psychological contributions must be taken into account. From an analysis of such literature he concludes that " 'human' cannot be defined in a genetic way *only,* or in a psychological way *only,* or in a cultural way *only;* it must be defined in such a way as to take account of all three elements in the 'human!' " (363) Any attempt therefore to define "human" only in terms of actualized cultural potentialities ignores the fact that such achieved humanity is possible only because of prior biological potentialities.

Callahan agrees with Grisez that our biological information clearly indicates that while the conceptus is dependent on the mother it is in itself independent as a discrete being. Yet this in itself is not sufficient to decide if human life has begun or even, granted that it has, that such life ought to be valued at that point. The latter question clearly involves wider moral policy decision; the former does in part but it also involves a philosophical policy designed to help answer the question of "the beginnings." (378) Exactly what Callahan intends by this distinction however is not clear, for as we shall see the latter question is determined by the answer he gives to the former.

Callahan distinguishes three basic schools of thought concerning both these questions: (1) the genetic, which attributes full humanity to the conceptus, (2) the developmental, which thinks some stage of morphological development is crucial, (3) and the social-consequence school which assumes the meaning of "human" can be determined by whatever criteria society finds most beneficial. Callahan finds the second alternative the more adequate because it (1) takes account of the biological evidence, (2) it allows for a consideration of a greater range of values at stake by providing the means of distinguishing different levels of "personhood," and (3) it is more open to the necessary weighing of the comparative value of the lives at stake. (396) He is hesitant to state exactly where the developmental line should be drawn, though he tentatively suggests the existence of brain activity as the basis to distinguish person from non-person.

Callahan does not deny that the genetic school is safer than the developmental in as much as it is a check against arbitrary discrimination among human beings on the basis of varying potentialities. However, it fails to do "nuanced justice" to the conflict of values in particular abortion cases. It is difficult to see why this follows. Simply to regard the conceptus as human life does not entail, as Grisez shows, the moral conclusion that under no conditions could such life be destroyed. By opting for the development school Callahan seems to be trying to substitute a descriptive argument for what ultimately only a moral position can give. Even though his adherence to the developmental position allows him to say that the destruction of the early fetus is not the destruction of a person but of an "important and valuable form of human life" (498), it is not clear that in any significant sense this qualifies the moral seriousness of taking such life.

Callahan makes another equally unfounded point against the genetic school when he criticizes Noonan for maintaining that once conception has occurred there is a sharp shift in probabilities toward saying this conceived being is a man. Callahan argues that this represents "a stipulation about what should be counted as 'a man,' thus begging the question of whether a particular conceived being is, in fact, a man." (381) But, as Callahan has so cogently argued, any attribution of humanity to the fetus is necessarily stipulative. He is right to indicate that the genetic school is placing great value on the physical aspect of our being by so stipulating the significance of the fetus. Moreover, this means that abortion decisions involve a conflict between body-life and person life. (398) But the genetic school forces those who wish to claim the primacy of person life over body life to show how such a "fuller humanity" excludes the physical characteristics that the fetus represents.

Callahan does not sufficiently treat the wider questions involved in "when does life begin?"—mainly, the significance of the body for any full account of man's fulfillment. Grisez's insistence that man's ability for self-determination is dependent on our capacity for embodiment (280) is a healthy check on the subtle gnosticism of many arguments that assume that there are no sufficient reasons why the fetus should be regarded as human life. It is obvious that the fetus lacks much that we associate with achieved humanity, but that descriptive condition is not morally decisive. The morally important question is whether we have denied significant aspects of our own being by our failure to regard the fetus as human life. It may be, for example, that bodily continuity is not the sole criterion of personal identity, but its significance at least establishes the intelligibility of conception as the starting point of human life.

When Can Life Be Taken?

Callahan's position on this question is not easy to state with exactness. This is not accidental since he intended that his position should be ultimately ambiguous. He wishes to leave in moral doubt a wide range of cases where abortion may or may not be performed. There are finally no automatic moral lines for or against abortion, as "each case has to be judged individually, taking account of all circumstances." (18) The only certainty is that any argument that abortion is always wrong or right, or that there are any necessary grounds for or against abortion, is wrong. However, his stated general policy, "sanctity of life," creates a general "bias" toward the preservation of life rather than its destruction. As a moral policy this "bias" also helps establish an ordering of more specific moral rules relevant to the general end of preserving life. These rules are not deduced from or entailed by the general principle; they are "implied, suggested, or hinted at" by the principle. (337) The indeterminate policy, sanctity of life, works in terms of Aiken's levels of moral discourse like an ethical principle that tests lower level rules of moral conduct. It has a procedural rather than a substantive function. What becomes crucial therefore are the more concrete rules that give specification to the general policy of sanctity of life.

Though admitting a variety of rules bearing on the policy of sanctity of life, Callahan enumerates five he thinks crucial: "(a) the survival and integrity of the human species, (b) the integrity of family lineages, (c) the integrity of bodily life, (d) the integrity of personal choice and self-determination, mental and emotional individuality, and (e) the integrity of personal bodily individuality." (327) Although such rules obviously overlap and under certain conditions could also conflict, Callahan does not think it likely "that a fixed ordering could be worked out which would be good for all times and in all circumstances." (336) It is normally assumed that the individual's "right to life" is the primary rule, since without human subjects all is beside the point. However, even this rule could come into question "if the survival of the species or of a whole people or nation were in danger from overpopulation, a scarcity of medical facilities or in time of war." (336) Thus the relationship between principle and rules should be kept flexible so that there can be a sensitive response to changing human contexts and shifting human needs.

Ignoring the why or where of Callahan's assumption that these are the crucial rules for the specification of "sanctity of life," there is still a serious question if this account is adequate. For contrary to Callahan's insistence that he is not trying to determine the priority of the rules, it seems clear he has done so by assuming in some circumstances the human species has a preemptive claim to existence. (328-330) This presupposes that the individual is subordinate to the interest of the survival of the greatest number which can determine what should and should not count for life.

The difficulty is that this provides a warrant for possible inhumanity in the name of an abstraction called "human species." It assumes that what is important about man is that he simply exist. Moreover, it implies that there is no good for which men might willingly die, even if it meant the end of them as a specific group, in order that the very meaning of what it is to be human be preserved. By leaving the content of "human species" empty and by refusing to indicate any subsequent priority in the constitutive rules, Callahan has come dangerously close to assuming that individual human life is always subject to the interests of the whole, no matter what those interests might be. It is hard to see what stops this line of reasoning from being applicable only to the abortion situation.

It may be objected that this criticism fails to do justice to Callahan's full position. For example, the arguments he makes against the moral policy of abortion-on-demand seem to qualify the above. He finds too ambiguous, for example, the idea that no unwanted child ought ever to be born; more importantly it implies that the value of the fetus is dependent on human interests. However, he leaves open the possibility of abortion on demand if hard statistical evidence could be produced which demonstrated that "unwanted conceptus" pose a danger to society. This makes sense only if Callahan is assuming that the interests of society take precedence over that of the continued existence of individuals. But what "interests" should count? Society and its interests are but abstractions unless we make clear what moral substance is implied by their use. There is at least the suggestion in Callahan's analysis that interest of society is simply the sum of the individual will, regardless of what is willed, of those that constitute society. But if society does not embody a moral good that offers a more fundamental conception of the nature of man, then it is very hard to see why any one person should be asked to be sacrificed for it. It may be the question of the protection of the fetus involves more than the conflict of interest groups, but rather it raises the question to what extent the good society should protect the rights of all its citizens.

Callahan himself feels very strongly that a general policy of abortion or any routine or unthinking employment of abortion is morally reprehensible. I have great sympathy with his attempt to formulate an ethical position that can deal with the tragedy that often results from the value conflicts in some abortion decisions; what must be asked is whether the ethical methodology he adopts involves implications he would not wish to draw.

I wonder if Callahan's major difficulty is not unlike the problems he associates with Roman Catholic arguments—a tendency to assume that the moral life is a highly formal and rationalistic affair. Men do not actually embody high level principles such as "sanctity of life" nor do they evaluate or test their actual moral practices in terms of such general policies. Maybe they ought to do so, but there may also be more wisdom in men just doing or not doing certain things than is immediately apparent. For such ideas as "sanctity of life" are not efficaciously sustained in our lives by intellectual argument, but by the fact that we inherit from the richness of human history certain practices that we simply do and do not do. It may be our hesitancy to have abortion is a good in itself that does not need further justification. Put another way, our notion of human life is not what determines our practices but our practices determine how we come to understand what human life means. The problem arises from the fact that our inherited language, which comes associated with the practice, is not sufficient to account for some of the more ambiguous abortion situations. By making use of conceptual abstractions to help us adjudicate these situations, we tend to forget that the prohibition against abortion itself does not need a wider theory in order to sustain its significance. Having once entered on such a program, our conceptualizations tend to undermine the practice.

My criticisms of Callahan would seem to entail a position similar to Grisez's, as it is his explicit intention to deny that our duties depend on the good consequences that an act might have. He wants to establish the inalienable right of all men to life and in so doing to deny any attempt to make discriminations based on our obvious differences or imputed worth. The question that determines his moral analysis is therefore whether it is ever ethically permissible for one person to attack another with the direct intention to kill him. (304-5)

The basic problem for all ethics, according to Grisez, is how moral freedom and moral standards can be reconciled, since the moral life is equally dependent on each. By freedom he means our capacity of self-determination that allows us to determine our own life through our power of choice. Such a freedom is not irrational, since it is possible only if we can rationally determine our actions by choosing among the alternatives open to us. Therefore, our ability for self-determination is not antithetical to basic human needs, but is only actual as we embody the drives for satisfaction inherent to our nature. At a minimum these essential human goods include: (1) life itself, including physical and mental health and safety, (2) activities engaged in for their own sake including those which also serve an ulterior purpose, (3) experiences sought for their own sake, (4) knowledge pursued for its own sake, (5) interior integrity and harmony among the various components of the self, (6) genuineness, that is, conformity between inner self and outward behavior, and (7) worship and holiness. (312-313)

These "needs" are not necessary constituents of each of our choices, but are possible purposes for our action. Thus Grisez's naturalism is not involved in the naturalistic fallacy, at least not immediately since these goods are understood to be like the "non-hypothetical principles of practical reason such as Kant wished to discover." (314) They are not what must be so but "what-is-to-be thought" in our action and therefore their "oughtness" is not the same as the "ought" of moral obligation. These fundamental goods are the principles of practical reason but cannot of themselves determine the morally good or evil.

Moral goodness is determined by the attitude with which we choose in so far as our attitude is conformed with reality. "To choose a particular good with an appreciation of its genuine but limited possibility and its objectively human character is to choose it with an attitude of realism. Such choice does not attempt to transform and belittle the goodness of what is not chosen, but only to realize what is chosen." (315) This is crucial, for no choice can embrace all the possible goods before man. Thus the basic moral attitude is one which tries in every choice not to deny one good in the name of another or subvert some principle of practical reason by appeal to another. An evil attitude is one which concentrates on one good to the exclusion of others. "The attitude of immorality is an irrational attempt to reorganize the moral universe, so that the center is not the whole range of human possibilities in which we can all share, but the goods I can actually pursue through my actions." (316) What Grisez seems to be recommending is what Nicolai Hartmann called the virtue of many-sidedness as one tries to act in such a way that no aspect of the reality of the realm of values is denied.

Thus the good man for Grisez always acts so as to remain open to all goods and avoids acting in any way which would inhibit other realizations of the good. One with a right moral attitude never acts directly against any basic good for this is to subordinate one good to another. Killing is immoral because human life is a basic good intrinsic to a person. "To choose directly to destroy a human life is to turn against this fundamental human good." (319-320)

It is not easy to understand exactly what kind of position Grisez is recommending. It has affinities to some forms of natural law positions but the notion of moral attitude and its relation to the realm of values seems to be derived from another source. It assumes the objectivity of moral values and goods but it is not clear exactly what ontological status pertains to such goods. Nor is it clear why Grisez concentrates on "attitude" as the very essence of moral behavior. However, even if one waives this, it is by no means clear that his account of what makes a "moral" attitude is the only possible one.

For example, Grisez's account does not seem to allow for the kind of single-minded pursuit of the good often associated with men of extreme moral seriousness. On Grisez's terms such men of purity appear to be morally degenerate since they fail to play life loose enough to keep all possibilities of the good open. Grisez seems to be very close to Callahan in wanting every decision to embody as many values as possible. It is interesting to ask how Grisez's recommendation of such a moral attitude differs formally from Callahan's idea of moral policy.

The significant difference between them, however, lies in Grisez's assumption that human goods "constitute a unified field for our choices" (317) in such a way that, ideally, they are not involved in significant conflict. Therefore, it is with some hesitation that Grisez admits that any moral system must ultimately consider the justification of killing human beings since certain hard cases cannot be ignored. This recognition would seem to qualify Grisez's general normative theory, at least to the extent that what it means to have a moral attitude is recognized as more complex than openness to the greatest possible range of human goods. Such a recommendation is far too general to account for the fact that the most significant aspect of our moral behavior centers in the necessity of making discriminating judgments which involve competing positive good. In other words, Grisez does not seem to provide the necessary theoretical account of why so many of our moral arguments take the form of choices between "lesser evils."

Grisez does not try to avoid considering certain hard cases, however, where it seems that we must directly take life. But in order to maintain his insistence that there is an absolute prohibition to any direct attack on human life he employs the principle of double effect to try to describe the taking of life in such circumstances as "unintended" consequence. For an act to fall under this principle four conditions must be fulfilled simultaneously: (1) the act must not be wrong in itself, even apart from possible bad effects, (2) an agent's intention must be right (one cannot aim at the death of the other directly), (3) the evil effect must not be the means to the good effect, (4) there must be a proportionately grave reason for doing such an act, since there is a general obligation to avoid evil so far as possible. (329). Grisez is aware that this last condition can easily lead to a limited form of utilitarianism and he is critical of attempts to expand the meaning of the principle to cover the agent's wider moral intention.

Grisez is also critical of the principle in so far as it only allows for abortion in a narrow number of cases—e.g., ectopic pregnancies and cancer of the uterus. An abortion cannot be performed where the fetus threatens the mother because of heart or kidney defect since the operation would directly intend the destruction of the fetus rather than the removal of a diseased organ. Grisez finds this too restrictive as "it demands that even in the order of physical causality the evil aspect of the act not precede the good." (333) From the "point of view of human moral activity" the act is an indivisible process throughout, with all that is involved in the process being equally immediate. Grisez argues that this does not qualify the inviolability of human life from direct attack but only extends the principle to situations where the mother's life is directly threatened. He refuses, therefore, to apply the same extension to cases where the very life of the mother is not in question—e.g., to those involving psychological indications, birth defects, social hardship, rape, and incest.

It is not clear exactly how Grisez can so limit the principle, for in his reinterpretation he has assumed the primacy of the "point of view of human moral activity." He has granted, therefore, exactly the point at issue, namely that the agent's description of the act has some claim to acceptance as a proper description of the act. No matter how he may deny it, Grisez has actually assumed the relative value of the lives involved, since the removal of the fetus from a heart patient obviously presupposes a judgment of the value of the mother over that of the fetus. Grisez no more than Callahan can avoid the kind of consequential reasoning that our human sensibilities seem to demand in such cases. Nor is it clear why only such extreme cases where the life of the mother is threatened may count as possible reasons for abortion.

In spite of this sophisticated and detailed argument, Grisez actually avoids the issue at stake. The extreme artificiality of the idea of intention associated with the principle of double effect suggests that there is a fundamental error in the basic normative position. In this respect I tend to agree with Callahan that double effect seems to be concerned not with what good can be grasped from tragic situations but at saving "the good conscience of those who might but do not act to save" those under such duress. (424) We can appreciate Grisez's attempt to expand the meaning of double effect, but it is doubtful he can do so without calling into question his basic presumption that life can never be subject to direct attack.

The question of abortion frustrates both Grisez's and Callahan's normative positions. Whether the development of more sophisticated normative theories can remove the ambiguities must be left an open question. It may be that issues such as abortion are finally not susceptible to intellectual "solution." I do not mean to suggest that we cease trying to formulate the problem in the most responsible manner possible, but rather that our best recourse may be to watch how good men and women handle the tragic alternatives we often confront in abortion situations. For Aristotle's insight that virtue is finally what the man of wisdom does may be all that can be said about such issues. For no amount of ethical reflection will ever change the basic fact that tragedy is a reality of our lives. A point is reached where we must have the wisdom to cease ethical reflection and affirm that certain issues indicate a reality more profound than the ethical.

8.

Abortion: The Agent's Perspective

Abortion is fundamentally a moral problem. Sociological, psychological, medical and legal information is necessary for any full discussion of abortion as an issue; but as Callahan has shown no amount of "facts" can determine whether abortion is right or wrong. To recognize this is to confront the hard issue concerning abortion, for it does not seem possible to hold a consistent moral position that does justice to the conflict of positive values often involved in this issue. For example the old textbook morality of Roman Catholic moral theology that assumed ethics was primarily a matter of following objective is insufficient for the hard cases that often seem to be involved in abortion. Callahan is hopeful that the "new moralists" who emphasize the significance of the situation, the conflict of value often involved in moral decisions, and the necessity of a flexible attitude toward moral decision will develop a moral methodology sufficient to the issue of abortion.[1]

Callahan is right to suggest that abortion is a basic test case for anyone's fundamental ethical and metaethical position; however, it is not clear that "the new ethics" is somehow going to be more sufficient for this issue. For as odd as it may seem, the new approach continues, like the "old morality," to assume that morally it knows what an abortion is. In this essay I will argue that it is just this assumption that must be questioned and analyzed. This has failed to be done in the past because we have inherited the language of abortion that seems to inform us quite adequately to the moral nature of abortion; yet our language is much more ambiguous than this, as our difficulties with the hard cases of abortion reveal.

In terms of this problem, those that argue for a policy of

---

[1]Daniel Callahan, *Abortion: Law, Choice, and Morality* (New York: Macmillan, 1970). 426-433.

pro-abortion have not faced up to the significance of their claim. For the very notion "abortion" carries a general prohibition against the taking of life derived from human experience. Thus, involved in the pro-abortionist argument is nothing less than a language reforming proposal, i.e., that abortion is not abortion. That is why the proposals that argue that abortion should be understood as the removal of tissue such as the appendix or some other such euphemism, no matter how we might be convinced that such an account is correct, still strike us as a bit odd. For such a suggestion seems to imply that we can possibly redescribe many possible moral evils as doing good.

The problem neither side in this debate address is what factors should be considered in morally describing an act as an abortion. How should I see or learn to describe what is in fact going on in the removal of the fetus from the mother's body before term? What should be the significance for the description of the act of the agent's understanding of what is happening? These questions make clear that the moral problem of abortion does not begin only when one asks, "Should I or should I not have an abortion" but rather with a more basic question "What is an abortion?" As we shall see these questions are interdependent, but they cannot be identified. Not to see this has caused much confusion in the discussion, because it has made it appear that what morally is at stake about abortion is a judgment about a clearly describable act. Those that want to argue for the possibility of abortion in some cases are then under an especially heavy burden, because in the very acceptance of the "description" of the act of abortion they accept a perjorative understanding of the practice.

One could of course argue that human experience and language are wrong in this respect and that abortion should be regarded in a morally positive manner. This is important as I do not wish to argue that we should simply accept what our language seems to imply is the case with abortion. The fact that men have called many extremely evil things good, is enough reason to call into question the acceptance of our inherited moral language as normative. In relation to the question of abortion, however, I shall argue that our languge is correct to understand abortion as a morally doubtful practice. But what is not clear is whether every act that has the physical characteristics of an abortion should be morally considered to be such.

As a way of indicating what I take to be some of the primary theological and ethical issues at stake in understanding what an abortion is, I will briefly consider two main questions: (1) When does life begin? and (2) When can life be taken legitimately? My general response to these questions will be that the fetus should be regarded as human life and that the range of exceptions for the possible taking of the life of the fetus is very narrow. Many who argue from a similar position seem to think that this is the end of the issue. However, I shall try to show that this fails to account for one other question that should be asked, namely (3) What does the agent understand to be happening?

This last suggestion may seem inconsistent with my position regarding the general practice of abortion. That is, it will make it appear that I must maintain with Callahan that there are "no automatic moral lines to be drawn against abortion; each case must be judged individually."[2] In one sense I agree with this as it is tautalogically true that each case of abortion insofar as it is judged must be judged individually, but I do not agree that each case must have unique aspects associated with it that would make inapplicable to it the notion of abortion. How I can maintain this and yet try to take account of the agent's perspective will be the primary burden of this essay.

I assume that this will have an interest beyond the immediate question of abortion, for we find in much ethical literature today, especially Roman Catholic, that a new appreciation of the significance of the agent in moral behavior must be taken into account in our moral reflection.[3] The unique history of the agent, his personal vision, his character cannot be excluded from consideration of the significance of any one act. I am in sympathy with this emphasis as it indicates the inappropriateness of abstracting and analyzing "acts" from moral behavior as if they were discreet units separated from the person who acts.[4] However, what is not clear is how this emphasis on the agent's history can avoid a vicious form of subjectivism or relativism. I hope to show in this essay that at least in relation to the question of abortion a proper understanding of the significance of the agent's perspective does not entail such conclusions.

---

[2]Callahan, op. cit., 18.

[3]For example see Charles Curran, A New Look at Christian Morality (Notre Dame: Fides Publishers, 1968).

[4]The old and new morality, especially as the latter assumes the form of situation ethics, agree insofar as each concentrates on atomistically conceived "acts."

First, however, I must consider the questions of the status of the fetus and under what conditions it might be justifiable to destroy it. Only when these questions have been discussed is the significance of the agent's perception properly raised.

When Does Life Begin?

What must be made clear about this question is that there is no sure way to remove the ambiguity that must surround any answer given to it. Any attribution of human life to the fetus is necessarily stipulative. Appeals to biological evidence of the uniqueness of the geneotype at the time of conception cannot change this.[5] Rather what is at stake in this question is whether we deny significant aspects of our own being by our failure to regard and treat the fetus as life.

It is my contention that even though the fetus has none of the characteristics we associate with "achieved humanity," its physicality represents the necessary basis for any possible form of what we think of as "fully human." The moral importance of the recognition of the fetus as human is a way of indicating our own essential physicality. Though this can be established on strictly philosophical grounds, I have special theological reasons for this position, as the physical is significant as the necessary basis for man's convenantal relation with God.[6] It is extremely important to understand this correctly, for there has always been a great temptation by theologians to give status to mankind's tendency to presuppose that only when a man is spiritualized is he worthy of God. The physical has often been treated

---

[5]John Noonan seems to assume that this is not the case; he is convinced that biology has established once and for all that the fetus must be considered as life from the moment of conception. See Noonan's "An Almost Absolute Value in History" in *The Morality of Abortion: Legal and Historical Perspectives,* edited by John Noonan (Cambridge: Harvard University Press, 1970). For an attempt to restate the delayed animation theory found among some scholastics see Joseph Donceel, "Animation and Hominization," *Theological Studies* (March, 1970), 76-105. The fact that during one period on the basis of bad biology some theologians held a late animation theory is not very significant. Noonan and Grisez both persuasively show that the primary direction of the church's teaching in this respect has been to protect the life of the fetus from its conception.

[6]Presupposed in this essay is an understanding of the relation of theological and ethical notions and reflections that would take far too long to make more explicit or defend. Generally it should be clear that I do not think that theological affirmation can directly determine the moral questions involved in the question of abortion.

as but a necessary stage that men must transcend in order to reach the "full humanity" God intends for them. The physical, however, is not the basis for man's "full humanity" before God as a platform to rise from; but rather we can come before God only as our "full humanity" is embodied through the physical. God does not will to love us as something more than men, but exactly as we are men who acquire our self-determination and creativity in and through the form of the physical. Salvation may be the intensification of the physical, but it cannot be its denial.

In less theological terms this means that we must recognize that our lives are inherently concrete and particular. I cannot be anyone I wish, but whoever I am and become will be done through the physical and biographical "givens" that make possible my being at all. I cannot love all women, but only the woman I am joined with in marriage. I cannot regard children as precious unless I learn to regard my own son as a marvelous gift. I cannot love or serve mankind, but I must serve this man and this institution with all the ambiguities of their historical existence. To recognize the significance of the physical means that we must constantly fight against our tendency to see the particular as but the manifestation of the universal, for the universal comes only in the form of the concrete.

In the current abortion debate the church is again being tempted by the cultural spiritualizers of our day to assume that real man is something more than and in spite of the physical. The call of these new gnostics is indeed tempting, as they appeal to our most refined aesthetic and ethical tastes to indicate what makes human life truly human. Theologians have often succumbed to this point of view in their interpretations of man's sexuality, as they assumed that only as our sexuality was ignored or denied was it acceptable before God.

These assumptions of man's flight from the physical seem questionable in the light of contemporary philosophical psychology, but theologically they must be resisted as but another attempt of men to deny the finite character of their existence. Man constantly attempts to make himself more than man by denying his limits. We fail to see that the limits of our existence, our physicality, our particular history, death, provides the necessary condition for regarding life precious and worthwhile.

Those who assume that abortion is a relatively insignificant

moral matter because the fetus is only "physical" are but
Manichees in a new form. What we tend to forget is that the
hard challenges to the faith come not in the forms of the crude
materialist, but rather as the defenders of the highest spiritual
goods in the name of ideal humanity. Insofar as the Catholic
position on abortion has resisted this attempt to free itself from
the peculiar claims of the physical it has made an important
contribution, for the theologian must resist any attempt to
suggest that the physical is but an incidental aspect of our
standing before God.

It is clear that the Christian should therefore have a strong
bias in favor of the fetus' development. Of course, this does not
answer the question of when life begins, for theological categories do not in themselves supply such information. Theological reflection does not supplant the necessity of human conceptualization and argument, but rather religious language only
creates the context in which such concepts and arguments have
significance. One must simply admit that there can be no
absolute certainty to any account of where physical life begins.
But if the significance of the physical is accepted, then I can see
no reason why the *conceptus* should not be regarded as human
life.

I want to be very clear about the nature of this assertion. I
am not trying to claim that the factual nature of the *conceptus*
necessitates attributing to it the status of human life; but rather
I am arguing that if the notion of human physical life I have
defended theologically is to be meaningful there are good reasons to consider the *conceptus* as life. The simply physical
nature of the *conceptus* does not determine what meaning the
idea of life has, but rather the idea of life determines why it is
significant to regard the *conceptus* as an important aspect of
life. Of course, there is no reason in principle that other accounts of life might not be possible that do not entail such an
understanding of the *conceptus,* but I would think that not
only would they be theologically doubtful but they would
appear extremely odd in terms of any common sense understanding of human life.

When the argument is put in this form it helps illuminate the
assertion some make that the fetus should be regarded as only
another piece of tissue in the mother's body. Against this many
call forth the factual nature of the fetus in terms of its genetic

and physical originality. But such appeals are only good insofar as one assumes that the idea of individual human life includes these kinds of physical characteristics. The hard question put to those who regard the fetus as tissue is not the factual one, but rather what view of life have they accepted by doing so. One must ask in what way their appeals to the "quality of life" to justify abortion include or deny the kind of aspects of life they refuse to recognize in the fetus.

When Can Life Be Taken?

No one needs to be told that taking the life of another is wrong. There is even something odd about our trying to give philosophical or theological reasons why we should hold that killing in almost all circumstances is wrong. It makes it sound as if the practice of respecting the existence of another is problematic depending on the formulation of reasons. Rather it is a fundamental assumption of our lives together. Without such an assumption the trust and love we think so important to meaningful human existence would prove to be impossible.

Insofar as the fetus is human life, then, it falls under this general prohibition against the taking the life of another. What creates difficulty for most of us about abortion is the hard cases where the taking of life seems to be a tragic but necessary act. In respect to these kinds of problems, what must be avoided is the possible arbitrariness of our subjectivities. The human capacity to give "good" reasons for being able to ignore the existence of the other, even to killing him, should never be underestimated. The more serious and basic the moral issue the more we are forced to make clear and justify our inchoate moral feelings that are sufficient for less significant issues. In relation to abortion, perhaps the best check against ourselves is to ask how the proposed abortion can be made nonapplicable to infanticide. In the light of such a question such criteria as dependency of the fetus, social stress, and economic deprivation seem problematic at best. For surely it is largely sentimental and cultural hesitancy that prevent such criteria from being applied to the four-month-old infant as well as to the four-month-old fetus.

It is, however, important to notice that this way of putting the matter makes clear that every case of abortion need not be subsumed under the category of murder, though some cases of abortion may be so described. While I should not deny that every case of abortion may have some physical similarities to murder, it is important to maintain the distinction as a way of indicating that there is often more descriptively and morally involved in an abortion than murder (insofar as murder involves more than killing life, but is an intentional unjustified attack on the innocent). The difference I think is not that the object of one act is usually thought of as a conscious individual while the other is not, but rather that the intentionality (which is not necessarily the same as the conscious intention of the agent) of the act of abortion is not the same as the intentionality of the act of murder. The mere fact that we tend to think of the former often in terms of the lesser of two evils is sufficient to distinguish it from murder.

Put another way this means that the physical characteristics of two acts may look exactly the same, but they may have different moral significance. If someone shoots me I am equally dead whether he did it purposively with malice or accidentally; but morally it makes all the difference. Thus I am suggesting that we need more sophisticated distinctions concerning the physical act of abortion to help us evaluate the kind of moral question involved in the various acts of abortion.

The best way to do this is through analogical comparisons of the abortion situations with other situations where the taking of human life seems to be unavoidable. For example, in abortion situations of life against life do we have a situation similar to justified self-defense? There are obvious analogies insofar as there seems to be a choice of one life or the other, but there is also the disanalogy of whether the fetus can be stipulated as an aggressor. It is only when we engage in that kind of reflection that the implication of the morality of direct abortion will be clear; or perhaps better put, it is then we will better understand ethically what abortion is. I suspect that the upshot of such a process for Christians will be to seriously limit the possibility of abortion, for it is just such a reflection that will make clear that the abortion situation involves not only the question of the life of the fetus but takes out a much more fundamental draft on the meaningfulness of all forms of human interdependency.

These kinds of arguments may appear at best irrelevant to the

young girl or mature woman who finds herself with an unwanted pregnancy, who feels that she is the suffering subject of
a masculine ethos and who feels nothing more toward the fetus
than revulsion and hate. I am not suggesting that perhaps the
best thing for all concerned in such a situation is to have the
fetus aborted. Rather I am trying to at least make clear that this
act of abortion cannot be seen as just an isolated act, but
involves fundamental options about the nature and significance
of life itself. What morally is at stake here is not the ability to
point a judgmental finger at a murderer, but rather what kind of
person we wish or ought to be.

In this connection I find some of the popular assumptions
about the morality of abortion rather shallow. For example,
many assume that in situations where there is a danger to the
life of the mother by the continued growth of the fetus not to
abort is positively immoral. To be sure, I should not wish to
deny such a possibility, but to assume it is the only alternative
is to limit too severely the moral possibilities. It may well be that
a woman is so committed to a particular understanding of the
nature of human life that she willingly suffers the possibility of
her own death in order to be faithful to that commitment
which her whole life as wife and mother has expressed to that
time. Of course, the situation may call for more complex
considerations in terms of the claims of the father, other children and wider social responsibilities. I should not wish to give a
warrant to any moral argument that could ignore these kinds of
considerations, but it may be that these claims are morally
based or at least interdependent with the ethical options involved in the attempts to protect the fetus.

In the context of these remarks, I wish to make clear I do not
agree with those who argue that once possible exceptions to the
taking of life are admitted in connection with abortion then
Auschwitz is somehow right around the corner. There is clearly
no logical relation between these, nor is it clear that there is
even a psychological relation. I must admit I have always found
rather unconvincing the argument that suggests that the
granting of possible exceptions for certain kinds of abortion
would be to undermine the value of "sanctity of life" in the
face of our nation's military spending alone, not to mention the
degradation of life we are willing to tolerate in our ghettos. If

what we have now is sanctity of life, then perhaps it could stand to be undermined.[7]

Yet I think there is some force to the anti-abortionist argument insofar as it asks on what basis one can render problematic the general recommendation against abortion as a practice.[8] Why should the fetus or a class be distinguished from other forms of life as being particularly open to destruction? There are many sentimental reasons that can be given for this, but I think this should not blind us to the fact that there has not yet been a good reason given for why the fetus should be so singled out. To maintain the significance of the fetus is not to assume it has an overriding right against all other claims; but rather its protection is an affirmation of life from which all other claims draw their significance, i.e., that we must learn to regard another's life as good insofar as it is, not insofar as it is useful.

Abortion and the Agent

The argument I have made to this point would tend to deny the possibility of abortion except in a few hard cases. It would be nice to be able to leave the case here and simply brand anyone who does not agree with it as morally obtuse. However, one cannot help but be impressed with the testimony of many who actually deal with women seeking or thinking about abortion and how foreign the theoretical considerations I have been making are to their actual difficulties. For example Howard Moody, one of the proponents of the change in the New York law, has said:

But the actual process of working with women compelled us to move beyond strictly theoretical hang-ups. In this process we always had to consider the moral questions of whether it is justifiable to force the unwanted upon the unwilling. In our anxiety to honor the theory of the sanctity of life in *general* we have played fast and loose with particular

---

[7]This is one of the reasons I avoid the phrase "sanctity of life" for it tends to become an ideological position, since it leaves very ambiguous what kind of life is to be sanctified. I also have theological reservations, since it often implies that man can and should create life sacred rather than responding to God's prior sanctifying of life.

[8]The distinction between abortion as a practice and as an act is as crucial as it is complex. However, the validity of the distinction is clear, for an act of abortion may be warranted as a moral but tragic possibility without entailing the conclusion that any abortion is morally permissible.

women's lives and forced them by legal fiat to bear children that they never intended to conceive.[9]

While there is much in this quote with which I disagree, it at least raises the question of what should be the status of the agent's point of view in establishing the description of what is going on.

Put in a more theoretical context I think that such a consideration is important as a way of indicating that moral behavior involves more than moral judgments. Iris Murdoch has argued that behaviorism in the philosophy of mind combined with the ethicist fascination with class words and the principle of universalizability has produced the idea that the essence of the moral life is made up of "external choices backed up by arguments which appeal to facts."[10] Against this she claims that there are kinds of moral outlooks and positive moral conceptions which are unconnected with or at least their moral significance is not determined directly by the principle of universality.[11] This is not meant to disparage the importance of the principle of universalizability for moral judgments; rather it is an attempt to show that there is more in an agent's deliberation and decisions that is morally important than is in the spectator's judgment about his decision.[12]

Put in a somewhat different way this is to argue that the moral life is best understood like an artist engaged in his skill than a critic making a judgment about the complete work.[13]

---

[9]Howard Moody, "Abortion: Women's Right and Legal Problem," *Christianity and Crisis* XXXI (March 8, 1971), 28.

[10]Iris Murdoch, "Vision and Choice in Morality" in *Christian Ethics and Contemporary Philosophy*, edited by Ian T. Ramsey (New York: Macmillan Co., 1966), 195-201.

[11]*Ibid.*, 207-208.

[12]It is of course true that morally serious men often use the principle of universalizability to guide their decisions and to guard against the temptation to make an exception for themselves in the face of a morally difficult choice. Kurt Baier has made this point persuasively in *The Moral Point of View* (New York: Random House, 1966). Baier argues that to be considered morally serious persons, we must always be willing to judge our action by the rules we hold, rules that can be meant for everyone (100-109). Though I think this is correct, the very fact that some men stand before such difficult choices seems to indicate that there is more to their moral life and decision than their willingness to constantly judge their own decisions by such criteria.

[13]See Stuart Hampshire, "Fallacies in Moral Philosophy," *Mind* 68 (1949), 466-67.

The processes of thought which are characteristic of the artist or the craftsman in conceiving and executing his designs are essentially different from the process of the critic who passes judgment on the artist's work. Our typical moral problems are not spectator's problems whether one should or should not do something, but rather what we are doing, under what description we are doing it, and with what consistency as to our history and peculiar experiences.

It is one thing, however, to point this out, and it is quite another to assess the agent's point of view for what it should tell us about the descriptions of the moral act. For I would not in any way want the emphasis on the significance of the agent to be taken as a warrant for the rather unthinking abortion on grounds such as the fetus' inconvenience. As a way of drawing the kind of issue we may have here, I want to take a concrete example offered by James Gustafson.[14] Not only is this a good example, but it has been criticized by Grisez in a way that should help us to be clearer about the significance of the agent's perspective. Gustafson describes the case like this:

The pregnant woman is in her early twenties. She is a lapsed Catholic, with no significant religious affiliation at the present time, although she expresses some need for a "church." Her marriage was terminated by divorce; her husband was given custody of three children by that marriage. She had an affair with a man who "befriended" her, but there were no serious propsects for a marriage with him, and the affair has ended. Her family life was as disrupted and as tragic as that which is dramatically presented in Eugene O'Neill's *Long Day's Journey into Night*. Her alcoholic mother mistreated her children, coerced them into deceptive activity for her ends, and was given to periods of violence. Her father has been addicted to drugs, but has managed to continue in business, avoid incarceration, and provide a decent income for his family. The pregnant woman fled from home after high school to reside in a distant state, and has no significant contact with her parents or siblings. She has two or three friends.

Her pregnancy occurred when she was raped by her former husband and three other men after she had agreed to meet him to talk about their children. The rapes can only be described as acts of sadistic vengeance. She is unwilling to prefer charges against the men, since she believes it would

---

[14]James Gustafson, "A Protestant Ethical Approach" in *The Morality of Abortion: Legal and Historical Perspectives* (Cambridge: Harvard U. Press, 1970), 101-122.

be a further detriment to her children. She has no steady job, partially because of periodic gastro-intestinal illnesses, and has no other income. There are no known physiological difficulties which would jeopardize her life or that of the child. She is unusually intelligent and very articulate, and is not hysterical about her situation. Termination of the pregnancy is a live option for her as a way to cope with one of the many difficulties she faces.[15]

Gustafson notes that one of the most compelling aspects of this girl's personality is her continuing positive orientation toward life in spite of the considerable adversity she has experienced in her life. She still wishes to achieve positive goals, plans to go to college or take up professional work of some kind that will give her some feeling of worthwhile work for others, each of which indicates she has not been defeated by her past. She can even articulate the possibility of keeping this child as part of her continuing project to secure some good out of this life.

In analyzing this case Gustafson tries to avoid two extremes: (1) that which assumes the matter is settled by the fact that there are no physiological difficulties present in the pregnancy and thus abortion should be denied; and (2) that which assumes that morally she should simply do whatever she feels is best for her. Gustafson would rather recognize that the moralist and the woman are in an interpersonal relationship and his first responsibility is to be open and attempt to understand her. However, as a

moralist he is to help her to objectify her situation, to see it from other perspectives than the one she comes with. He is to call to her attention not only alternative courses of action with some of the potential consequences of each, but also the value of life and those values which would have to be higher in order to warrant the taking of life.[16]

Gustafson is therefore quite aware that as a moralist he comes to this situation with definite presuppositions and judgments that determine how he relates to this girl. For example, he assumes the viability of the fetus as life from the moment of conception. Moreover as a Christian moralist he has a basic perspective determined by his belief in God's reconciliation and redemption and His special relation to the weak that creates a

---

[15]*Ibid.*, 107.
[16]*Ibid.*, 109.

moral bias that "life is to be preserved, the weak and the helpless are to be cared for especially, the moral requisite of trust, hope, love, freedom, justice and others are to be met so that human life can be meaningful."[17] However, as a moralist his decision is also informed by his view of human life that knows a child born within stable conditions of love is more likely to have a better quality of life than one born under other conditions. He must therefore recognize that the human in such situations involves more than the physical, thus whether the conditions necessary to sustain and heal the humanity of the child and the mother in the future must be considered.

Given this description of the agent's and the moralist's perspective, Gustafson concludes that if he were in this woman's human predicament he could morally justify and give moral propriety to the possibility of her attaining an abortion.[18] Though such a decision cannot be based solely on "logic," it clearly does not involve the assertion that "the situation determines everything." Rather the two special conditions that provide the moral viability of this woman's decision to have an abortion are the fact that the pregnancy is the result of a sex crime and the social and emotional conditions for the well-being of the mother and child are not advantageous for each one's humane development.

Germain Grisez points out that Gustafson has not completely taken the point of view of the agent in this example, because he

has actually presented us with an abstraction which might occur in an indefinitely repeated set of cases. Moreover, in stating his belief that he could justify abortion in this instance, he is making a judgment the validity of which is independent of whether one is involved or not. Whoever makes an ethical judgment affirms that if he or anyone else were in the position of an agent, that ethical judgment would be a sound guide for acting.[19]

This is not however a devastating critique, since Gustafson is quite ready to admit that his account involves such "abstraction" that is based on moral and theological judgments. Moreover, Gustafson in fact indicates his two conditions are applicable to similar cases. (In this respect his second condition of "well-being" would need much fuller explication.)

---

[17]*Ibid.*, 114.

[18]*Ibid.*, 117.

[19]Grisez, *op. cit.*, 269.

However, what is especially important to notice is that Gustafson has not said that every woman in such a predicament (whose case meets his two conditions) can or ought to have an abortion. That is quite another matter. Rather what he has said is that *these* conditions for *this* girl at least establish the moral possibility of abortion. By using the word "moral" in this context Gustafson is not implying that "abortion is therefore a good thing to do." An abortion is no occasion for rejoicing, for just as the morally conscientious soldier is convinced life can and ought to be taken "justly" but also "mournfully," "so the moralist can be convinced that the life of the defenseless fetus can be taken, less justly, but more mournfully."[20]

This is extremely important, for it means that abortion morally is justified under an ethical perspective that tries to pull as much good as possible from the situation. Thus I assume there are a number of different conditions which if present might have made a difference in Gustafson's ultimate decision. For example, if he could have presupposed a community to morally and physically sustain this girl and her child, he could have perhaps encouraged her to carry the fetus to term. By community I do not mean just her immediate associates, but also a general societal ethos and institutional arrangement that encourages the enhancement of life beyond simply having laws against abortion. In the absence of such community abortion becomes a tragic option.[21]

Moreover the girl's own biography limits and enhances the moral possibilities of the decision, for it might be that the presence of the child can be seen as a lure of hope in a world in which violent acts of rape can occur. Thus it might be possible to help the girl regard the fetus as a moral opportunity to come to terms with herself and what has happened to her. It would be her way of affirming what had often been denied in others' treatment of her, that is, that the life of another, regardless of its doubtful beginnings, is a precious gift that contains the seeds of each of our own humanity.

---

[20]Gustafson, *op. cit.*, 122. Gustafson does not deny therefore that what is going on in this case still has aspects to it that make it appropriate to call this an abortion. The girl's own perception does not provide the grounds for changing the moral description of the act, but rather aspects of her perception provide the grounds for broadening the moral framework in which the abortion takes place.

[21]One of the troubling aspects of those who argue against reform of abortion laws is their unwillingness to follow out the implication of the phrase "respect life" for other social and institutional forms beside the law.

Yet Gustafson does not think such moral possibilities are present in this girl, at least not at this time. Rather he is obviously impressed with her grim determination to hang on in the face of unbelievable adversity, and he fears that the continuation of the pregnancy might be the last straw. Thus as a way of affirming as much life and humanity as possible in this situation he thinks it justifiable to entertain the tragic possibility of abortion for this girl.

At the heart of Gustafson's decision is a profound assumption about the context in which theological and ethical reflection must go forward, namely that "the good and the right are found within the conditions of limitations. Present acts respond to the conditions of past actions, conditions which are usually irrevocable, unalterable."[22] Our moral choices do not occur in ideal conditions where right and wrong are apparent, but rather the right must be wrenched from less than ideal alternatives. Moral risk is fundamental to human action for there is no assurance in such contexts that we have "done the right thing." The Christian can only be sustained by his confidence in the forgiveness of God in whose light all our decisions appear less than full of grace.

What Gustafson has attempted to provide is a larger context for the understanding of what is morally at stake in abortion. The context of the abortion involves not only the physical destruction of the fetus, but also at least why the fetus is being destroyed, the conditions of the mother, the situation of conception, the larger societal context, and the limitation of the moral situation. He has tried to give theological and ethical warrants for "seeing" the abortion situation in this way. It is my conviction that he has opened a fruitful line of investigation for increasing our understanding of what is involved in abortion, but I want to raise three questions about his position.

First, there is a slight hint in Gustafson's argument that the moral good involves trying to avoid, as in the case of this woman, "potential tragedy, suffering and anguish." There is also his concern for the environment into which the child is to be born. I do not mean to suggest that we must pursue tragedy, but rather that the good and our being good often come only through suffering and anguish. Particularly troubling in this

---

22Gustafson, *op. cit.*, 115.

respect is the rather shallow happiness ethic that seems to underlie many pro-abortionist arguments. Such an ethic takes as the primary good individual satisfaction. The fetus as well as others appear in such an ethic as but an unwanted bother to be removed. In such a context I am extremely suspicious of any talk of "no unwanted child should be born," since the criterion of "want" tends at the very best to be horribly trite. While there is nothing in Gustafson's position to give comfort to such an ethic of abortion, it seems worthwhile in the contemporary context to make this as clear as possible.

Secondly, it seems to me that in assessing the various points of view involved in this case, Gustafson has paid insufficient attention to that of the fetus. Since he grants the fetus viability it cannot be ignored. Gustafson is surely considering the fetus in terms of the kind of future care that can be anticipated for it, but the question can still be meaningfully asked if the fetus itself would choose not to live rather than be born into such an environment. Gustafson seems to think of the issue primarily in terms of a choice between qualities of life; but the issue is more complex, for it involves the sacrifice of one life by others in the name of a higher good. Would it make a meaningful difference in the argument if the fetus were one day old?

Finally, the note of judgment is missing from Gustafson's account of the moral structure of this abortion situation. I have no interest in defending the strong sense of the moralist as judge that Gustafson is reacting against, that is, of the ethicist who assumes perfect understanding of the morality of abortion so that he is able to pronounce the "right" thing to do regardless of the situation. Rather I mean by judgment the importance of the moralist saying in context that an abortion attitude toward the fetus is fundamentally immoral. Not to do so is to fail to meet the other as we allow the girl to continue in her self-imposed necessities. Moral judgment correctly understood and employed is not self-righteous certitude, but rather a call to the other that there is more to existence than she has possibly allowed. Judgment so understood is the necessary presupposition of a healthy counseling situation, for unless the counselor is willing to judge he does not properly respect the moral being of the one he is trying to help.

What I have tried to do is present the theological and moral presuppositions necessary to understand what an abortion is in terms of the kind of life implied by abortion decisions. It is not a simple picture that gives one a satisfied feeling of understanding how to handle the issue. Rather I hope it has at least served to indicate that the moral significance of how we should see abortion and the language associated with it involves far more than just our opinion on when life begins, but rather is part and parcel of our fundamental perspectives and commitments.

The Individual and Social Problem Of Abortion

In conclusion I want to make a brief point concerning the social problem that abortion represents. Nothing I have said has immediate application to the issue of whether there ought to be or ought not to be a law against abortion, or whether abortion is or is not an acceptable social practice. Each of these issues involves independent questions apart from the morality of abortion in and of itself. It is not my intention to try to enter into this kind of discussion this late in this essay.

Rather I wish only to comment on what I consider to be a rather dangerous tendency to confuse the social, legal and moral issue. This is not the confusion that usually occurs where the former two questions are assumed to be settled by the latter, but rather the confusion I am concerned with is the reverse of this. Many seem to be arguing or suggesting that the moral agent should assume the perspective of society in "responsibly" deciding whether to have or not to have a child. This is often bound up with the problem of overpopulation and the necessity to find acceptable ways of limiting population growth.

It is not my intention to deny the seriousness of the latter problem; nor do I wish to question the importance of taking account of wider social responsibility in our decisions beyond our immediate self-interests. Rather what I wish to call into question is the assumption that a personal moral decision such as abortion should be determined in terms of some vague criteria such as the "needs" of society. Such a position involves a dangerous assumption concerning the supremacy of society over the individual. If society does not provide the context in which the individual can do the good, the conclusion to be reached is that the society should be changed and not the individual's decision.

The persuasiveness of the pro-abortion argument often depends on the assumption that we cannot depend on society to alleviate the conditions of poverty, racial discrimination, etc., that make another birth seem tragic. It seems we should be willing in such a context to morally approve of abortion because it is the best we can do. But the good of society must be determined not by what is possible, but by what men should be. Morally, men ought to be able to live so that they respect the being of the other in a community of trust and fellowship. I cannot see how a recommendation for abortion as a way of ameliorating immediate social problems will contribute to the social good inasmuch as such a good embodies the good for each man. For abortion as a practice implies a denial of the very trust that is fundamental to the individual and societal good.

9.

The Ethics of Death:
Letting Die or Putting to Death?

The most unavoidable aspects of our existence, such as sex and death, seem to present us with our greatest difficulties. These difficulties often arise just when we think we have sex or death under control. Perhaps their familiarity lulls us into forgetting that mighty forces reside in their everydayness. For sex and death are always potentially destructive, especially if we rely on convention to contain and direct their power. It is therefore necessary, if we are to save sex and death from pornographic perversion, to constantly engage in the task of rethinking, animating, and embodying their facticity in forms appropriate to our humanity.[1]

In our cultural context it seems especially important to be able to deal with the meaning of death. For our attempt to avoid death has tended to pervert not only our living but also our ways of dying. There has been a good deal of moral reflection about death in terms of such issues as euthanasia and suicide, but there has been little sustained ethical reflection on death as a necessary aspect of our life project; such reflection is

---

[1]There has been a recent avalanch of books and articles on death. The best discussion of the ethical issues is Ramsey's *The Patient as Person* (New Haven: Yale, 1970). My obvious debt to Ramsey will be evident throughout. For a good collection of essays on the social-psychological issues around death see *Death and Dying*, edited by Leonard Pearson (Cleveland: Case Western, 1969). This book also contains a good bibliographical essay on the subject. Two recent journals have devoted whole issues to the theme: *Dialog*, II (Summer, 1972); and *Social Research*, 39 (Autumn, 1972). It is hard to know how to explain this sudden upsurge of interest in death and dying. Death, like the poor, we always have with us and why it suddenly becomes an object of intellectual interest is a subject in itself. Of course the kind of fascination with death that is embodied in newspaper headlines is the result of the unmentionableness of death in our society. We are only perversely willing to have death displayed when it is abstracted from its natural home of grief and sadness. William May's discussion of this point and his general analysis of death is the most insightful writing about our current views of death I have found. "The Sacral Power of Death in Contemporary Experience," in *Perspectives on Death*, edited by Liston Mills (New York: Abingdon Press, 1969), pp. 169-196.

necessary if we are to be able to deal with death in its everyday form. Moreover, few ethicists have analyzed the meaning of death in its empirical and moral dimensions. Without this kind of conceptual work our judgments about such issues as organ transplants and the care of the dying will appear at best adhoc and at worst arbitrary. In this essay I intend to discuss some of our immediate practical problems as a way of raising the issues necessary to clarify the moral significance of death.[2]

Cases such as Mr. Bruce Tucker are often used to illustrate why today we need more refined thinking about death. Mr. Tucker was used as a heart donor after he had suffered massive brain damage in an accident. His brother brought suit against the doctors who performed the transplant, contending that Mr. Tucker was alive when the heart was taken, since machines were maintaining respiration and blood flow. There are even more confusing cases such as those in Newcastle and Houston, where men, who had suffered irreversible brain damage as the result of a criminal attack, were kept "alive" so that their kidney and heart could be used. The assailants then maintained that they had not killed the men, since they had been kept alive up until the time of the transplants.[3] Because of such difficulties, many doctors are suggesting that we need to update our understanding of when the moment of death occurs.

Transplants are but one aspect of this problem. We have all become aware that modern medicine possesses an amazing arsenal of weapons to keep a person alive almost indefinitely. Thus, most of us look forward to a death surrounded by sophisticated equipment, tubes, and other paraphernalia that manage to keep us alive when our physiological system can no longer spontaneously sustain our existence. Dr. William Poe, one of the increas-

[2]This point is a correlative of my general position that ethics is more a matter of coming to see than it is of deciding. For example see Chapter 1, "Situation Ethics, Moral Notions, and Moral Theology." In the terms of that chapter this essay is an attempt to establish the formal meaning of death in relation to its material content— i.e., the correlation of our moral understanding of death with its physical characteristics.

[3]This essay avoids entirely the legal problems surrounding death. It is safe generalization however that our legal definitions of death need to be brought into line with actual medical practice. For a good discussion of recent legal decisions concerning the legal standing of a patient to determine the nature of his death see Jonas Robitscher, "The Right to Die," *Hastings Center Report,* 2 (September, 1972), pp. 11-14; see also A. M. Capron and L. R. Kass, "A Statutory Definition of the Standards for Determining Human Death," *University of Pennsylvania Law Review,* 121 (1972), pp. 87-118.

ing number of medical men who advocate providing for a dignified death, criticizes those "surgical residents that do radical neck
dissection on octogenarians. We put feeding tubes in poor old
bodies that should be allowed to die. Rehabilitation people
break their backs to get old hemiphegics to take feeble steps for
no purpose."[4]

Apart from the inhumanity of the death modern medicine
seems to have destined for us, this kind of death poses problems
in the use of our medical resources. As Beecher says,

Inevitably, with more and more bold and venturesome and commendable
attempts to rescue the dying, more and more patients will accumulate in
the hospitals of the land—patients who can be kept "alive" only by
extraordinary means, in whom there is no hope of recovery of consciousness, let alone recovery to a functioning, pleasurable existence, and all this
at a cost of 25,000 to 30,000 per patient per year. Burdensome as this cost
is, it is the less of the two. Another cost: if the average hospital stay is two
weeks, the irretrievably unconscious patient then occupies space that
could have been used by 26 others in a year's time. There are today great
delays in hospital admissions owing to bed shortages, even of patients with
cancer. A life could be lost owing to delay in getting definitive hospital
care—lost because a bed was occupied by a hopeless patient.[5]

Therefore Beecher suggests that we must reexamine our responsibility to keep people alive. For "money is human life.
The money spent to maintain unconscious and hopelessly dam-
aged persons could be used to restore those who are salvage-
able." What are our responsibilities to the 21 year old woman
who has been in a coma since a traffic accident 12 years before?
Beecher realizes that it is difficult to answer such questions
because we know that the "hopelessly ill" have a disturbing
tendency to get well. Therefore he urges that we develop some
mechanism for deciding in these cases what is just for all.

If we are going to be able to say anything worthwhile about
such issues, it is imperative that we first attend to some distinctions and separate some issues. The latter is of utmost importance especially in the matter of transplants. For as I have

---

[4]Quoted in *New York Times* article, "New Medical Specialty Urged to Help One
'Die with Dignity,' " (May 16, 1972), p. 42. See also Lucy Morgan, "On Drinking the
Hemlock," *Hastings Center Report*, 3 (December, 1971), pp. 4-5.

[5]Henry Beecher, "The Hopeless Unconscious Patient," *New England Journal of
Medicine*, 278 (June 27, 1968), pp. 1425-26.

indicated, many recent proposals for updating the definition of death have had this issue in mind. But, with Ramsey, I think that this is clearly a mistake and a morally reprehensible one.[6] I do not wish to deny that we may need a better criteria for determining the moment of death, rather, I want to deny that any definition of death should be but a correlative of the patient's potential as a donor of organs.

The felt necessity for updating our definitions of death comes from the fact that for a patient who is dead by traditional criteria a kidney must be removed almost immediately, i.e., within 30 to 45 minutes after the heart stops beating.[7] Some ethicists sympathetic with this suggest that we cannot afford to waste this valuable tissue and argue that "surely it is ethical to speed things up."[8] They generally approve of the new criterion of brain death as an attempt to move the time of death up so that organs can be taken before the dying person's heart and respiration may have stopped functioning.

However, there are at least two problems with this proposal—one ethical, the other factual. The ethical question has been well discussed by Hans Jonas in his article "Philosophical Reflections on Human Experimentation." In response to Beecher's suggestion that "society can ill afford to discard the tissues and organs of the hopelessly unconscious patient," Jonas argues, "Discarding implies proprietary rights—nobody can discard what does not belong to him in the first place. Does society own my body?" Jonas assumes that unfortunate people with kidney and heart disease cannot afford to do without a kidney or heart, but this does not give them a right to it. Nor does it oblige society to procure it for them, especially if this means that one man is put to death in order to secure parts for the life of another. "Society cannot 'afford' a single miscarriage of

[6]Paul Ramsey, "On Updating Death," *The Religious Situation,* edited by Donald Cutler (Boston: Beacon Press, 1968), pp. 253-275. For a radically different position in the same volume see Joseph Fletcher, "Our Shameful Waste of Human Tissue: An Ethical Problem for the Living and the Dead," pp. 223-251.

[7]R. Y. Calne, "Transplantation: Existing Legal Constraints," in *Ethics in Medical Progress,* edited by G. E. W. Wolstenholme, (Boston: Beacon, 1966) p. 96. This volume is an excellent source to set most of the issues surrounding transplantation and dying.

[8]Fletcher, p. 243. For some reason even beyond his adherence to crude utilitarianism, Fletcher seems to have a penchant for finding reasons to say what modern medicine does and wants to do should be done.

justice, a single inequity in the dispensation of its laws, the violation of the rights of even the tiniest minority, because these undermine the moral basis on which society's existence rests. Nor can it, for a similar reason, afford the absence or atrophy in its midst of compassion and of the effort to alleviate suffering—be it widespread or rare—one form of which is the effort to conquer disease of any kind."[9] In short society needs members virtuous enough to sacrifice beyond defined duty, but it cannot enforce such heroic ethic as duty without becoming an unjust society.[10] This is especially pernicious if society tries to substitute for a moral argument a supposed technical redefinition of death that hides the fact that we are taking the lives of some in order to provide replacement parts for others.

Nothing Jonas has said implies that it is impermissible to let a patient die, but he is objecting to mixing two questions by determining the meaning of one patient's death with reference to other patient's need for organ transplant. However, Jonas concludes that if it is rightful to allow the patient to die, he should be let die all the way through the gamut of definitions since the indeterminacy of the boundary between life and death bids us lean toward a maximal rather than a minimal determination of death.[11] For finally the patient must be absolutely sure that his doctor does not become his executioner, and that no definition authorizes him to become one. His right to this certainty is unqualified, and so is his right to his own body with all its organs. Respect for these rights violates no one else's right, for no one has a right to another's body.

The issue of whether brain or heart death is the best criterion of death is separable from the ethical issues involved in the transplant situation. Traditionally it has been assumed that when the heart stopped a man was dead since the brain would also die in a few minutes. However, with the new methods of resuscitation and heart machines, we can now restore "life" as

---

[9]Hans Jonas, "Philosophical Reflections on Human Experimentation," *Daedalus*, (Spring, 1969), pp. 228-229. This issue is entitled "Ethical Aspects of Experimentation with Human Subjects," and many of the articles have direct importance for the ethics of death.

[10]This is an interesting example of why a heroic ethic cannot be made obligatory without moral injury. Of course even prior to this issue is whether we have the right of self-mutilation for the good of another.

[11]Jonas, p. 244.

judged by respiration and heartbeat—even when there is not the remotest possibility that consciousness can be recovered after massive brain damage. Thus many doctors are urging that a flat EEG is better proof of death. A few points about this issue are worth exploring because widespread misunderstanding surrounds the meaning of brain or heart death.

The so-stated alternative, is misleading. Doctors do not depend on a flat EEG alone as a sign of death; there are cases where patients have had a flat EEG for several hours and recovered. Dr. Alexandre, one of the leaders in transplant surgery, notes that almost no one takes the flat EEG as sufficient in itself; other signs—such as falling blood pressure, absence of reflexes, and lack of spontaneous respiration—are also considered. However, Dr. Calne states that even on his own criteria Alexandre has removed kidneys from live donors, for Calne argues that as long as a patient has a spontaneuous heartbeat, he is alive.[12] For example, would you bury a man whose heart is still beating? At the very least, given the ambiguity surrounding this question, the use of two different medical teams to care for the respective patients is imperative; the prospective donee must be cared for by those doctors not responsible to the patient needing the organ. For example, some of the "dead" being prepared for transplants have recovered due to the better care and skill of the physicians preparing them for transplants.

Ramsey is quite right in his discussion of this matter: the issue of whether heart versus brain death is really a procedural matter occasioned by our use of life-supporting techniques.[13] What the proposals for updating the definition of death then try to do is make clear that artificially sustained signs of life are in themselves not signs of life—in other words, that we should stop ventilating and circulating the blood of an unburied corpse because there are no longer vital or spontaneous functions really alive or recoverable in the patient. Thus the famous Harvard report is really a set of guidelines about how to use a respirator—it is an attempt to define the limits of rescue technology. If, however, with prior patient consent or consent of the family,

---

[12]Calne and Alexandre in *Ethics in Medical Progress*, p. 73.

[13]Ramsey, *Patient as Person*, pp. 88-89. For an excellent discussion of the Harvard Report and the criteria of death see "Refinements in Criteria for the Determination of Death: An Appraisal," *Journal of the American Medical Association*, 221, No 1 (July 3, 1972), pp. 48-58.

the doctors are given permission to continue artificially certain life processes in the unburied corpse for purpose of transplants, I do not see why there should be any decisive objection to this. What is important is that we are clear what we are doing—i.e., we are keeping certain organs functioning in a corpse—we are not taking the organs from a man that is living but on the road to death. This may seem to be casuistrical double-talk but I ask you to remember that we are what we say. The choice of our vocabulary is a moral act.

Though I have argued that the issue of determining the moment of death must be separated from the patient as an eligible donor, the issue of when death occurs cannot nor should not be ignored for the issue of the care of the hopelessly ill patient. Here again we must be clear at the start to distinguish two separate issues: the necessary attempt to determine the criteria of the moment of death is not the same as the question of whether a life is worth prolonging. Put differently, the issue of when to discontinue life-saving technology is not and cannot be determined in terms of whether a man is dead. Definitional wizzardry determining the moment of death cannot relieve us of facing the moral problem of deciding when life should no longer be prolonged. Several important controversies that revolve around this point bear fuller discussion—they might be described as conceptual issues of moral significance.

For example, Robert Morison has argued that death cannot properly be understood as an event, but is more correctly seen as a process that begins with birth. While he is sympathetic with the attempt to update death by new definitions, he thinks that these will only prove to be arbitrary and scientifically unsound.[14] Life and death are a continuum and therefore death cannot occur at a specific moment. Practically this means that we must face the fact that the practical problems around death and dying occasioned by our technological skill can only be solved by a cost-benefit analysis concerning the value of the lives that might be or might not be prolonged. Morison observes that respect for life is fundamental to our society and such respect must be preserved, but this respect does not need to be

---

[14]Robert Morison, "Death: Process or Event?" *Science*, 173 (August, 1971) pp. 694-698; and the reply by Leon Kass, "Death as an Event: A Commentary on Robert Morison," pp. 698-702.

based on the assumption that life is an absolute value. (While I agree with Morison about this point, I think he fails to appreciate why life is so often treated as an absolute; it is not because we feel our society embodies respect for life, but because we think it does not and only by making life an absolute in certain contexts can we draw a line against possible arbitrariness.)

While I am sympathetic with Morison's argument that the moral question of when it is permissible for a physician to withhold or withdraw treatment from a patient in order to allow him to die cannot be settled by definitional fiat, I think his own argument has serious flaws. For even though it may be true in a poetic sense that our dying begins with birth, ethically this is nonsense; it would make our living synonymous with dying. As Kass suggests in a response to Morison, this would at least open up the possibility that murder could be considered a far-sighted form of euthanasia, a gift to the dying of an early exit from the miseries of old age. Morison has in effect confused aging with dying and the process of death with death itself.[15]

However, Morison's argument is important because it forces us to consider the relationship between the meaning of death and determining the criteria of the time of the event of death. For of course Morison is quite right to insist that death from certain perspectives is a process or at least involves various levels. For example there is cellular death which we in fact may not ever endure, since human cells can be maintained in tissue cultures for years. In effect, this means we cannot define death as the loss of all vital functions. Then there is physiological death, which occurs when the vital activities have ceased—that is, the death which occurs when integrated tissue and organ functions cease. Finally, there are what might be called the higher forms of death associated with our intellectual, social, and spiritual existence. In these terms much of the problem is that medically we can keep parts of the physiological organism functioning even though the integration necessary for life can only be sustained artificially. At another level the question can be put as the relationship between the higher forms of death and the doctors pledge to keep the physiological system functioning.

---

[15]Perhaps the reason Morison confuses the categories of aging and death is that we tend as a society to see aging as an illness. See for example Eric Cassell, "Is Aging a Disease?" *Hastings Center Report,* 2 (April, 1972) pp. 4-6.

Thus the concept of death is crucial to the whole issue. By death I mean simply that transition from the state of being alive to the state of being dead; but what dies is the organism as a whole, not various organs or cells. Men can have a death of a part without it being somatic death, or death of the whole. As Ramsey contends, "life means the functioning of the integrated being or physiological organism as in some sense a whole. Death means the cessation of this functioning."[16] This in turn depends on the integrated function of the great organs of the heart, lungs, and brain. While conceptually this understanding of death does not necessitate any one set of empirical criteria that will stand as evidence that death has occurred at a particular point in time, it does provide at least a workable indication of when we can say a person is dead. For example I think we can claim that it is a necessary condition for the ascription of death that one of the major organs has ceased to function to the extent that it cannot through therapeutic means or continued aid (artificial lungs, pace makers, dialysis machines) be returned to near normal activity. Thus, a person with their brain split in half in an accident is dead even if their heart continues to beat. Moreover the extent and amount of continued aid necessary is relevant to the determination of death as the person who can be sustained only by a heart-lung machine but with no hope of improvement beyond the machinery's ability to keep the physiological machinery functioning is dead.

It may be thought I am spending far too much time over the rather meaningless issue of being able to determine the time of death. But the attempt to determine the criteria of the moment of death is not unimportant if the essential trust between the patient and doctor necessary for the practice of medicine is to be preserved. Without some general understanding and public discussion of this issue we would enter the hospital only under the greatest duress, since the criteria of life would be left to the subjective preference of the individual doctor. I am sure any criterion of the moment of death will have difficulty with some borderline cases, but if we abandon all standards because of these cases, we will simply leave ourselves to the tastes and

---

16Ramsey, *Patient as Person,* p. 59. It is not clear why Ramsey uses the confusing phrase, "in some sense."

prejudices of the contemporary opinions about such matters. Thus the question "Is he dead?" is still a "factual" question, although it is one with great moral and social consequences, and there is good moral reasons to resist those who would try to make the question one of cost-benefit analysis for the society. In other words our death cannot anymore be subject to definition by the needs of society any more than the value of our living can.

This understanding of death helps put in better perspective the growing criticism of doctors for prolonging life beyond all reasonable expectations. Even though I am sympathetic with aspects of this criticism, it is important to understand and appreciate the positive moral values embodied in the doctor's attempt to sustain life.[17] The physician's commitment to keep the patient's physiological organism functioning apart from the patient's other qualities is an affirmation of the doctor's duty to care for all patients equally, regardless of their value for others. In other words, the doctor's insistence on concentrating on the physiological condition of his patient is a necessary, though not sufficient, condition if our medical practice is to care for all equally. It is a way of assuring the autonomy of medical ethics against the more provincial values embodied in society.

Moreover, by insisting on the significance of the physical in formulating any "fuller" or more comprehensive understanding of human life, the medical profession embodies the essentially Christian affirmation of the goodness of the body. The great evils that men perpetrate on each other are often done because we have forgotten this: we cannot affirm the higher aspects of our being without also affirming that without our body we would have no further potential.[18] By insisting that whatever else health may mean, it must at least include the functioning of our physiological system, doctors embody more wisdom than is articulated in their explicit ethics. The doctor's contention that death at least means the cessation of the integral function of the major organs is a healthy corrective to the subtle gnosticism of

[17]For an insightful article analyzing the religious and value commitments that inform our medical practice involving death see Parsons, Fox, and Lidz, "The 'Gift of Life' and Its Reciprocation," *Social Research*, 39 (Autumn, 1972) pp. 367-415.

[18]For a more extended discussion of the significance of the physical related to the issue of abortion see Chapter 8, "Abortion: The Agents' Perspective."

many of the calls for a new more "existential" conception of death.[19] To be sure, concentration on keeping the physiological machinery operative, combined with medicine's growing technological skill, has led to perversions, but this is not an argument against the wisdom assumed in the doctor's basic assumption that his first duty is to sustain our physical being.

But this conceptual-definitional (or criteriological) issue of when death occurs does nothing to inform us about the ethics of prolonging life or the care of the dying. Morison is right to raise such issues in terms of the suffering that often results from slavish and limitless attempts to prolong life. His mistake is to try to answer it by denying any significance to determining when death has occurred except from a societal point of view. The question of when life is worth prolonging cannot be avoided. Of course there has been much reflection on this issue in the past, such as Pius XII's use of the distinction between ordinary and extraordinary means; he says only the former are obligatory in the care of the sick. The problem with such a distinction is its highly relative nature: what is ordinary procedure for one kind of patient would be extraordinary for another. Modern medicine has been primarily characterized by making ordinary what was extraordinary but yet a year or a few short months before. The issue is not really whether we can draw a distinction between "ordinary" and "extraordinary," but whether in all circumstances even ordinary measures ought to be employed to keep the hopelessly ill patient alive.[20]

Of course this kind of distinction was occasioned by the necessity of distinguishing the withdrawal of medical support from euthanasia which the church absolutely condemns. However, this whole discussion is better carried on in terms of the distinction between putting to death and letting die. For such a distinction makes it clear that the church has no stake in the

---

[19]For example see Daniel Maguire, "The Freedom to Die," *Commonweal,* XCXI (August 11, 1972), pp. 423-427. Catholics are especially open to this temptation because of their reaction to the conclusions drawn from the physicalist assumptions associated with their sexual ethics.

[20]Ramsey has an excellent discussion of this distinction as he shows the difference between how doctors and moralists understand it. *The Patient and Person,* pp. 118-124.

absolute preservation of life as an end in itself. The prohibition against euthanasia tends to give the impression that there are no limits to the obligation to sustain life. This, however, is wrong; there is nothing in Christianity that teaches the preserving of life as an end in itself—not even the preserving of the life of another. Rather, the Gospel demands the care of the weak, which is quite a different matter.[21]

The limits of this essay prevent any developed general theology of death to support this contention.[22] Briefly, I think that the kind of ambiguity found in the New Testament—where death is at once seen as an enemy yet accepted as necessary and natural aspect of our lives—sets the boundaries for any general discussion of death.[23] In this respect, many of the recent theological recommendations that we view death as a friend I find artificial and full of false courage. Death is an enemy that cannot be defeated by human doublethink, theologically rationalized or not. I prefer the realism of the New Testament; otherwise we only fall deeper into the illusions that constantly threaten to engulf us in our fear of death. The message of the gospel does not remove the fact of our death; it only gives us language and the skill to see it for what it is—that is, the Gospel teaches us the appropriate kind of fear of death.

Death should be avoided. Death should be feared. It should be avoided and feared exactly because of its positive contribution to our living. Without death our lives would have no height or depth, for nothing is precious in a world that literally has time for everything. For example, death makes precious the ones I love by forcing me to regard them as finite beings. Put differently, life faced with death is a resource which I can only use up. Death creates the economy that makes it necessary to choose between life projects, between that which is valuable

---

[21]See my "The Christian, Society, and the Weak," Chapter 10.

[22]Generally I find Karl Rahner's *On the Theology of Death* (New York: Herder and Herder, 1961) to be one of the most balanced theological discussions of death. See also May's article above. For an excellent critique of "eternal life" as a symbol for the Christian's understanding of life after death, see Milton McGatch, *Death: Meaning and Mortality in Christian Thought and Contemporary Culture* (New York: Seabury Press, 1969).

[23]Leander Kech, "New Testament Views of Death," *Perspectives on Death*, edited by Liston Mills (Nashville: Abingdon, 1969), pp. 33-98.

and that which is not.[24] As such, death is a precious gift which
we literally cannot live without. However, death's power to make
our life precious is why we cannot grasp it to our bosom as a
friend. For death paradoxically becomes the enemy of its own
creation as it negates all it has taught us to love. Thus death is at
once friend and enemy, brother and stranger. Any theological
affirmation that overlooks either of these polarities will distort
our ability to see our life as that destined and formed by death.

Death is, then, to be feared. On the other hand, the proper
fear of death can be perverted, especially if it takes the form of
the ideology of the absoluteness of life. Moreover, modern
medicine often seems to embody such an ideology as it fights
death as an unmitigated evil and a sign of the physician's failure
at his task. For example sociological studies show that physicians respond more negatively to death than men in other
professions. Whether medicine attracts a certain personality
type or this is part of the training of the profession is not clear.
However, it is at least a sign that our medical practice as it is
now institutionalized embodies less than a morally healthy
ethos about death.

Ideally the aim of medicine is not and should not be to help
us to live forever; the aim of medicine is to provide us with
health. To be able to do this, we need to recover a more
accepting attitude toward death and a greater concern for the
needs of the dying patient. Often our job may not be to cure
but to help the other cope with terminal illness. We must do
this especially if the technological interventions and institutional practices we employ to cure deny the dying the right to
die in the community of those who care and love him. To do
this we must restore to the practice of medicine the ethic of
allowing a person to die.[25]

Modern medicine's embodiment of our avoidance of death
has created the conditions for the inhuman death we allow
ourselves to suffer. Our unwillingness to face death has tended
to turn medicine into magic that is presided over by a white

---

[24]James Laney, Ethics and Death," in *Perspectives on Death*, pp. 231-252. See
also, Charles Fried, *Anatomy of Values* (Cambridge: Harvard University Press, 1970),
pp. 166-69; Rollo May, *Love and Will* (New York: Norton, 1969) pp. 99-121; and
Merle Longwood, "Ethical Reflections on the Meaning of Death," *Dialog*, 11 (Summer, 1972), pp. 195-201.

[25]Leon Kass, p. 701.

frocked group of priests. Like all priests, these men mediate to us regular mortals the secrets of the universe dwelling in that mysterious realm we have come to call "science." We look to them to use this marvelous new magic to work miraculous cures that save us from suffering and death. As priests they are, of course, hesitant to tell us the truth about our condition since it is their heavy burden to carry the knowledge of good and evil. Moreover such ignorance is necessary to sustain the proper aura of the miraculous cure. If this were not the case, the horrible doubt might be given reign that perhaps the doctor is not as all-conquering as we demand that he be. For we give ourselves to the medical profession with abandon because we need to have an island of safety amid the storms of sickness and death.

I do not mean to imply that doctors consciously or maliciously assume the role of priests of the new magic, for it is we who thrust it on them. We expect this of the doctor; for otherwise we might have to face the reality that no profession can insure our life from pain and destruction. We thus charged these men in the name of the marvel of science to act as if we live in a new day where we can grow old without fear of disease. Woe be he who fails to fulfill his role once he has the sacred title of doctor, for he will be accused of the worst sin: unprofessional behavior.

Of course doctors benefit enormously from this kind of development; it legitimizes their elite status and all the monetary benefits that accrue to it. Moreover, it opens their profession to the manipulation of society's "haves," since they have the coin necessary to persuade these wonder-workers to exercise their magic.

Of course it's true that this analogy is overdrawn, but I fear it is far too close to the truth.[26] We must reject modern medicine's fundamental assumption that the designation of illness is a technical and morally neutral judgment. "The concept of illness is inherently evaluational. Medicine is a moral enterprise like law and religion, seeking to uncover and control things that it considers undesirable."[27] The designation of illness as a

---

[26]For a more extended discussion of medicine as religion see Roy Branson, "The Secularization of Medicine," *The Hastings Center Studies,* 1, 2 (1973), 17-28.

[27]Eliot Freidson, *Profession of Medicine* (New York: Dodd, Mead and Company, 1970), p. 208. For a discussion of this point from an ethical point of view, see

social-moral act cannot be ignored by a retreat to the "neutral" world of science—the form, description, and kind of our illness are a correlate of the values we hold.[28] Modern medicine is the institutional means through which we legitimate and recognize sickness. That is why medicine's jurisdiction extends far beyond its capacity to cure—it exists not only to cure but to establish the bounds between sickness and health. The tendency to describe any malfunction of the individual and society as "illness" is but a sign of medicine's hegemony in this respect.

To recognize medicine's moral and social function is not to suggest medicine should be otherwise. Rather it is to require that the practice of medicine be defended and formed by values consistent with the normative demands of being human. There is a new upsurge of writing about "medical ethics," but, as currently conceived, it is almost exclusively concerned with the hard and dramatic cases that result from our modern technology. However this kind of endeavor is far too narrow; what is called for is a much more general analysis and justification of the everyday practice of medicine as a moral art.

This is especially important for the ethics of the medical care of the dying. For there is a strong tendency for doctors to assume that care is synonymous with cure—thus no procedure is left undone that might lengthen our stay on this earth. Therefore just as medicine tends to define sickness as that which can be cured or controlled, the dying person becomes the one who the doctor can no longer help.[29] As soon as it becomes clear that the doctor can no longer cure, he then retreats from the patient, as he assuming that he can no longer care for him—medically speaking, the patient is already dead.

Yet, properly understood, caring is the refusal to abandon

Alexander Capron, "Genetic Therapy," in *The New Genetics and the Future of Man,* edited by Michael Hamilton, (Grand Rapids: Eerdmans Publishing Company, 1972), pp. 133-156.

[28]Talcott Parson, "Definition of Health and Illness in the Light of American Values and Social Structure," in Talcott Parsons, *Social Structure and Personality* (New York: Free Press, 1964), pp. 258-291.

[29]Eric Cassell, "Being and Becoming Dead," *Social Research,* 39 (Autumn, 1972) p. 522. Of course it may be argued that it is not the doctor's responsibility to take on the burden of this alternate sense of care, but if this is the case it still must be someone's job. However, I think such care should be given by doctors if for no other reason than to provide a check on their assumption that medicine can be reduced the technique.

the patient simply because he is dying.[30] Caring is not to be identified with curing but with our willingness to be with another even though he is dying. Care is the insistence that human community is not destroyed at the first sign of death, but extends to and through the moment of death. The current suggestions about returning death to the home have much to recommend them in this respect.[31] For to be allowed to die among our fellows and amid the familiar is one of our most significant ways of affirming care. Neither we nor the doctor should delude ourselves that we can substitute for this the technological forms of uncare with which we often surround the patient as our substitute for personal presence.

No one can read Kubler-Ross without appreciating her sensitivity to the importance of not abandoning the dying.[32] However, I think a world of caution is necessary for many of those influenced by her work. They rightly react against the manipulative and inhuman prolongation of a life through technological means. But their insistence on teaching us to die well can be just as manipulative. If I wish to die without reaching the stage of "acceptance," that is my right, whether others think I am dying a "good death" or not. The development of medical and social specializations in the art of dying may well be important, but we must be careful not to get so taken up with securing a good death that we forget that our aim is to live. Death is not a romantic adventure; it is what we do not know and it is seldom pretty. The issue is not whether we have a "right to die," but whether we and our community are morally healthy and can face death in the spirit of human solidarity.

For example, some of the recommendations about "good death" imply that the Christian should celebrate the death of those close to him. But this is false and pretentious faith. It is God's prerogative to rejoice in the death of one of His own, but

[30]William May, "The Sacral Power of Death in Contemporary Experience," *Social Research,* 39 (Autumn, 1972) pp. 482-3. This is an excellent revision of the essay in *Perspective on Death.*

[31]Robert Neale discusses the development in England of the hospice as a home for the dying in "A Place to Live, a Place to Die," *Hastings Center Report,* 2 (June, 1972), pp. 12-13. That death is now almost entirely something that happens in the hospital may be the most single important factor that contributes to our inability to deal with death.

[32]Elizabeth Kubler-Ross, *On Death and Dying* (New York: MacMillan, 1969).

He can do that because He is God. By His grace we do not have to try to be like God; thus death for us is rightly an occasion of grief and sadness. To treat it otherwise is to rob death of its human significance. Of course the sadness of the Christian is bounded by hope, but such hope is only truthful when it takes seriously the reality of death as acute separation from the human community.

In fairness it should be said that for the medical profession to embody an ethic of "only caring for the dying" would place it in sharp tension with its society.[33] For our development of exotic life-saving means is but the correlate on this side of life of our exotic funeral practices on the other. In our society, we live and act as if death is to be avoided, and our medicine faithfully serves our wishes. If our medicine is to provide for more humane forms of dying, it will have to find the source of its medical ethics not in its culture generally but in the development of its own moral ethos. While individual physicians may be up to such a task, the medical profession as a whole is not.

In the context of this kind of problem, we might seriously consider the possibility of developing a Christian practice of medicine and supporting institutions. Modern medicine has tried to give the impression that it is a seamless garment, that there is a consensus about what should constitute the practice of medicine, that the only variations occur in terms of the skill of individual doctors. This impression is illusory but if medicine is trying to serve a pluralist society with impartiality, it is a necessary illusion. For example, doctors are prone to take an absolutist stance concerning the protection of life because they do not wish to be placed in the position of having to decide between competing sets of values about who is and is not valuable.

In such a situation it may well be that Christians as a people who live with their peculiar readiness to die will have to begin to find new means to institutionalize this ethic.[34] It may mean

---

[33]Ramsey uses this phrase in the *Patient as Person*, pp. 125-132.

[34]What is disturbing about the recent bishops directives for Catholic hospitals is how little they wrestled with this larger issue. What makes a hospital Christian is not that certain things are not done there, but the way the institution is organized for the enhancement of life. For the directives and two excellent critical responses by Richard McCormick and Warren Reich, see *The Linacre Quarterly*, 29 (February, 1972), pp. 8-29.

that Christians organize their hospitals to allow for an open awareness and sharing of the experience of death rather than a closed.[35] It may mean that they insist that their hospitals be institutions where the truth can and must be spoken; for Christians we can afford the truth because as a community we will stand with those who must bear the reality of dying. It may be that because the Christian people have a special obligation to care for the weak, we must use our limited resources not to develop larger and better units for rescue medicine to prolong life, but preventive medicine that aims at helping us live morally worthy lives rather than keeping us alive as an end in itself.

Of course there are extremely vague suggestions that deserve more detailed argument than the limits of this essay allows. However, I wish to say more about the primary distinction between putting to death and letting die. This distinction is alive with philosophical and ethical issues. For example, at the heart of the distinction is the assumption that there is a real difference between acting and refraining from action; that morally it is wrong to act to put someone to death, but legitimate to neglect to take steps which would prevent his death. Of course this is a generalization that will not hold up under analysis; it is clear from reading murder mysteries where the murder is accomplished by withholding needed medicine that to refrain from giving care is the same as directly acting to kill. [36] The distinction's moral relevance for this essay therefore is dependent on the ability to distinguish the dying process from the ability to sustain life over a period of time. In other words to refrain from acting is simply a way of saying that you will not prolong the dying process, it is not to cease to try to cure when life has the possibility of being sustained.

In practice, however, it is extraordinarily difficult to determine when the dying process begins, especially since we can

[35]For an elaboration of these two institutional options see Anselm Strauss, "Awareness of Dying," in *Death and Dying*, pp. 108-132.

[36]For an excellent discussion of the distinction between acting and refraining see Jonathan Bennett, "Whatever the Consequences," in *Situationalism and the New Morality*, edited by Robert Cunningham (New York: Appleton-Century-Crofts, 1970, pp. 139-143. This distinction is extremely important for any attempt to ethically analyze suicide and euthanasia. Though I think what I have done in this paper has implications for these issues I cannot begin to investigate these complex matters here. However see *Euthanasia and the Right to Die. The Case for Voluntary Euthenaria*, edited by A. B. Downing (London: Peter Owen, 1969).

184 VISION AND VIRTUE

seemingly put off some forms of our dying indefinitely through the use of artificial means. I would resist any attempt to draw hard and fast lines concerning this kind of decision. Rather, I would make the plea that the patient himself be consulted about his dying—namely, that his dying be considered not just a matter of when the physiological machinery is run down, but under what conditions he wants to place himself as it runs down. I think that this can and should vary from one person to another. Consistent with the life plan they have embodied in their character, some may wish to fight to the end, using all the available means of medical technology. But others may form their death in quite a different way consistent with their character, not fighting but calmly accepting death as an affirmation of their willingness to provide a place for new life among us.

The importance of determining when the dying process has begun is crucial for another reason. Up until this point in the essay I have spoken of death at the end of a fully lived life, but it can also occur at the beginning of life. For example Bernard Bard confesses that when he became the father of a mongoloid son he wished the boy would die. He explicitly requested that the doctors do nothing to extend his son's life artificially, and he was assured that the sanitarium to which he committed his son contained no oxygen nor did it provide inoculations against childhood disease.[37] Mr. Bard was relieved when his son finally died of heart failure and jaundice.

Was this simply a form of the ethic of letting die, or is it putting to death? I think that there is no doubt that this is killing, and it should be so described. There is little difference between this kind of case and the cases of mongoloid children born with digestive obstructions that parents are refusing to allow doctors to operate on and thus condemning these children to the slow death of starvation. This can hardly be called cooperating with the dying process. Though I certainly would agree that the question of what means ought to be used to sustain the lives of children (not just those "sub-normal")

---

[37]Bernard Bard, "The Right to Die," *Atlantic Monthly*, 221 (April, 1968) pp. 59-62. See also Joseph Fletcher's praise of Mr. Bard's decision, pp. 62-64. It is a mystery as to how the article was so mistitled, since it is really concerned with the "Right to Put to Death."

cannot be settled in principle; surely our pledge to care for the weak exerts a greater pressure here than at the other end of life.

One of the interesting things about cases where they let the mongoloid child starve to death is that for some reason they refrain from acting to put the child to death. Surely in such circumstances it would be easier on everyone concerned if an air bubble were shot into the child's veins. The nurses on the ward would not be upset, the doctor could cease worrying and agonizing, and the parents could cease calling every day to see if "it" had died. I suspect however that we do not do this because we want to preserve the illusion that we are simply allowing what is natural to take place. But I would maintain that we will be much more moral if we honestly face what we are doing in such cases—putting a child to death—and then do it in the quickest and easiest way. The murderer is more humane who does not live under the illusion that he is letting nature take its course for the good of humanity.

Finally the ethic of letting die must be based solely on the consideration of the welfare of the dying patient, rather than considerations of the benefits that might accrue to society or his family through his death. It is one thing to take one's bearings as I have suggested should be done from the patient's own interests, but it is quite another to allow his death because of the costs to society. The doctor's duty remains to the patient, not to secure the overall health of society. If this is not the case then we open the medical profession to the perversions of a society that often kills in the name of its own good. In a society that already is so murderous this seems to be an "advance" we can scarcely afford.

I cannot pretend that there are no dangers in the institutionalization of an ethic of "letting die." It is a phrase that is morally intelligible as it is informed by a set of background beliefs concerning our obligation to regard our life as a gift of God. It may be that in a society such as ours it is more prudential to order our language and institutions concerned with death in terms of more absolute standards such as "right to life." Yet it is my presupposition that for Christians our basic symbols are still operative to the extent we can take the risk to think about and live with death in a way that does justice to its ambiguous form in our lives. If this is not the case, if our community and symbolic universe is too weak to provide such a background, then I fear that the power of death will indeed reign over us with a tyranny that is all the more pervasive because we have forgotten that it is not we, but Christ, who reigns over death.

10.

The Christian, Society, and the Weak:
A Meditation on the Care of the Retarded

As a meditation, this short essay neither provides comprehensive analysis nor suggests all the ethical issues raised by the care of the retarded. The arguments presented here are not designed to satisfy those skilled in ethical and theological matters. This is a personal attempt by one weak Christian—who incidentally happens to be a theologian and ethicist—to understand what it means to live in a world peopled by those born retarded.

Therefore this is not written for everyone; it is written for men and women who find themselves both Christian and confronted by the retarded. Those who do not share the Christian conviction may find what I say here at best incredible and at worst morally irresponsible. For some, including many Christians, the fact that unbelievers will stumble over the Christian perspective is a decisive argument against any attempt to understand the obligation to care for the retarded from a "narrowly" Christian viewpoint. There seem to be at least two reasons for this reluctance: (1) Christians are increasingly aware of their obligation to avoid the scandal of the inhumanity and self-righteousness often associated with those who claim special "religious" obligation; and (2) Christians feel a duty to serve the needy; in a pluralist society, this seems to entail downplaying our differences in order to join in a common effort for human betterment. Thus, in the interest of a good society, Christians impressed by the bad faith of our own society have tended to write their ethics from a broadly humanistic perspective; thereby, they hope to be able to formulate for institutional structures clear policy entailments that all men of good will can jointly pursue.

Even though I am not unsympathetic to every aspect of this style of ethical reflection, I do not think it adequately permits the Christian to articulate his obligation to care for the retarded. For the humanism which the Christian accepts in the name of the good society all too quickly seduces him into accepting the good which is humanly possible rather than the good we must do as Christians. Thus, in the name of humanity we begin to entertain the sacrifice of the few for the many, the weak for the strong. We try to calculate the "rights" of the "retarded" against the "rights" of the "normal," or to determine who shall live and who shall die in terms of the "quality" of their lives. Moreover, by accepting the humanism of the day, Christians betray their unique contribution to the good society; this leaves unchallenged the humanist assumption that there is no good beyond what can be accomplished in this existence. The question of the care of the retarded is the most compelling example illustrating this general contention. (However, the care of the retarded in many ways is but an aspect of our care for all children. Any full attempt to treat the ethics of the care of the retarded should be a subdivision of the more general ethics of responsible parenthood. Our inability to face the retarded is but a specific and intense form of our society's distaste for children and its failure to properly respect and care for them.)

For the presence and necessary care of the retarded raise harder and deeper problems than the optimism necessary to sustain any humanism can entertain. These harder questions were best articulated for me by a young man through a song he sang during the reception of the Eucharist at the University of Notre Dame. He had written the song after a friend had shared his agony about learning to live with a retarded brother. It goes like this:

(For Rick)

I. I have a brother, forgotten child
   I ask myself why? I get no answers.
   Does anyone know, in God's name, why
   Some are retarded?

   Refrain
   Give me strength to face the madness.
   To be able to say there was some
     purpose.

Give me strength to face the madness.
Why? No it's happened.
Why? No it's happened.

II. He's older than I, I've always thought
We should have grown up together
Playing baseball, going swimming
Enjoying summer, like other brothers.

III. He does not know me, He can say nothing.
I have no reasons, but I love him.
We could have been friends, learned together
I only ask, *where is he?*

(Steve Campbell)

We are seldom able to ask the questions raised by this song; they remind us too much of the fragility and ambiguity of our existence. Therefore, it is not accidental that such a song was sung in the presence of the sacrifice of the Mass. For only if such a sacrifice is good, only if such a sacrifice sustains and constitutes our own existence and the existence of the world, can we be free from our fear of meaninglessness to look honestly at our retarded brothers. The sacrifice of the Son of God affirms that our existence is bounded by a goodness we can trust; Calvary reveals that we, even the weakest among us, are valued in ways not dependent on our human purposes and strengths.

The God we Christians worship is the God of the sacrifice, the God of weakness and suffering, who draws us to his table not by coercive power but by sacrificial love. Such love is formed by a weakness that is not of this world. God's weakness is strong enough to resist the temptation to be just another (more subtle) method of controlling others. For we know from our experience that as men we cannot even will to be weak without using that weakness to gain power over another person; this power is even more destructive than force since it has the form of a renunciation of power that controls completely since it does not appear to control at all. But the weakness of God is no sham; this is fully manifest in the absolute commitment

which leads him to become a man and to suffer even to dying
on a cross. Such weakness lures us from our pretentious attempt
to make our lives meaningful through power and violence; it
draws us to trust in him who has suffered much in order to
make peace possible for us.

In his weakness, God comes to us not to dominate in the
name of the good, but to serve in the reality of goodness, to
reveal the nature of the good. Jesus did not come with new
political alternatives in the sense that Caesar or those that
opposed Caesar would understand; he came proclaiming a new
Kingdom where men would share in the very life of God. He
came not to the rich and the powerful, but to the poor, the
weak, the dying, and the sinner. Through such as these the
nature of his kingdom is revealed as the freedom to feed the
poor and forgive the sinner. God, therefore, refused to establish
himself through the violent power of this world with its many
deceptions; his rule can be established only through the gentle-
ness that comes from genuinely being weak and not just from
taking the form of the weak. Only such a God could be the God
of the Mass; through his Church, he continues to give himself in
weakness so that his people will have the strength to renounce
the power of this world.

When we have been joined to this God through this meal of
weakness, we cannot get up as the same people. This meal fills
us with the power to trust God and to serve the weak of the
world who are his special concern. In each other, in the weak,
we find Christ; like him, they love us even though they do not
have the power to preserve themselves. We become transformed
exactly to the extent we learn to accept this love without
letting it turn to self-hate because of what it reveals of our
wretchedness.

The Christian's task to care for the weak is but an aspect of
his call to love God. Serving the weak in the name of man is not
enough; God calls us to love and care for the weak just as He
has loved and cared for us. Surely this is the force of Jesus'
admonition to be perfect as his Father is perfect.

The Christian songwriter who asks "Where is he?" knows his
retarded brother is in Christ, but this "answer" does not provide
an easy explanation that can relieve the anxiety of the question.
Rather, this answer provides the pattern of obedient love and
care in conformity to the one on whom any genuine purpose in

this life must be dependent. The retarded are the sign that all men have significance beyond what they can be for us—our friend, our playmate, our brother; each of us is previous and significant because his being is grounded in God's care. The retarded, the poor, the sick, are but particularly intense forms of God's call to every man through the other. Thus, God calls us to regard each other as significant as we each exist in Him, as we are each God's gift to the other.

Thus to see the retarded honestly is to remind ourselves that we cannot earn significance for our lives; it is a gift of God. In this context it makes sense to say that I must live in such a way that only one thing matters: that my life manifest God's glory. I do not gain significance by trying to relieve all suffering; that would be another form of trying to establish my power. Rather, my hard task is to learn to love this one retarded brother who can never understand the very opportunity of love he offers. From his presence I learn the radicalism of refusing to deny love and care for him; I cannot deny this care for my retarded brother even in the name of creating a better world for all "humanity" or for "my already existing family." A world so created or a family so sustained cannot be "better"; it deafens me to the call to humanity this one retarded child offers me.

Christ makes it possible for me to love my retarded brother in a way radically different from the possessive love that thrives on the need to be needed. Christ's love creates the conditions for respect of the retarded. A respect that frees us to care without stifling sentimentality. For it is sentimental love which builds the uncaring institutions where we enclose the retarded in invisibility in the name of their own good. To love the weak in Christ is to dare to free the weak from our dependency on their need. This love respects the being of the retarded so much that it is willing to allow them to experience the pain and frustration of using their capabilities to come to terms with the world. I do not need to protect my retarded brother with the smothering care that only reinforces his retardation; I can love him with the love that sustains his efforts. He knows this love will not abandon him when he has gone through the struggle to fashion a will independent of mine.

Moreover, such love reveals the perversity of those theodicies which try to save God's honor by attributing the existence of the retarded to his will. It is certainly true that the existence of such children may provide the occasion for producing much good; they call us to a fuller humanity by challenging our notions of what makes life meaningful. But these possible good fruits do not warrant the implication that God wills these children for such purposes; this would make the Lord of this world into a weak and petty monarch who would stop at nothing to get his way. Such children are not directly willed by God; rather he is the kind of God who makes it possible for them to be present among us in a nondestructive way. In their presence we learn how difficult, how terrible, and how wonderful it is to say that God is love and that his love is most perfectly revealed on a cross.

Please note that I have not attempted to base the Christian obligation to the retarded on such principles as the "right to life" or "respect for life." Such principles embody moral wisdom that the Christian has an interest in preserving, but these very principles are sometimes used to justify forms of life foreign to the gospel. But the Christian is not obligated to protect human life as if life were an end in itself. To do so would belie the affirmation that because God gives life, the existence of ourselves and others is but a relative good within his providential care for us. Divorced from this proper theological context, principles such as "right to life" tend to become ideologies supporting some men's feverish attempts to sustain their existence at all cost in preference to others. It is therefore, the Christian's task to care for the retarded in ways that make clear that there are much worse things in this life than death.

I am aware that some will interpret my insistence on the care of the weak as a religious justification for societal irresponsibility. It seems unjust to argue such care of the retarded in a society with so many needs. For example, in an article discussing the genetic aspects of therapeutic abortion, Dr. James Neel describes the tremendous and exorbitant cost to society that the care of the retarded and other genetically deficient children entails. Moreover, despite this expenditure, these children can have only a "very marginal performance in our complex society. While I do not for one moment wish to place a price tag on a human life, I cannot help wondering how that same sum spent on normal children might advance the interests of society." ("Some Genetic Aspects of Therapeutic Abortion," *Perspectives in Biology and Medicine,* Autumn, 1967, pp. 133-134.)

Dr. Neel's question is not unfair. It is not inhuman; the question embodies much humanness and charity. But it is a charity run wild and gone crazy because it is unable to totally relieve the world of its suffering. This charity tries to join hands with the powers created by men; thus it is willing to destroy some in the name of the "quality" of life. This charity no longer has the patience to attempt to act justly in a world racked with suffering. This charity blinds itself to the existence of the one retarded child in the name of a better way of life for the many; but this way of life can only be empty if it fails to meet the needs of such a child. Neel's question assumes that there is nothing to live for apart from relieving the suffering we experience in this life. For all of its great humanity, it is therefore a godless question.

It is not a question we can contemplate as Christians. For the Lord who spreads his table before us requires more than this question even envisions. The Christian's duty is to care for the weak, and no limits can be placed on that demand. The Christian can hold nothing back in his care for the weak; he may even have to sacrifice his dream of "advancing the interests of society." If the Christian must sacrifice even his own life so that the weak may be cared for, he will do so; for he does not live as if he were placed on earth to exist forever. The Christian cares little for existing; his aim is to learn to live. Nor must he care for others as if their care were but a means to the existence of an even-higher quality of the human species. The Christian's care for the weak embodies no grand humanistic vision, but only the idea that regardless of its accomplishments, no society that fails to care for retarded will be worthy or humane. It is just this kind of vision that exposes the sinful and power-hungry pretensions we hide behind our claims to serve others in the name of humanity. No such humanity exists except as it is found in a child who must struggle to speak his name.

We Christians must admit that we have hesitated to recognize this demand plainly, because we know how unfaithful we have been to it. We have tried to help the poor and the weak through the philanthropy of thanksgiving baskets or government programs, programs which do not require us to give of ourselves. We have deluded ourselves that opposing the repeal of abortion laws was sufficient even though we were unwilling to sacrifice to meet the needs of the child born in poverty. We have so trapped ourselves through our bad faith that we eagerly grasp the latest technique that does some good as if it expressed the full demand of Christ. By so doing we buy cheaply into the reigning humanism; we turn the uncompromising Christian demand to love all men into the possibility of being kind and helpful to some men. And Christians wonder why men no longer think belief in God relevant to learning to live in this life! Only as Christians refuse to avoid the existence and care of the retarded will men realize faith makes a difference. For we have failed to realize how radical our position is for even though we help the retarded we do not embody the implications of that kind of help for our total existence. To genuinely support the care of the retarded as Christians is bound to put us in much greater tension with our society than we now envisage.

It is therefore the Christian's task and the Church's responsibility to provide care for the retarded beyond what is considered to be "socially responsible" at the time. For in its faithful worship the Church provides the vision of existence within which we can articulate our obligation to care for others; this clarity of vision is radically different from the blindness produced by our attempts to avoid self-hate. Only thus will we be able to admit that it is our own uncare and self-assertion which often produce the retarded (environmental retardation is more prevalent than genetic), yet such knowledge need not force us deeper into the defenses of our self-interest. For the demand of Christian love can be radical exactly because it frees the self from defensiveness; we are freed from the necessity of creating and sustaining the significance of our own lives.

What I have said does not mean the Christian must refuse to support what can be done through the wider society; it does mean he must recognize that the demands laid on a member of the human species or a citizen of a nation are not the same as the demands laid on him as a member of the church. It seems a trivial observation that the church and Christians feel deeply at home in the civilization created by them. But I suspect that the more Christians consider the fundamental issues raised by the care of the retarded, the stranger they will feel as they go about amid the glories and the ruins of their own building. As we live with such strangeness, perhaps we will be better able to comprehend and love those who exist as strangers among us; they cannot understand as we understand, but these retarded brothers are no less members of God's kingdom.

III.
Vision and Society

11.

The Nonresistant Church:
The Theological Ethics of
John Howard Yoder

Pacifism and Contemporary Christian Social Ethics

In spite of significant theological and ethical disagreements among modern Christian ethicists, they continue to share the basic conviction that the Christian's attitude toward socio-political reality cannot be one of indifference. Often this presupposition is based on an interpretation of the gospel that refuses to limit theological categories to concern for the individual. God's work in the world is not aimed only at changing individual hearts, but encompasses the institutional structures of our lives. Therefore the Christian has the warrant or perhaps better the imperative to engage in work for the betterment of society. This is a common presupposition regardless of whether the socio-political structures are theologically construed in terms of God's creating, preserving, or redeeming activity. In this respect the current political theology and theology of revolution are but further developments of these more basic theological commitments.

A corollary of this presupposition is for the Christian to responsibly act in society he must be willing to combine with the good forms of evil or less good. The ethical issues of the socio-political realm seldom come in such a way that the good can be clearly distinguished from the bad. In order to make limited gains for the social good it is necessary for the Christian to use means that he would not employ under ideal circumstances. This insight is the substance of "Christian realism" as the Christian is forced to face the situation as it is if he is going to work for a more tolerable state of affairs. The only other alternative is to retreat to an ethic of intention where the concern is our own righteousness rather than the need of the brother.

Put in less theoretical terms this means that the Christian must be willing to employ force and violence to secure the good. The problems of society are not solved by simple moral suasion but by using the various kinds of force available to us. Thus the Christian, if he is really interested in effective action, must be willing when it is necessary to balance force with force, meet conflict with conflict, and violence with violence. The extent or kind of force used will vary with the problem that is being confronted. It may be organizing the political power of one group against another, it may be the willingness to kill as a soldier, or it may entail joining a revolution in the interest of a downtrodden social class. Regardless of the concrete form it can generally be said that the notion that the Christian has a responsibility to work for a better society involves a denial of pacifism.

That this has become a kind of "conventional wisdom" is evident from the fact that these questions are seldom argued for or discussed explicitly in contemporary theological ethics. Such a discussion is long overdue for when such significant assumptions are accepted as true in themselves the original qualifications and nuances surrounding them become lost. As a result implications are drawn from the now established orthodoxy that was not envisaged as a possibility in the original formulation. The current advocacy of violence as a good in itself rather than a lesser evil is an example of the kind of development I have in mind.

My primary intention in this essay is to try to help us feel the oddness of the theological legitimation of the Christian use of violence. In order to do this I will analyze John Howard Yoder's defense of Christian pacifism. Even though much of the paper will consist in an exposition of Yoder's position my major interest is systematic. I shall therefore argue that: (1) Yoder has developed and defended a form of Christian pacifism that the conventional arguments against pacifism fail to meet; and (2) in so doing he has provided a basis for and a form of Christian social criticism that is theologically more defensible than that assumed by the various forms of "Christian realism." In terms of this latter thesis I hope to show that Yoder has made a particularly valuable contribution to theological reflection by raising the question of the special nature of Christian ethics.

Though I shall first discuss the nature of Yoder's pacifism, the main argument of this essay will involve simultaneous discussion of both of these theses. This is necessary in order to provide a fair presentation of Yoder's thought since these questions are not sharply distinguished in his work. I must also state that my short explication of his position here cannot do justice to the subtlety of Yoder's thought, but I am so convinced of the importance of the issues his position raises I want at least to try to make clear the broad outlines of his theology.

There is also an ecumenical reason for attempting a serious theological analysis of Yoder's position. Yoder has taken the time as a Mennonite to write disciplined theological critiques of the theology of Barth, Reinhold Niebuhr, and Richard Niebuhr. However, as yet no one from the more "orthodox" tradition has attempted a similar assessment of Yoder's positive theological position. We continue to be content with the stereotype of the "sectarian" as irrelevant pacifist. I at least hope to make clear in this essay that Yoder's theological position cannot be so easily dismissed and that if we engage it openly it will provide a valuable contribution toward the development of a genuinely ecumenical theology.

The Theological Basis of Christian Pacifism

In order to understand Yoder's theological defense of Christian pacifism it is first necessary to remove some possible misunderstanding concerning the nature of pacifism. Many assume that pacifism involves a denial of all violence as an inherent evil and an absolute prohibition against the taking of life in any form. Such a pacifism is usually based on vague and rather sentimental appeals to the essential goodness of man, the nature of love, and the ideal of universal brotherhood. This kind of pacifism is often defended in terms of political strategies that place great faith in the development of world government, general disarmament, or the optimistic assumption that a nation can renounce the use of military force as an instrument of national policy. It is this kind of pacifism that came under the devastating criticisms of Reinhold Niebuhr for its romantic assumptions about man, its unrealistic analysis of the behavior of social groups, and especially for its concern for personal righteousness rather than responsible social action.

Yoder, however, is careful to distinguish Christian pacifism from this that is based on such broadly humanistic affirmations. He agrees with many of the criticisms that realists make against pacifism understood as a political program in the sense that they have not been able to establish that it would actually be successful.[1] His more basic objection to this form of pacifism is theological rather than pragmatic since it assumes a constantinian view of the world as it attempts to conform states and statesmen to the demands of the gospel.[2] Such an assumption confuses the church with the world and fails to see that theologically it is wrong to think the state is open to that kind of commitment.

Christian pacifism does not make any such assumption about the state. Rather Christian pacifism stated in its simplest form is that Christians cannot see how war can be an imperative of the Christian life.[3] Yoder does not try to argue that pacifism, so understood, is the central question of Christian faith and ethics.[4] There is no suggestion or attempt to translate the gospel into a moralistic program of nonviolence. On the contrary Yoder is insistent that pacifism is meaningful only in the larger framework and structure of a Christian social ethic.[5] Therefore to understand Yoder's defense of pacifism we must look at his basic theological commitments.

---

[1] J. H. Yoder, "Reinhold Niebuhr and Christian Pascifism," (Pamphlet) *Concern*, Scottdale, 1968, p. 16. For example Yoder is critical of placing all faith in an organization such as the U.N. since the desirability of one central world government with unchallengeable coercive power has dangers of its own. Moreover when pacifism is so defended the assumption is that if it is not successful then violence is permissible, a conclusion that is unacceptable to the Christian.

[2] J. H. Yoder, "Peace Without Eschatology?" (Pamphlet), *Concern*, Scottdale, 1959, p. 17. See also, *The Christian Witness to the State* (Newton: Faith and Life Press, 1964), p. 30.

[3] J. H. Yoder, "Karl Barth and Christian Pacifism," Working Paper No. 4: Peace Section of the Mennonite Central Committee, 1966, p. 19 (55). This work has been reissued in a somewhat revised form as *Karl Barth and the Problem of War* (Nashville: Abingdon Press, 1970). When their work is footnoted the page number in parenthesis will be the reference from their latter work.

It should be noted that their understanding of pacifism is only provisionally suggested by Yoder as a way of discussing Barth's own view of pacifism. I have repeated it here for methodological reasons as Yoder's full meaning of nonresistance involves his complete theological framework and in particular his ecclesiology.

[4] *Ibid.*, p. 2.

[5] J. H. Yoder, "The Pacifism of Karl Barth," (Pamphlet), Scottdale: Herald Press, 1968, p. 1. This is a historical study of Barth that is quite different from Yoder's treatment of Barth above.

201 THE NONRESISTANT CHURCH

For Yoder the fundamental fact from which the Christian faith springs is God's action in Jesus Christ. By Christ's coming and action a new kingdom has been established as God declares his Lordship by reclaiming his creation and subduing the powers to his will. God's will for man has been clearly revealed in the figure of Jesus Christ. As such, God's command does not consist in adherence to ideals that cannot possibly be fulfilled, but rather involves the real conformation of the Christian to the norm of Christ. To base the Christian life on any other assumption is to deny the incarnation of Jesus Christ, for such obedience is based on the affirmation

that in Jesus human history knew a fully obedient human being; he was not simply a divine figure masquerading as a man whose apparent obedience was therefore irrelevant to the rest of us; he was the true human being. Faith in Jesus Christ is not an arbitrary or magical inscription on the heavenly ledgers; faith is rather participation in the being of God, incorporation into the body of Christ. The possibility of obedience is therefore a statement not about our own human capabilities, but about the fullness of the humanity of Jesus and the believers identity with him through the Spirit in the church.[6]

The Christian life is therefore nothing less than an imitation of the way of Jesus. It is a participation through discipleship in the divine love. Thus what becomes crucial is the form that divine love took in Jesus Christ. According to Yoder the essence of the incarnation is the nonresistant love that reached its most intense reality on the cross. Christ indeed brought a new life that has immense social implications, but all through his life he refused the political means, i.e. the coercive techniques, that were offered him to accomplish his purposes.[7] This was necessary because the very essence of the incarnation, the meaning of the victory of the resurrection, and the subsequent form of the Christian life is that God deals with evil through self-giving, nonresistant love. The meaning of the cross is the rejection of political means of self-defense, that "agape seeks neither effectiveness nor justice, and is willing to suffer any loss or seeming defeat for the sake of obedience."[8] Thus the Christian's refusal

---

[6]J. H. Yoder, " 'Christ and Culture,' A Critique of H. Richard Niebuhr," Mimeographed Paper, p. 16.

[7]Yoder, "Peace Without Eschatology?" p. 7.

[8]Ibid., p. 7

to use violence is not based on legalistic abhorence of violence or as absolute commitment to life as an end in itself, but rather it is a matter of "as he was, so we must be in the world." Pacifism is not an independent norm that determines the meaning of Christ, but Christ and discipleship to him requires a stance of nonresistance to evil.

The Christian is not surprised therefore if he is called upon to suffer in the face of evil. Moreover he must reject all attempts to distinguish between killing a just and unjust foe as it is impossible in the light of Christ to determine who is the enemy. Indeed one of the worst sins the church commits is endorsing certain nationalist aims, even in terms of the just war criterion, and thereby giving legitimation to an understanding of the other as an enemy. Moreover in so doing it denies the unity of the body of Christ by entertaining the possibility of one Christian killing another.[9]

Thus Yoder's pacifism is in no way based on prudential calculation of its possible success, but rather on the theological affirmation that the norm of the Christian life is to be obedient to the form of Christ—i.e., the essence of discipleship is the nonresistance to evil made possible by Christ's death and resurrection. "The good action is measured by its conformity to the command and to the nature of God and not by its success in achieving specific results."[10]

Yoder does not try to avoid the hard question that such an ethic necessarily involves an apparent complicity with evil. He does not deny that this is in fact the case, but defends such an attitude as a correspondence with God's patience to allow the sinner freedom to separate himself from God's love even to letting his son be killed on the cross. Any doctrine of redemption that denies the sinner the liberty of refusing God's grace in reality denies human choice has any meaning at all. Moreover this willingness to let sin work its worse through nonresistance is in accordance with the New Testament message that the final triumph of evil will not be brought by human means, but the victory will be God's. The task for the Christian is to obey and it is ultimately God's business to bring the kingdom of this

---

[9]Yoder, "Reinhold Niebuhr and Christian Pacifism," p. 21.

[10]Yoder, *The Christian Witness to the State*, p. 49.

world into his realm. But God does not do this by accepting the coercive means of the world, but rather by the creation of a people who refuse to meet the world on its own terms—i.e., through the creation of the nonresistant church.[11]

This is the main thrust of Yoder's theological defense of Christian nonresistance. It is clear that the kinds of arguments made against political pacifism simply do not meet Yoder's position. If his Christian pacifism is to be countered it would entail arguments against the doctrine of God and Christology on which his position is based. I suspect however that rather than such a direct attack on his basic theological affirmations the primary means of challenging this kind of Christian pacifism is to claim that he has not done justice to the complete reality of God or human experience—i.e., there is some truth here but it is not the whole story.

The most natural response to this position is to point to its failure to provide a responsible stance for the Christian in the world. By implication it seems to require a withdrawal ethic by the Christian and the church in a way that the Christian fails to show proper love for his neighbor in wider societal structures. Theologically this bad social strategy is the result of an insufficient doctrine of God's creating and preserving activity which fails to legitimate the Christian's proper concern with the world and the world's justice. It is therefore asserted at best that such a Christian ethic stands as a reminder to the horror of violence and war, but at worst it is a denial of Christian charity in the interest of preserving personal righteousness.

However Yoder refuses to accept this as a proper presentation of the implications of his Christological formulation of the ethic of nonviolence. Rather he argues that that kind of ethic of nonresistance is not nor should not be irrelevant to the social order. The form of nonresistance required of the Christian is not just a negative ethic in the face of evil, but a positive form of life that obligates the Christian to confront the world in its socio-political reality. In order to understand how Yoder can at once advocate nonresistance yet affirm the Christian's duty toward society we must look at his more general theological understanding of the Christian's relationship to society.

---

[11]Yoder, "Peace Without Eschatology;", p. 11.

The Problem of Christian Social Ethics

Yoder's understanding of the place of the Christian in society begins by rejecting what he calls the constantinian formulation of the problem, that is, the problem posed as if the only alternatives for the Christian were "responsibility" or "withdrawal."[12] Such a statement of the problem presupposes the fusion of church and world and destroys the vital dialetic between these two distinct sociological and theological realities. Those who use the slogan "responsibility" assume the most effective way for the church to be responsible for society is by losing her visible specificity in order to leven the whole lump. As a result the church tries to formulate an ethic that will work as well for non-Christians as Christians.

The idea of responsibility therefore actually hides a commitment of the Christian to take charge of the social order in the interest of its survival. " 'Responsibility' becomes an autonomous moral absolute, sinful society is accepted as normative for ethics, and when society calls for violence the law of love is no longer decisive (except in the 'discriminate' function of preferring the less nasty sorts of violence.)"[13] Substituted for the nonresistant love of the gospel, the value of the survival of civilization becomes an absolute imperative on the assumption that the church has a stake in the survival of the going social order. It is only on such an assumption that it seems rational for the church to engage in an altruistic pragmatism that ends up weighing the number of lives lost at Hiroshima against the number that would have been lost in a military invasion.[14]

Yoder's basic criticism of this position is its failure to make Christian revelation the sole norm of the Christian's witness to the state.[15] The Christian theologian must view with great suspicion all ideas that come to him that claim to have author-

---

[12]Yoder, "The Otherness of the Church," *Mennonite Quarterly Review*, XXXV, (Oct., 1961), p. 289.

[13]Yoder, "Reinhold Niebuhr and Christian Pacifism," p. 18. Yoder criticizes H. Richard Niebuhr's famous typology, Christ and Culture, on the same grounds. He argues that Niebuhr's humility, while genuine in itself, works in fact like a cover for his acceptance of culture as an abstract and autonomous norm which creates the artificial problem of Christ's relationship to it.

[14]Yoder, "The Pacifism of Karl Barth," p. 29.

[15]Yoder, "Karl Barth and Christian Pacifism," p. 1b. (P. 18)

ity apart from and over against Jesus Christ. It is clear that all ethics that emphasize the idea of responsibility, the order of creation, or natural law do just this as they lay standards of justice on men prior to those derived from Jesus Christ. "They claim that within the realm of the state's responsibility there are insights or understandings or principles or ways of working at problems which have the same kind of authority over men including Christians, that Christ himself claims, yet which calls men to do things that Christ does not call men to do."[16]

In contrast to these alternatives Yoder maintains that Christian ethics must be based on a clear statement of the necessary dualism between the norm of Christ and the form of this world. The kind of life assumed by the faithful Christian is not the same as the secular man of good will. The Christian's duties are not the same as those laid upon him by the modern welfare state. This means that there are simply some aspects of society in which the Christian will not be called to participate.[17] It is to be noted that Yoder puts the issue in terms of calling to avoid the legalistic question of "What can we no do," which is only a way of avoiding the hard obligations of being a Christian.

However the dualistic nature of an authentic Christian social ethic cannot be construed in terms of the classical Lutheran distinction between the order of creation and redemption. This is not simply because this position has tended historically to be socially conservative as the order of creation has been identified with the current institutional arrangements, but because such a dualism is based on a fundamental theological error. Not only does such a dualism presuppose, like natural law positions, a norm of justice apart from Christ, but it turns a condition made necessary by human sin into a theological principle that even determines the subsequent doctrine of God. The reformation rightly affirmed the ethical value of vocation, but wrongly gave theological legitimacy to the idea that the proper behavior in a vocation is not decided by Christ but by the inherent norms of the vocation itself.[18] In doing so Lutheran theology wrongly

---

[16]Yoder, *Christian Witness to the State*, p. 18. Though Yoder's Christological starting point is similar to Barth's he does not have Barth's tendency to deny the importance of other forms of knowledge and ethical reasoning for moral decisions.

[17]Yoder, "The Otherness of the Church," p. 294.

[18]*Ibid.*, p. 290.

attributed revelatory value to an autonomous sphere separate from Christ's redeeming work.

In contrast to this Yoder maintains that the fundamental form of the duality in Christian social ethics is the difference of faith and unbelief as the presupposition of the ethical message.[19] The Christian is dependent for his knowing and doing of the good on the forgiveness and regeneration of the gospel, but not all men share this knowledge and experience. Because of this the Christian cannot speak to society as if it were capable of acting in terms of the demands of the gospel. The Christian must learn to regard wider society as the institutionalization of structured unbelief and sin. Thus there must be a clear distinction between ethics for the Christian and for the non-Christian and their institutions, not because there is a duality of realms or orders, but because of the difference in the agents. This is not to imply that non-Christian society should not ideally act in accordance with the gospel, but it is to realistically admit that it cannot so act as long as the resources for making such redeemed behavior possible are lacking. Thus the Christian social ethic presupposes a duality of response, without implying a duality of orders.

By defending this form of dualism Yoder has no intention of legitimating a withdrawl by Christians from their societal context. Such a withdrawal is not theologically possible since in spite of the obvious reality of continued unbelief in institutionalized form the church continues to confess that Christ is indeed Lord over all the world.[20] This belief in Christ's defeat and subjection of the "powers" (*exousiai*) of this world enables and requires the church, in spite of her distinctiveness from the world, to call the world back from its estrangement from God.

Moreover such a withdrawal ethic would fail to be obedient to the gospel which is primarily the proclamation of God's redemption of society. The evangelism of the gospel is not just a witness to individuals, but rather it is the message that the kingdom, that is the true and just community, has come near. This does not mean that the gospel can be in any way construed as a plan for social betterment or that it contains a blueprint of the ethically ideal society. Rather it is to make clear that "the

---

[19]Yoder, *The Christian Witness to the State*, p. 29.
[20]Yoder, "The Otherness of the Church," p. 287.

good news to the world has to do with the reign of God among men in all their interpersonal relations, and not solely with the forgiveness of sins or the regeneration of individuals."[21] It is wrong to say there is no social ethic in the gospel, for the gospel is a social ethic of interpersonal love. The problem is not that there is no social ethic in the gospel but that we do not wish to practice the one that is there because it is not relevant to the social concerns determined by the world.

It may be objected at this point that Yoder seems to have come full circle as these last two points would seem to commit him to some kind of "social responsibility" ethic for the Christian. In order to understand in what sense this is true we must look at his more concrete understanding of the relation of the church to the society. For ultimately the question of the form of a Christian social ethic for Yoder is the question of ecclesiology.

Eschatology, Ecclesiology, and the Function of the State

In order to understand the relation between church and society according to Yoder it is necessary to see each in terms of their eschatological context. Human history is to be characterized by the simultaneous existence of two aeons that are radically opposed. The old aeon points backwards to human history before Christ; the new aeon points to the fullness of the kingdom of God which we now only have a foretaste. The old (and present aeon) is characterized by sin and centered on man; the coming aeon is the reality of redemption which can be found in a decisive way only in Jesus Christ.[22]

Each of these two aeons have a social manifestation. The old aeon can be identified with the world and society in general. It has its most intense manifestation in the workings of the state. The new aeon can be found in the church as it is the foretaste of the ultimate triumphant redemptive work of God. Even though in the present age these two kingdoms must remain antagonistic there is no ultimate dualism between them. For the world, even though still rebellious, as much as the church, points forward to its ultimate subjection to the kingdom of

21Yoder, *The Christian Witness to the State*, p. 23.
22Yoder, *The Christian Witness to the State*, p. 9-10: "Peace Without Eschatology?" p. 7.

Christ. This does not mean that the old aeon is changed essentially, but rather that the new aeon in Christ has now taken primacy over the old, explains the meaning of the old, and will finally vanquish the old.

The primary characteristic of Christ's Lordship over the old aeon in the present time is that evil without being destroyed is now used by God to serve his purposes.[23] Vengence, for example, instead of creating chaos is harnessed through the state in a way to preserve order and give room for the growth of the church. Such a rechanneling of evil does not make evil good, but rather renders its subservient to God's providential order as an anticipation of the ultimate defeat of sin.

This is the basis for the relative positive evaluation of the state in Romans 13 even though the essential coercive nature of the state is not forgotten. The state is God's instrument for preserving order in society. The state thus uses its force legitimately as long as it serves to protect the innocent, punish the evil doer, and preserve peace so that the church might have the opportunity to confront all men with the Gospel. Such an evaluation of the state does not nor should not be used as a legitimation for any possible existing state, but rather each historical state must be reevaluated in terms of the existing alternatives. The fact that the state legitimately can use violence does not mean that the Christian must accept every form of violence done by the state.[24] The main problem is not that state officials will fail to do their job of policing, but rather the temptation on the part of the state is to give its violent work religious significance by claiming the state's ultimate importance.

Against all attempted self-glorification of the state the church must constantly stand on guard. It must make it clear that the church does not exist primarily for the ends of society, even when such ends are worthily understood, but rather it is for the church's work of preaching the gospel that society and the state continue to exist.[25] The church's task is to constantly call the state to its legitimate function, for the church knows why the state exists, in fact better than the state itself, and this under-

---

[23]Yoder, "Peace Without Eschatology?" p. 9.

[24]Yoder, *The Christian Witness to the State*, p. 42.

[25]*Ibid.*, p. 13.

standing gives her both the justification and standards by which she judges the states action. This form of the church's witness to the state does not depend on positing any source of good apart from revelation, for it is based solely on the work of Christ as He established his Lordship over the state.

This cannot mean that the Christian criticism's of society and the state depend on some "theory of the state" found in the gospel. The Christian does not have a special Christian theory for the legitimate state, but rather he simply accepts the fact that the state exists.[26] Because of this the Christian witness to the state will always express itself in terms of specific criticisms to concrete injustices. The Christian does not assume it is possible to create an ideal society, since that is only the future kingdom of God, and thus no societal order can be accepted as adequate.[27]

Christian criticism of the state must operate without universal moral principles presupposed in natural law theories or social ethics based on general anthropological assumptions. Christian social criticism is based only in Christ and such concrete principles of social criticism can be known only mediately. Thus the Christian's witness to the state must take the form of certain "middle axioms" which "translate into meaningful and concrete terms the general relevance of the lordship of Christ for a given social ethical issue. They mediate between the general principles of Christological ethics and the concrete problems of political application."[28] In terms of particular analysis of political events, the Christian's judgment may not differ greatly from the judgment of other social critics. The distinctive nature of the Christian's witness is not necessarily in terms of his suggestions about concrete issues, but rather how he as a Christian relates to the situation in terms of his loyalty to Jesus Christ.

Put in terms of the Christian's relation to the state this means that the Christian's obligation to call the state to its legitimate function does not necessarily mean that the Christian himself assumes the burden of the state. For example we have seen that Yoder accepts the police function of the state as an aspect of God's providential ordering to secure relative peace. Christian's

---

[26]*Ibid.*, p. 78.

[27]*Ibid.*, p. 32.

[28]*Ibid.*, pp. 32-33.

cannot therefore ask for governments to be nonresistant, but they can ask and in fact demand that the state take the most just and least violent action possible in order that there be a reasonable harmony of interest established. Thus the use of force by the state can take place only when it is guided by fair judicial processes, subject to recognized legislative regulation, and safeguarded in practice against its running away with the situation.[29]

On such a criterion Yoder argues that the Christian cannot in any way participate in modern war waged by the state, as such war occurs in the absence of superior legislative and judicial control and it kills without discrimination between innocence and guilt.[30] Attempts to limit war in terms of just war criteria, which are in effect the extension of the limited violence of police authority, are useful in as much as they try to control the extent of violence. But though there is justification for the "logic" of the just war pattern of thought there is little realism as it is clear that modern war is not nor cannot be carried out in such limits. In this context the Christian pacifist can base his absolute refusal to participate in international conflicts on just war grounds.

However this is not the true basis of the Christian's attitude toward violence, for this would make it appear that the Christian might thereby be able to legitimately involve himself in the police function of the state. However the ethics of the police function necessarily involves the ethics of the lesser evil, for the basis of justice for the state is finally the falleness of men. [31] Such a justice is perfectly adequate for the state in its current sinful condition, but it is completely inadequate and illegitimate for guiding Christian discipleship whose sole norm is self-giving and nonresistant agape.[32] Therefore the Christian, while affirming the theological significance of the relative justice secured by the police function of the state, is called to serve a justice not secured by force.

Yoder admits that the most compelling argument against this

---

[29]*Ibid.*, pp. 36-37.

[30]Yoder, "Karl Barth and Christian Pacifism," p. 41, (p. 102).

[31]Yoder, *The Christian Witness to the State*, p. 49.

[32]*Ibid.*, pp. 49, 83. Yoder does not in principle rule out the possibility of a Christian policeman, but he clearly thinks that a Christian has not yet shown clearly to the Church why he should take on this strange work of God's wrath.

position that the Christian's necessary concern for the protection of his neighbor against the relatively unjust interest of another neighbor, seems to be lost. When the issue involves a third party it seems the Christian's duty must be, through the function of the state, to contribute to the maintenance of order and justice. This understanding of the function of the state is perfectly legitimate in terms of the logic of the police function of the state, but this is exactly the reason that the Christian cannot be persuaded to participate in the state's use of violence. For such an analysis of the state is based on the old aeon and knows nothing of the new. "It is not specifically Christian, and would fit into any honest system of social morality. If Christ had never become incarnate, died, risen, ascended to heaven and sent his Spirit, this view would be just as possible, though its particularly clear and objective expression results from certain Christian insights."[33]

The crucial question is not whether the church should or should not be responsible for society, but rather what that responsibility is. It is surely being irresponsible if it attempts to change the world through the shortcut of using means unfitting to its ends. The church cannot attempt to become another power group among others in society that seek to dominate in the name of the good. Rather the first duty of the church for society is to be the church, i.e., the body of people who insist on the primacy of faith by refusing to accept obligations that might lead them to treat in an unbrotherly way an "enemy" of the state. Such a "withdrawal" from the police function of the state is not a bad faith confession that Christ's redemption has not been fully effective, but rather is based on the conviction that God has changed the essential reality of human affairs by his work in Christ. For the church to act in any way that contradicts this faith means that she has failed in her central responsibility of pointing the world toward where its salvation ultimately rests.

It is the duty of the church to be a society which through the

---

[33]Yoder, "Peace Without Eschatology?" p. 20. Yoder counters the argument that such a stance would leave the state open to exploitation by demonic men by arguing: (1) the police function is not demonic but under the reign of Christ; (2) that by osmosis Christianity has humanized most men; (3) the prophetic function of the church is more effective against specific injustice than political machinery itself; and (4) that other egoisms always check the power of other egoisms.

way its members deal with one another demonstrates to the world what love means in social relations. So understood the church fulfills its social responsibility by being an example, a witness, a creative minority formed by its obedience to non-resistant love.[34] Only as the church is a disciplined community who embodies in her own life the love of the other does she have the right to speak to the world. It is assumed therefore that the church will be composed of a relatively small minority who have accepted nonresistance as the form of the Christian witness to the fact that indeed Christ has defeated the powers of evil by submitting to their power in the cross.

As an example the life of the church cannot be applied directly to society as the latter does not function on the basis of repentance and faith. However by analogy certain aspects of the church may be instructive as stimuli to the conscience of society in such matters as mutual caring for duties, the significance of equality, and by "piloting" new ways to meet social needs.[35] Moreover the Christian will call society to the greater justice not only by his conscientious refusal to conform to certain prevalent patterns of behavior, but also by his "conscientious participation" on those roles and jobs of society which he can assume. There is thus an indirect way that Christians help raise the standards of their societies as through osmosis their moral values are slowly accepted by the world at large even though it has no basis for such a commitment.

The church therefore does not fulfill her social responsibility by attacking directly the social structures of society, but by being itself it indirectly has a tremendous significance for the ethical form of society. Yoder finds particularly significant the historical irony that those churches that did not claim direct social significance or concern for society have always had the greatest social significance. This does not mean that the church must not at times witness directly to the state on specific issues that have particular significance in terms of its own commitments, but the church cannot and should not attempt to speak on every issue confronting the body politic. This is not only because it has no particular insight into a general form of the good society, but moreover it knows there are limitations to

---

34Yoder, "The Pacifism of Karl Barth," p. 30.

35Yoder, *The Christian Witness to the State*, pp. 17-19.

what the state can do in its fallen form. The church does not ask the state to eliminate all evils, but those that are particularly significant. Therefore the church always addresses itself directly to the state in terms of specific injustices and in terms of the available alternatives.

When the church speaks to the state in this direct manner it does not assume that the statesman has become faithful to the gospel. Rather it is necessary for the church to address him in terms that he can understand through the cloud of his unbelief.[36] Thus the church may appeal to such secular terms as liberty, equality, democracy which are as high of standards as the world of unbelief can conceive. Also there are general cultural values the church may use in its direct witness, such as honesty, mutual respect, hard work, unselfishness, and tolerance which have been "somehow subject" to the Christian formative influences.[37] Moreover the church is aware that there has been progress in human history and that it is therefore possible to make some distinctions in terms of the relative justice of various states. However in making such judgments the church must never forget that they are limited to the ethics of prudence and self-preservation and less than the ethics of discipleship that the Christian is obligated to follow. Such judgments are in effect the functional equivalent of judgments based on natural law or the order of creation, but it is now clearly perceived that they have no ultimate theological claim on the Christian's form of life, but rather are significant for the Christian only as they can be used for his service to the neighbor in Christ.

Evaluation and Criticism

I think it is clear that Yoder's position cannot be easily dismissed as a withdrawal ethic that is morally irresponsible and theologically unsound. Rather he has given a sustained and disciplined theological argument concerning the special nature of the Christian's responsibility for society. It is a position that resists easy stereotyping and subsequently easy dismissal. It combines in a creative way the classical Protestant options of

---

[36]*Ibid.,* p. 73.
[37]*Ibid.,* p. 40.

the relation of church and society. It shares the Luthern concern to distinguish between the kind of response called for in society from the obligation of the gospel. It thus can embody the realism of Reinhold Niebuhr about societal activities and the limitations of the justice achieved in the world. However it is Calvinist in its refusal to admit an ultimate separation between God's order of providence and redemption thus avoiding any suggestion that the ethic of the world is autonomous or sufficient in the light of the gospel. However it has the sectarian refusal to link church and society so that the dialetic between these two entities is maintained, but in a way that it is clear the Christian cannot withdraw completely from societal responsibility.

Yoder's thought is particularly significant when it is compared to most forms of contemporary Christian social ethics as he has challenged its basic presupposition that the issue of a Christian social ethic is the question of withdrawal or responsibility. He has argued correctly that the issue is not whether the Christian is to be responsible or not, but rather what form that responsibility is to take in the light of God's action in Jesus Christ. Christian social ethics that failed to put the issue in this way did affirm the norm of Christendom under the rubric of "being responsible." In other words it accepted the idea that the basis of the ethics of society and the church are not essentially different. It is interesting to note that the current forms of Christian social ethics that attempt to give legitimation to revolution and other forms or societal disruption also share this assumption. Their radical form is not a denial of the past formal commitment of Christian ethics to a Christendom model, but what has changed is the form of society they want the Christian to serve. As such, its radicalness is not that of the gospel demand to face evil in the form of Christ, but rather it is the radicalness of a new power group that seeks to dominate in terms of its particular conception of the good society.

In this connection I think Yoder has also served to remind us that Christian social ethics is not to be determined solely in terms of the interest of the poor and the disadvantaged. To be sure the Church has a special relation to the poor as it is obedient to the call of its Lord, but this does not mean that it is its job to simply identify with the self-interest of the poor in terms of the power strategies necessary to achieve a more relative justice. For the church to do this is for it to fail to bring the healing word of the gospel to the poor by drawing back from the judgment that the political tactics used by the poor, while perhaps achieving a greater justice according to the world, only makes them as men more subject to the powers of this world.

This is indeed a hard thing to say in our contemporary context without being misunderstood. For too many times the church has used the perversion of this message to still the just indignation of the poor while not equally applying the judgment to those who have possessed the poor. However, such bad faith as this should not prevent us from arguing anything less than the truth of the gospel—i.e., that true justice cannot be achieved by engaging in action that forces us to join hands with the devil as we work for good ends.

The authenticity of these kinds of questions Yoder is putting to the major assumptions of Christian social ethics depends finally on the question of the distinctiveness of the Christian claim. Yoder I think is right to say that almost all contemporary Christian social ethics has been written as if Jesus' death, resurrection, and establishment of the kingdom did not decisively change the world and the Christian's relation to it. Theologically, in one way or another, it has presupposed that whatever Christ did was not directly relevant to the concrete world of societal affairs except as an indiscriminate judgment on our lives together. This is not to deny that much of what has been said from this perspective has not been of great value, but rather that it is hard to determine what makes it specificially Christian. Yoder's work can be seen as an opportunity to reconsider the question of whether there is not an authentic *Christian* social ethic.

It is important to distinguish this question from a concern to somehow make Christ relevant to the socio-political problems of our lives. This kind of concern can only arise from a basis of bad faith that assumes that there is a reality more significant than the redemption that has been wrought in Jesus Christ. The proper theological question is rather that of what form the Christian witness to his society must take in the light of the fact that Christ has decisively changed the character of our social existence through his death and resurrection.

Yoder has suggested rightly that at least this means that the

Christian cannot participate in every form of life he finds present in his societal context. This nonparticipation cannot be simply identified with a refusal to stand against an "establishment" in the name of a more radical cause as this assumes the gospel has no word to the radical. Rather the nonparticipation of the Christian has a more radical form than the current forms of radicalism can know. For it is based on a form of life that points beyond the nature of the loyalities present in this life. The life of nonresistance is only a rational possibility as it is grounded in the hope that there is a deeper form of justice than is immediately apparent in our everyday world.

In terms of concrete strategy this means that the contemporary attempt to enliven the church by tying it to the engines of the current social causes is doomed to failure. Such a strategy is not only pragmatically doubtful, but more importantly it is theologically unwarranted. The first question of significance in Christian social ethics cannot be which social cause should the church support, but rather what form the church must assume in order to be true to the Lord of all society. In a sense the church is most relevant to society when it is self-regarding, for the criterion of such a concern for its own life must be the gospel of Jesus Christ.

Thus I suspect that theologically today the most vital form of Christian social ethics must actually be a concern about the kind of community that Christians form among themselves. In other words, the church will serve the world best as it serves its Lord through the depth of its doctrinal affirmations, its liturgical experience, and the kind of moral concern the members of the church share among one another. If it does this well the church cannot be content with its institutional affairs and an end in themselves, for the content of its doctrine, liturgy, and communal form will not let it forget that it exists only as mission to the world.

It is obvious that I have deep sympathies with the major direction of Yoder's thought. However Yoder has said that, "Ethics should deal with arguments, 'cold-bloodly,' critically, and without respect of persons. The measure of the brotherly character of Christian polemics will be not the mildness, but the clarity, accuracy, and objectivity of the appeal to the criterion of revelation."[38]   In that spirit I should like to raise a few

---

[38]Yoder, "Karl Barth and Christian Pacifism," p. lc.

questions about Yoder's theology of social criticism. I will
concentrate of the more explicit ethical aspects of his thought,
even though I think there are interesting questions that should
be raised about his doctrine of revelation and scriptural authority.[39]

My first question concerns Yoder's interpretation of the
nature of the dualism between faith and unbelief. My concern
at this point is not that descriptively it is hard to distinguish the
men of faith from the men of the world for I assume that
Yoder's argument is meant normatively—i.e., that men of faith
ought to be different from men of unbelief. In response to any
descriptive objection, e.g., that Christians do not mean to act
greatly different from other men, he can rightly respond that
this situation is the result of bad theology that legitimates a way
of life for Christians that is less than the gospel's demand.

Rather my question is whether some forms of justice based
on the possibilities open to unbelief do not have a more positive
relation to the life of faith that Yoder's account provides. In
this connection one must question whether Yoder can ultimately free Christian social ethics of "principles" or "ideal patterns"
as much as he seems to suggest. The use of the idea of "middle
axioms" seem to be too easy in this respect, as it avoids making
clear what criteria and conception of the just society is used for
the individual judgments about society. For example Yoder says
the state has the responsibility of protecting the innocent from
the guilty, but he never makes clear on what grounds the state
judges which is the innocent. Or he says the church must speak
directly against the most significant forms of injustice, but how
are we to know a significant from insignificant form? If such
criteria were made more explicit it might be possible to suggest
in a more positive fashion what stake men of faith have in the
maintenance of such criteria of justice: or at least it might make
somewhat problematic Yoder's assertion that a sufficient Christian ethic can be based solely in revelation. Yoder may object
that such criteria are not necessary as the Christian simply
works within the alternatives of the historically contingent

---

[39]What I have in mind here is Yoder's assumption that revelation is not subject to
historical relativities in the same way other forms of human knowledge seem to be.
He seems to assume a kind of revelational positivism somewhat similar to Barth's
without feeling the need to defend such an assumption in regard to such questions as
the relation between scripture and revelation, the nature of revelation in respect to
other ways of knowing, and how the content of revelation is determined.

state, but then it seems that the Christian is always in danger of accepting the status quo as normative—i.e., just the problem that Yoder most wants to avoid.

Yoder's position I think is not as devoid of "principles" or criteria of justice as some of his statements would seem to imply. He explicitly assumes certain positive principles and societal models (the fellowship of the church) are normative for the wider society. Of course he can respond that they are normative only in an analogical way since such criteria are dependent on the presupposition of the gospel which the wider society does not share. However one must ask if the very idea of analogy does not depend on the theological affirmation that the forms of justice possible in the realm of unbelief do not have affinities to the redemptive work of God. Does not the very idea that "middle-axioms" can bridge the gap from Christological ethics to the justice possible in the world depend on the theological understanding that redemptive reality of God's work is effective in the socio-political realities of our lives? Is it not possible to allow for the possibility that the achievement of more progressive forms of justice, which Yoder admits has occurred, denotes a dimension of justice that is more than that derived from the basis of sin?

In this connection one must ask if Yoder's theological predisposition has not prevented him from considering a more positive understanding of the nature of political community. Yoder's assertion that violence is the essence of the state fails to appreciate that the state as a form of community cannot be explained or reduced to a Hobbesian mutual protection society.[40] Violence is necessary not as the essence of community, but when community is no longer sustained by the common wills of those that make it up.[41] True authority does not need violence as it is the recognition and obedience given by the citizen to the governers who legitimately lead in accordance with the common good of that society.[42]

---

[40]Yoder, *Karl Barth and Christian Pacifism*, p. 45 (P. 109). Yoder says, "The fact that certain agents are chosen by relatively democratic procedures does not modify the fact that the state is still defined by its claim to the use of violence for the maintenance of order."

[41]Hanah Arendt, *On Violence*, (New York: Harcourt, Brace and World, 1969), pp. 40-47.

[42]For a fuller exposition of this understanding of civil community see Yves

This does not mean that power is excluded from the state, but it is a power that is nonviolent in the sense that the individual is directed to the good of the society in the context of his own wider loyalty to the society. For power is the essence of the state, not simply because some refuse to obey from evil intention, but because of the richness of the various visions of the good that must be directed toward the whole of the common good. Power is not necessary because men are inherently deficient in some way, but because men have sufficient resources to see part of the good. Yoder by reducing all power to physical threat fails to appreciate the tremendous significance of the forms of community that men share that are based on mutual trust and aspiration for the good. To be sure the acts of violence that the state perpetrates are so dramatic and historically vivid it is tempting to assume that the essence of the state is manifested in them. But no state can long exist that depends on the threat of violence alone. The state, like all communities, must continue to depend on the willed initiative and sentiment of those that constitute the society if it is to endure.

Perhaps I can make this point clearer by stating the issue in terms of the relation between the language of faith and the language of justice rather than actual institutional arrangements. Yoder seems to assume that the language of justice is completely determined by sin and thus from the perspective of faith can only be negatively understood. The justice of the state is limited by the inhumanity, especially as it assumes the form of violence, that of necessity constitutes it in this life. Thus the language of faith can have no positive relation to the language of justice.

Yet it must be questioned if any discriminating social judgments by the Christian can be made without buying in at some point to the language of justice. But this does not necessarily mean that the Christian's use of the language of justice is limited to the form as he receives it from the world. Rather the Christian must realize that it is exactly his task to transform the language of justice by refusing to accept it as given and by insisting that justice is only properly understood under the

---

Simon, *Philosophy of Democratic Government* (Chicago: U. of Chicago Press, 1951) pp. 30-34.

norm of Christ. This suggestion contradicts Yoder's insistence that Christian ethics can only be based on revelation, but it is consistent with his refusal to accept as normative language that is independent from revelation. Christian ethical reflection cannot completely divorce itself from the world's categories of justice, but this does not mean, as Yoder seems to suggest, that it must necessarily be limited by them.

To put the issue in Yoder's own terminology I am suggesting that his theology of the Church's form of witness to society is not supported completely by the distinction he draws between the old and new aeons. To be sure he says both are redeemed in Christ, but if this is the case can he draw the line between them quite as sharply as he seems to do in terms of the Christian's stance toward the society and its cares? Or put in a somewhat different way, how is he sure where the line between them is to be drawn? The virtue of understanding the dualism of Christian ethics to be one primarily of possible response of agents is that it allows for a dynamic understanding of God's redeeming work and the Christian's response to it. Yoder seems, however, to have severely qualified this aspect of his theology of social criticism by assuming an exact parallel between faith and the new aeon, unbelief and the old aeon.

There would be no difficulty in this if Yoder's understanding of the relationship between the two aeons were more dynamic. Yoder wants to claim that Christ has in reality defeated and harnessed some forms of the powers of the old order, but does not the New Testament affirm that God's work is continuing to bring in reality all the affairs of the old aeon under his rule. Such an affirmation need not be translated into the idea that God's kingdom is quickly reaching its climax on earth in the sense that the form of this world perfectly reflects his rule. Rather it affirms that some developments in the socio-political forms of our existence may be more appropriate of God's redemptive purposes than others. If this is the case then some forms of Christian direct action in the name of creating a responsible society perhaps has a deeper theological significance than simply a contantinian rejection accounts for. At least it can be suggested that if Yoder's position is finally to avoid the idea of orders or realms, then it seems he must allow for a more dynamic conception of the interrelation of faith and unbelief, the new and old aeons, than he has in fact done.

Such an affirmation should not be taken as a warrant for the church to take sides in terms of the battles of this world. The establishment of the kingdom by Christ is wider than the confines of the church. The church's job in relation to the kingdom is not to act toward society as if the kingdom's realization depended on its direct action. The church no more than the world knows where or how the kingdom is finally coming. Rather the church's job is to be a people who witness in their lives that in fact the kingdom has come and is a reality. The church is not directly God's agent for the realization of the kingdom, but rather it is God's harbinger of the kingdom by being the fellowship of the faithful in which the reality of the kingdom is manifest.

Finally I should like to raise a question concerning the norm of nonresistance as the form of the Christian life. Even if one accepts this as the essence of the incarnation, it still remains problematic how the Christian in fact embodies it in his life. For the nature of evil is broader than the questions of violence in itself. We constantly confront and perpetrate on others subtle forms of aggression and injustice that are all the more fatal for their nonviolent forms. What form would nonresistance take in the face of this kind of problem in our lives?

It is wrong, as Yoder I think also believes but fails to make explicit enough, to interpret the idea of nonresistance as a good in itself. Rather Christian nonresistance is an integral part of a more general affirmation of the nature of how our lives should be ordered together in the light of Christ's work. If that is the case then surely nonresistance can take the form in certain contexts of a vigorous defense of the good. That the forms of such a defense is limited is true, but if nonresistance is not a stance based on a profounder sense of right then it is an ethic of capitulation rather than redemption. However, surely Yoder is right that the burden of proof for such active resistance, especially as it approaches the use of physical violence, must fall on him who takes it up.

12.

Politics, Vision, and the Common Good

The Contemporary Situation and the Theological Response

To say that we are living in a time of crisis has become a cliché that does little to inform one about the state of the world. Generally it seems to be a way of indicating that such specific issues as the war, race, poverty, pollution, and population have clustered together to raise deeper questions about the viability of our contemporary institutions. Politically it is the youth that seem to feel this crisis most intensely and are willing to employ the means to bring it to our attention. They are not content to work within the established procedures of our political polity but are choosing means to bring pressure against what they consider to be an unresponsive establishment. Many of us who have identified ourselves as liberal are a bit taken aback when we find that we are declared the enemy by these new scions of righteousness.

Many theologians, ethicists, and social philosophers have responded to the new radicals by identifying with their ends but raising questions about their tactics. They have been appalled by the rhetoric of the movement, its self-righteous character, its too easy acceptance of marxist or anarchist ideals, its anti-intellectualism, and its romantic penchant for revolution. More importantly, they have expressed concern for some of the totalitarian tendencies that seem to be present in some of the new radical groups.[1]

This has not, however, been the only response to this reemergence of radicalism; some try to give a theological justification for the new movement. For example, Michael Novak says that he wishes "to bring a radical Christian theology to the support of the student movement of the present generation."[2] The

---

[1]The best critique of the new radicals is by Peter Berger in a book co-authored by Richard Neuhaus called *Movement and Revolution* (New York: Anchor, 1970).

[2]Michael Novak, *Theology for Radical Politics* (New York: Herder and Herder, 1969), p. 17.

222

theological supporters of this "new politics" suggest that the above negative considerations fail to appreciate the fact that we are living in a radically unique age in which the struggle for social justice must be worked out in new terms.[3] It is not the new radical that is guilty of utopianism but the old liberal who thinks the present system can find solutions to our contemporary problems.[4]

It is interesting to notice that this new theology of radicalism is primarily interested in giving a warrant to a kind of style rather than an explicit political position. Style is significant for the new radicals because they are not concerned with simply trying to formulate new political programs but they are attempting to render problematic a whole way of life. A change in style denotes the assumption of a whole new stance toward our contemporary world. The problem with the liberal is not just that he continues to adhere to traditional political techniques, but primarily that his whole way of seeing and understanding the world is wrong. For the liberal is inextricably committed to a technological social order that is of necessity dehumanizing. Therefore what must be created is not just a new political order; in effect, a new "counter-culture" must be born that is based on personalism rather than the tyranny of technological society.[5]

It is not my purpose to try to evaluate this kind of general claim about modern society. (I must admit I am extremely uncertain as to how one would go about assessing the truth of such broad statements about contemporary life. I suspect that whether one is persuaded by such arguments is ultimately dependent on prior dispositional characteristics.) Rather, I want to concentrate here on the kind of dissatisfaction that the radicals find in the American political community. It may be charged that it is impossible to separate this one concern from their general critique, but I think that it is at least possible to distinguish certain political themes from their general rejection of contemporary life.

---

[3] Richard Schaull, "Liberal and Radical in an Age of Discontinuity," *Christianity and Crisis* (January 5, 1970), pp. 339-345. See also Stephen C. Snyder, "Rhetoric and Life-Styles," *Christianity and Crisis* (February 16, 1970), pp. 15-20.

[4] Schaull, p. 342.

[5] Theodore Roszak, *The Making of a Counter Culture* (New York: Anchor Books, 1969). By speaking of the "new radical" in a general way I do not mean to ignore the significant differences among the radical groups. What I am trying to characterize here is but a general tendency of the contemporary discussion.

In the political context the new radicals are principally attempting to call an end to the liberal era of "political realism." Issue politics is no longer sufficient to solve our problems. Liberal welfare programs are but further delays to preserve an essentially corrupt society. As an editorial in as staid a journal as *Christian Century* suggests, what is being forced upon us is that we must again learn to think in utopian terms.[6] It points out that those of us who cut our political teeth on Reinhold Niebuhr's understanding of the political process, though appearing liberal at the time, really managed to exist quite easily with the essential conservatism of the American scene. In contrast to this, they counterpose the work of Ruban Alves (*Theology of Human Hope*) who argues that the task of Christian ethics is "the liberation of man's imagination so that it can build new utopias different from all current models of society and therefore be capable of contemplating the liberation of the world. When utopias are not imagined, ethics is reduced to solving problems within the established system."

I think this attack on "political realism" is significant for at least two reasons. First, it reveals the nakedness of the king, for too often "realism" has been used as a magic incantation to avoid analyzing what ethically is at stake. The appeals to "realism" are sometimes nothing more than the assertion of the "facticity" of the status quo and its necessary acceptance. It may be a good thing to accept such "facticity" but such an acceptance must be dependent on wider ethical grounds than an appeal to "realism" as though it is clear what it means.

More importantly, their rejection of "political realism" reminds us that our political philosophy and ethics is and always has been an attempt to learn a way of "seeing" political phenomenon, not just in the sense of seeing what it is, but in the sense of being able to evaluate the "what is" in a wider context of significance. Imagination is the means through which the political ethicist attempts to express his fundamental values and thus to transcend his historical contingent place. As Sheldon Wolin suggests in his book, *Politics and Vision,* the great political theorists were aware that they were injecting imagination or fancy into their theories, and they did so because they believed that fancy, exaggeration, even extravagance, sometimes permit

---

[6]*Christian Century* (March 25, 1970), p. 347.

us to see things that are otherwise not apparent.[7] For them, imagination was significant because political philosophy must be committed to lessening the gap between the possibilities grasped through political imagination and the actualities of political existence. The more comprehensive vision provided a way to think

about political society in its corrected fullness, not as it is but as it might be. Precisely because political theory pictured society in an exaggerated, "unreal" way, it was a necessary complement to action. Precisely because action involved intervention into existing affairs, it sorely needed a perspective of tantalizing possibilities.[8]

Problematics of the Theological Response

I think we must be thankful to the new radicals and their theological counterparts for reminding us of this aspect of political thinking. The radical theologians, however, seem to think that this necessarily entails the acceptance and support by the church of the current radical vitalities and causes. Such an identification of the cause of the church with political radicalism seems perilously close to making relevancy an end in itself. One cannot help but get the feeling that those who are so willing to identify the gospel with the current forms of radicalism are turning theology into a rationalization for decisions they have made on other grounds.[9] They seem to think that the language of God's action in history or the recovery of the eschatological dimension of the gospel entails that change must always be viewed as good. Little consideration is given to the ethical questions involved in distinguishing between various forms of changes in the socio-political process and the relationship between means and end in such change.

---

[7]Sheldon Wolin, *Politics and Vision* (Boston: Little, Brown, and Co., 1960), p. 18.

[8]*Ibid.* pp. 20-21.

[9]Thus Jacques Ellul says, "What troubles me is not that the opinions of Christians change, nor that their opinions are shaped by the problems of the times; on the contrary, that is good. What troubles me is that Christians conform to the trend of the moment without introducing into it *anything* specifically Christian. Their convictions are determined by their social milieu, not by faith in the revelation; they lack the uniqueness which ought to be the expression of that faith. Thus theologies become mechanical exercises that justify the positions adopted, and justify them on grounds that are absolutely not Christian." *Violence* (New York: Seabury Press, 1969), p. 28.

As they put the issues before us it seems the main focus of the church's social ethics is put in terms of the necessity of taking a side. Hopefully it is urged that in this new situation the church will for a change side with those against the status quo. Not only does this seem to imply that the church should be regarded simply as another sectarian power group,[10] but it assumes that all issues are such that it is appropriate to take sides. It is the "either you are for me or against me" mentality in radical form.

While I do not wish to deny the unfaithful tendency of the church to identify with the status quo; nor do I wish to deny that there are not at times issues on which the church cannot fail to take a stand even risking the danger of being identified as simply another political power group;[11] I do wish to deny that all issues can be understood this way. Not only does such a stance assume a new form of self-righteousness about the church, but it also seems committed to claiming an infallible insight for the church on societal matters that simply is not appropriate. Moreover, such a social action ecclesiology fails to consider the integrity of the church's mission as primarily the proclamation of God's act in Christ as any aspect of such a proclamation that is not politically relevant is ignored.

The new "political theology" seems to be open to this kind of danger because of its tendency to lump all issues together under the one rubric of the rich against the poor.[12] Since the current situation continues to favor the rich, the conclusion is

---

[10]See Paul Ramsey's critique of this in *Who Speaks for the Church* (Nashville: Abingdon Press, 1967).

[11]I find unconvincing Ramsey's argument that the church should influence the direction of policy by influencing a society's ethos but not attempt to formulate directions of specific policies. It simply is not clear that such a distinction is possible in the socio-political realm. *Ibid.*, p. 38.

[12]I use the word tendency here deliberately as I certainly would not attribute this to all those developing this position. What I wish to call attention to is a possible misuse of "political theology," not necessarily its essential intent. For examples of this development, see the Autumn issue of *Dialog* (1969) on "Theology and Politics"; Jürgen Moltmann, *Religion, Revolution, and the Future* (New York: Scribner's, 1969); *Faith and the World of Politics*, edited by Johannes Metz, (New York: Paulist Press, 1968); Johannes Metz, "Religion and Society in the Light of Political Theology," *Harvard Theological Review* (October, 1968), pp. 507-523; Frederick Herzog, "Political Theology," *Christian Century* (July 23, 1969); Larry Fishback, "Man Comes of Age: Hope and Ethics," *Listening* (Autumn, 1969), pp. 221-227; and *New Theology*, 6, edited by Marty and Peerman (London: Macmillan Co., 1968).

drawn that anything that causes change is good. Any attempt to make discriminating judgments or to ask how a decision is ethically justified is interpreted as a delaying strategy by the "established." It seems to assume that once theological terms are seen to have a social dimension, the ethical task is done. This presupposes that right and wrong on political issues is fairly easily determined and that the only problem is to put the power of the church on the right side. There is little appreciation for the importance of trying to delineate a framework within which serious political questions can be adjudicated with fairness and rigor.

This seems paradoxical in the light of their demand for vision and imagination in the socio-political realm. The assumption seems to be that one's "vision" is relatively subjective and therefore cannot be analyzed or evaluated for its strength or weakness. Vision and utopianism are equated in a way that places one's ends beyond the scope of rational discussion. (What is interesting about this is that it shares the positivist assumption that value questions are basically nonrational.) One simply assumes one's feelings of dissatisfaction are morally worthy and that the only issue is which political stance best exemplifies one's feelings.

Contrary to this, I want to suggest that the "vision" we have of our political questions is open to debate and adjudication. For the content of vision is not simply "subjective" experience, but the way we see is formed by concepts and language which can be argued about and defended. Moreover, I will try to show that our current problems are not totally new in that they are open to analysis in terms of some of the categories of traditional political theory. What is in effect happening is that our contemporary problems are opening up the possibility of a renewed appreciation of some traditional categories of political theory or, if one prefers, "visions."

By attempting to do this, I want to suggest that at least one of the important contributions of the church for social issues is the attempt to elucidate the framework within which the problems facing us can be discussed and argued about in a way that reveals what is at stake. Such a task falls on the church as it is required to be an honest institution, that is, an institution that

uncovers the limitations of all present forms of social and political life and which brings man into relation with the ultimate reality that comprises his own ultimate destiny. This relation must be effected by confronting candidly—not by evading—the shortcomings and limitations of man's present life.[13]

This can be done by the church because her loyalty is not centered in a cause of this world but in the final destiny of man, the kingdom of God, which has been revealed in Jesus Christ. (The fact that the church's criterion of honesty is centered in Christ does not mean it necessarily has special insight in these matters. It must engage in the same kind of hard critical work that all men of good will must attempt in seeking understanding in these kinds of complex issues. The only difference is that the church has no reason to fear the truth, no matter how destructive it may be.) The church that serves such a truth may find itself the object of scorn as much by the left as the center and right.

Critique of the Pluralist Ideal

Even though much of the criticism directed at the new radicals today is just, I think that they have hold of the central issue before the American polity.[14] They often fail to state the issue in intellectually coherent terms, or their conceptualization of the issue may only tend to obscure rather than enlighten what they intuitively feel. Simply stated, the central question they are raising is whether substantive change in a democratic polity is still possible and if some new alternative to democratic

---

[13]Wolfhart Pannenberg, *Theology and the Kingdom of God* (Philadelphia: West minster Press, 1969), pp. 82-83. For a similar understanding of the church as critic see Julian Hartt, *A Christian Critique of American Culture* (New York: Harper and Row, 1967).

[14]It should be noted that I am not trying to deal with the political-ethical questions of developing countries or the third world. There is a tendency in the radical literature to connect such questions with the concerns of American polity under the general rubric of liberation. It seems to me that this causes an unavoidable confusion of issues and prevents real argument. Of course this is an assertion that must be defended, but such a defense is not possible in this context. Briefly, however, it entails a rejection of the revolutionary alternative in the American situation. By revolution I do not mean just substantive social change but the use of armed force to effect social and political change. In the current American situation revolution is neither normatively justified nor practically possible. (See Richard Neuhaus, *Movement and Revolution,* for the best discussion of this.) Since this is the case, the serious practical question becomes how the current American society is moved toward substantive reform.

society is not needed. I shall try to show that they are rightly calling into question a current model of democratic polity that is and has become the main ideology of political realism. I shall argue, however, that such an ideology does not encompass the richness of possibilities in the democratic experience, and that the crucial question for us today is how to make efficacious a substantive notion of the common good within a democratic framework.

It is now generally agreed that the political battle-lines of the past are no longer relevant. Due to the increasing necessity and importance of administrative procedures the old issues of more or less government are no longer debated. The old capitalist model of the self-regulating society of free competition between individuals has lost its descriptive power, if indeed it ever fit the factual situation. The death of this old model according to Theodore Lowi has occasioned the birth of a new public philosophy that he calls "interest-group liberalism."[15] The essential core of this new philosophy Lowi identifies as "pluralism," which assumes the primary political unit is not the individual but the group.[16] This new public philosophy, however, like the old capitalism, assumes that society is self-regulating, only now the equilibrium is established politically, not economically, between competing interest groups. This does not prevent the assumption that such a philosophy is liberal, as positive government action is regarded as necessary in order to maintain societal order.

William Connolly gives the best short description of the liberal's idea of pluralist society.[17] Pluralism, he says,

portrays the system as a balance of power among overlapping economic, religious, ethic, and geographic groupings. Each "group" has some voice in shaping socially binding decisions; and all major groups share a broad system of beliefs and values which encourage conflict to proceed within established channels and allows initial disagreements to dissolve into compromise solutions.

15Theodore Lowi, *The End of Liberalism* (New York: W. W. Norton and Co., 1969), p. 29.

16For a similar analysis, see Robert Paul Wolff, *The Poverty of Liberalism* (Boston: Beacon Press, 1968), pp. 122-138.

17William Connolly, "The Challenge to Pluralist Theory" in *The Bias of Pluralism,* edited by William Connolly. (New York: Atherton Press, 1969), pp. 3-4.

As ideal, the system is celebrated not because it performs any single function perfectly, but because it is said to promote, more effectively than any other known alternative, a plurality of laudable private and public ends. Pluralist politics combines, it is said, the best features from the individualistic liberalism of John Locke, the social conservatism of Edmund Burke, and the participatory democracy of a Jean-Jacques Rousseau.

The individual's active involvement in group life enables him to develop the language, deliberative powers, and sense of purpose which make up a fully developed personality.[18] His access to a multiplicity of groups promotes a diversity of experience and interests and enables him to reach alternative power centers if some unit of government or society constrains him.

Society as a whole also benefits from pluralism. The system of multiple group pressures provides reasonable assurance that most important problems and grievances will be channeled to governmental arena for debate and resolution.[19] The involvement of individuals in politics through group association gives most citizens a stake in the society and helps to generate the loyalties needed to maintain a stable regime with the minimum of coercion. Stability is further promoted, in the long run, because public policy outcomes tend to *reflect* the distribution (balance) of power among groups in the society. Yet, the theory goes, innovation and change are also possible in pluralist politics. New groups, created perhaps by changes in economic processes or population distribution, can articulate new perspectives and preferences which will eventually seep into the balancing process, affecting the shape of political conflicts and the direction of issue resolution.

In short, pluralism has been justified as a system which develops individual capacities, protects individual rights and freedoms, identifies important social problems, and promotes a politics of incremental change while maintaining a long-term stability based on consent.

---

[18]Wolff shows that the theory of pluralism tries to combine in an ingenious way the individualism of Mill with the conservative sociology of Durkheim. *The Poverty of Liberalism*, pp. 143-149.

[19]In terms of such a model, government is seen primarily either as a referee whose function is to lay down "ground rules for conflict and competition among private associations and to employ its power to make sure that no major interest in the nation abuses its influence or gains an unchecked mastery over some sector of social life"; or as a "vector-sum" where the pressures are exerted by interest groups throughout the nation which results in Congress resolving these interests into a single social decision. (Wolff, pp. 128-129). In either of these views, government is regarded only as another interest group as there is no "public good" for the government to serve beyond the necessities of maintaining order.

It is obvious that for many this is more than just a description of how our society works but is a normative ideal. Moreover, there is good reason for such a position: (1) it seems to embody the traditional concern of Americans for the limited state; (2) it provides for a relatively open society; (3) it recognizes the necessity of establishing peace between competing groups;[20] (4) it makes our politics relatively nonideological, as the politicians' job simply becomes the resolving of conflicts between groups; (5) it avoids the question of public authority, as it implies that power is not power at all, since sovereignty is parceled out among groups, and no one is then at a disadvantage;[21] (6) moreover, it provides a way of adjudicating the classical question of the nature of democracy in an empirically verifiable way, as the distinction between democracy and dictatorship can now be seen not so much as a distinction between government by a majority and government by a minority as one between government by a minority and government by *minorities.*[22]

Lowi is right, therefore, to suggest that this pluralist model now forms a strong system of belief on which public policy is formulated.[23] That is, now public decisions are made in accordance with what enhances the inherent pluralism of our society. Any causal reading of most contemporary books in political science will show their immense indebtedness to this model of society. Nor can it be denied that it is just this understanding of democratic polity that most Protestant social ethicists after Niebuhr presupposed as the warrant for political realism.[24]   I

---

[20]In effect, the pluralists are strongly Madisonian, as one of their major fears is majoritarian democracy. Paradoxically, they see what Madison feared, "factionalism" as the way of insuring that no one group dominates the social order. We will see that the issue that the critics raise is that, while to be sure this is not pure majoritarian tyranny as there is conflict between groups, the established equilibrium works the same as the oppression of a majority.

[21]Lowi, pp. 76-77.

[22]Robert Dahl, *A Preface to Democratic Theory* (Chicago: University of Chicago Press, 1956), p. 133.

[23]Lowi, p. 3.

[24]For example Niebuhr says, "Christianity knows that a healthy society must seek to achieve the greatest possible equilibrium of power, the greatest possible number of centers of power, the greatest possible social check upon the administration of power, and the greatest possible inner moral check on human ambition, as well as the most effective use of forms of power in which consent with coercion are

think that many of us were convinced by Niebuhr's use of the pluralist model not only because we thought it theologically appropriate and descriptively correct, but more importantly, we thought it gave us a warrant to become moralistic Machiavellians—that is, we could use any political means possible in the established political game in order to achieve what we considered to be morally good ends.

In spite of the pervasiveness of this model of democratic polity, it has come under decisive attack today from several different directions. Some of those attacking the pluralist ideology do not deny it had and perhaps still has valuable aspects in the development of democratic government. Nor do the critics wish to question the considerable descriptive force this model has for understanding American society. It is not its descriptive potential they question but its normative status.[25] The criticism of the pluralist model can be distinguished in terms of those that concentrate primarily on internal aspects of the system and those which raise external questions. The former is concerned primarily in contrasting the real operation of pluralism to the ideal, while the latter questions the sufficiency of the ideal itself.

---

compounded." *Reinhold Niebuhr on Politics,* edited by Davis and Good (New York: Scribner's, 1960), p. 182. The current critique of the pluralist model raises the question of the relation between Niebuhr's political theory and his theological position. At the time, the model of society as countervailing powers seemed completely appropriate to Niebuhr's doctrine of sin. It can now be asked if Niebuhr's theological position might not allow for a more positive analysis of the possibilities of society than the model of society he assumed. If not, then it might indicate an insufficiency in Niebuhr's theological program.

For an example of how pervasive Niebuhr's influence still is, see Joseph Hough's *Black Power and White Protestants* (New York: Oxford, 1968). Even though Hough wants to develop a social ethic that embodies the more positive and humanistic aspects of the gospel, it is clear his primary assumption is still the Niebuhrian model.

[25]One aspect of this general critique of the pluralist model involves an attack on the so-called "neutrality" of contemporary social science. The "behaviorist" social scientist is accused of assuming a normative commitment of the status quo under the guise of objectivity and empiricism. Evidence of this is the kind of research they undertake in terms of social "problems," and the fact that their conceptual framework assumes some form of an equilibrium as a norm for society. The idea that there is now an "end of ideology" is being questioned not in order to suggest that the social scientist should become a political ideologue, but rather that he cannot avoid investigating the normative issues of "what kind of government, what ends of government, what forms of government, what consequences of government," simply because they are not empirical. (Lowi, XI.) See also *The New Sociology,* edited by I. L. Horowitz, (New York: Galaxy Books, 1965); *Readings of the Philosophy of Science,* edited by May Broadbeck, (New York: Macmillan Co., 1968); Gibson Winter, *Elements for a Social Ethic* (New York: Macmillan Co., 1966).

The internal form of criticism is found embodied in a wide range of opinion and literature of extremely uneven quality. Some of this literature seems intent on trying to show that there is some form of explicit conspiracy among the military, business, and the middle class to maintain favored position. However, the more responsible critics of pluralism do not assume that it is necessary to hypothesize a demonic "establishment." Rather, their point is that the pluralist system creates an inherent bias that bestows advantages on portions of the society.[26] They do not deny that competition occurs in America, but it is not true competition among all the groups in society but competition among the elites. To be sure, a "consensus" is reached in the society, but it is a consensus which works to the detriment of those who are currently the outcasts. Since the rules of fair play are instituted by the prevailing consensus, while perhaps just in themselves, their institutional embodiment always means they work to the disadvantage of the powerless.

That such a bias is operative in a pluralist system is evident by the fact that certain groups and issues simply do not get adequately represented. By assuming all group interests are equally good—the segregationist, industrialist, the black, and the poor are all given equal standing—the system works necessarily against those who were not part of the original balance and against those who are unorganized. Moreover, many viable alternatives and issues do not reach the arena of government simply because they are not seen as significant by the ruling consensus. As a result, the disadvantaged often do not have an adequate perspective with which to locate the structural causes of their vague feelings of anxiety, frustration, and resentment. The linkage between private troubles and public issues is highly biased: some segments of society, such as the impoverished, the blacks, unorganized laborers, have not developed a way of being efficaciously heard in our society.[27] The space that such groups gain in the mass media is not an indication of their power but

[26]The best substantiation of these kinds of criticisms is found in the essays in the *Bias of Pluralism* edited by Connolly and in Lowi and Wolff's writings. Also see, Charles McCoy and John Playford, eds., *Apolitical Politics: A Critique of Behaviorism* (New York, 1967). For more popular treatment of some of the same issues that concentrates on our more obvious problems see *The Great Society Reader,* edited by Gettleman and Mermelstein (New York: Vintage Books, 1967); *The Radical Papers,* edited by Irving Howe (New York: Anchor, 1965); Michael Harrington, *Toward a Democratic Left* (Baltimore: Penguin, 1968).

[27]Connolly, p. 15.

their powerlessness, as they are forced to use tactics that make "news" but which cannot achieve their real aims.

It is interesting that many of the contemporary radicals concentrate on these kinds of criticisms as justification for their claim that our social order must be completely overturned. For these issues are open to adjudication in terms of the pluralist model. Rather than rejecting pluralism, these criticisms simply suggest that we do not have enough of it. If these kinds of issues are going to call into question the very structure of our societal order, then they must be shown to reveal the limits of pluralism in a more profound way. The reason much of the current criticism of our society has more the appearance than the substance of radicalism is the tendency of the critic to stereotype the society and its processes. Thus the radicals' criticism often fails to raise the hard questions because they are in effect tilting at windmills. All substantive criticism requires the honest gaze at the object in order to see fairly its moral strengths as well as its weaknesses.

What must be called into question is the fundamental assumption of the pluralist ideal—namely that the balance of interest achieved by the free bargaining of groups in society will achieve the greatest possible justice and common good. Such an assumption is but the old capitalist-utilitarian idea that the common good equals the greatest sum of individual satisfactions translated into the group model. The problem with such a presupposition is that justice is only conceived as a procedural requirement. There is no substantive understanding of justice or the common good to allow the state to plan or act in the interest of forming the good society. For the pluralist theory of society simply does not allow for the legitimation of such authority, as its whole presupposition is that coercion is not necessary for the creation of the good society. Pluralism by organizing and legitimatizing a society that prevents any one set of interests from dominating all other interests also prevents the possibility of the society from serving the interests of the whole.

Our current social ills in America are forcing us to recognize that they cannot be cured by the techniques of pluralist politics.[28] As Robert Paul Wolff says,

---

[28]Probably the most sensitive analysis of the ideal of pluralist social change is still Dahl and Lindblom's *Politics, Economics and Welfare* (New York: Harper Torch-

For example, America is growing uglier, more dangerous and less pleasant to live in, as its citizens grow richer. The reason is that natural beauty, public order, and the cultivation of the arts are not the special interests of any identifiable social group. Consequently, the evils and inadequacies in those areas cannot be remedied by shifting the distribution of wealth and power among existing social groups. To be sure, crime and urban slums hurt the poor more than the rich, the Negro more than the white—but fundamentally they are problems of the society as a whole, not of any particular group. That is to say, they concern the general good, not merely the aggregate of private goods. To deal with such problems, there must be some way of constituting the whole society a genuine group with a group purpose and a conception of the common good. Pluralism rules this out in theory by portraying society as an aggregate of human communities rather than as itself a human community; and it equally rules out a concern for the general good in practice by encouraging a politics of interest-group pressures in which there is no mechanism for the discovery and expression of the common good. . . . Pluralism both as a theory and as a practice, simply does not acknowledge the possibility of wholesale reorganization of the society. By insisting on the group nature of society, it denies the existence of the society-wide interests—save the purely procedural interest in preserving the system of group pressures—and the possibility of communal action in pursuit of the general good.[29]

The Nature of the Common Good

If this argument is correct, then it would suggest that the primary problem with political realism is that it has failed to see the significance of community for political behavior. To be sure, political realism may have had too limited imagination and vision, but this does not mean that the imagination necessarily must be given over to utopian speculation. The idea of the common good may not be as dramatic as utopian ideals, but it is no less morally exacting.

When understood in this context, the meaning of the current "crisis" in our nation is that our contemporary political experi-

books, 1953). For them, the ideal form of change is incrementalism, which is "a method of social action that takes existing reality as one alternative and compares the probable gains and losses of closely related alternatives by making relatively small adjustments in existing reality, or making larger adjustments about whose consequences approximately as much is known as about the existing reality or both." (p. 82.) The criterion of knowledge here is scientific verifiability. One cannot help but feel that the radicals are right in assuming that, in spite of appearances to the contrary, most liberals have a very pessimistic view of the possibilities of substantive social change.

[29]Wolff, pp. 159-160.

ence is forcing us to appreciate the significance of the traditional idea of the common good. As such, it should be viewed as an important opportunity, for I think it is fair to say that this concept has not played an important part in the explicit (implicitly is another question) public philosophy of our country. Our democratic institutions have been justified and formed more with the idea of limiting evil than as means to the good.[30] We must now recognize, for example, that the toleration that we have institutionalized through societal checks and balances is not an end in itself but one aspect of the good community. It may well be that tolerance understood in an absolute way will need to be qualified if we are to achieve the good society. Niebuhr is right to say that democracy must begin with a confession of sin, but it cannot stop there if democracy also entails striving for the good society.

It is important to make clear the nature of the concept of the common good as I am using it here. The common good represents that good of society beyond the individual or group interests that may happen to comprise it in fact. The common good is not simply the sum of individual or group interests, but it is genuinely a good that is common.[31] Implied in this idea is a view of man that sees man as essentially social—not just descriptively, but normatively. We are not individuals who come to the social order to get what we can from it, but rather in being fully individuals we must be socially constituted. Politics as a moral concept in this context takes on a wider significance than simply the question of satisfaction or balancing of interests. Politics is again understood in its traditional meaning as the art engaged in to achieve the good society. What is envisaged is a moralization of politics. American political behavior has been very moralistic but not very moral. "Political realism" by denying the "moralistic" abuse failed to appreciate the real morality of the political as the creation of the good community.

Such an understanding of the common good has often been

---

[30]For a good example of the defense of democracy on the grounds of man's failure to know the good see T. L. Thorson, *The Logic of Democracy* (New York: Holt, Rinehart, and Winston, 1962). Interestingly enough, although Thorson analyzes to great lengths the various justifications of democracy, he never feels the necessity of defining the nature of democracy.

[31]For an excellent discussion of this distinction in relation to Rousseau's "general will" see A. D. Lindsay, *Modern Democratic State* (New York: Galaxy Books, 1962), pp. 230-248. I should also like to give special thanks to my former colleague, Dr. Ross Paulson, for his stimulating suggestions about the nature of the common good.

interpreted to mean the death of democratic polity. For the genesis of democratic institutions is that they allow human society to function though no one is in possession of the good or the truth.[32] Benevolent totalitarians have always justified their action by claiming to have a special insight into the good. Paradoxically, men who have defended most fervently rational discussion as the good itself have tended to deny or limit the possibility of genuine political dialogue. Thus Plato, *in the name of the good society,* had to deny the true political art of conciliation necessary to maintain the ongoing activities of real men.[33]

However, the substantial conception of the common good I am arguing for is not an abstract model of the good society which only the chosen understand. There is nothing about the idea of the common good that entails that it must not be worked out in the contingencies of each society's historical circumstances. There is an inescapable "contextual" dimension to any genuine understanding of the common good.[34] The fact that the common good cannot be abstractly determined, however, does not mean the idea of the common good does not add a dimension to our political discussion, for it is required that any society policy must be genuinely public. To insist on the importance of the common good is to argue that if the political is to have significance, it must deal with those things that are general for the society in a general way (not just as a problem of harmonizing interests).[35] That is, the demand of the common good is the demand to seek, form, and maintain rational community, community not seen merely as the

efficient means to such desirable political ends as peace, order or distribu-tive justice. It is an activity, an experience, a reciprocity of consciousness among morally and politically equal rational agents who freely come together and deliberate with one another for the purposes of concerting their wills in the positing of collective goals and in the performance of common actions.[36]

---

[32]"Democracy in short is not a method which is effective only among virtuous men. It is a method which prevents interested men from following their interests to the detriment of the community." *Reinhold Niebuhr on Politics,* p. 184.

[33]Wolin, pp. 42-43.

[34]For a good explication of this see Richard Flathman, *The Public Interest* (New York: Wiley and Sons, 1966).

[35]Wolin, p. 429.

[36]Wolff, p. 192.

Democracy is that form of government that allows for such collective deliberation. Freedom and liberty are the institutional prerequisites for the development of democratic discussion. Such freedom is not, however, an end in itself, but the means to achieve the good society. Political freedom is not just the absence of limitations; it is freedom to do the good.[37] Thus, the democratic state is not necessarily committed to preserving absolute "freedom" of the individual at the cost of the development of the community. The function of the democratic state is to work for the enhancement and growth of wider community. The fact that coercion may be necessary for such work does not deny the basis of democratic polity as long as the coercion can be legitimated in accordance with the good determined by the community.

The task before America is whether we can collectively formulate and envision such a good and make it efficacious in our political life. To develop such a vision does not necessarily mean that our differences must be denied or our pluralism qualified. It is not our actual pluralism that is at stake here but a certain conceptual picture of that pluralism that has held our will captive.[38] To stress the importance of the common good means that we must try to develop a more profound unity that will undergird our differences. Not a unity that imposes the boredom of mediocrity and sameness in the interest of peace and order, but a unity that demands excellence and creativity in the interest of moral good. Only once it is clear that this is the morally substantive issue facing our body politic can we seriously ask what kinds of political strategy will work best in order to

---

[37]John Bennett, in his discussion of democracy, reflects a general tendency to characterize it as a way of avoiding the excesses of totalitarianism and anarchy. *Christian Ethics and Social Policy* (New York: Scribner's Sons, 1946), pp. 84-85. My argument here, while wanting to preserve this kind of consideration, tries to suggest that this kind of dichotomy is too simple to take account of all the significant issues of our political experience. Put in our historical context, the problem is one of how to move to an appreciation of a more substantive understanding of democratic community while preserving the gains of the past.

[38]Presupposed here is an understanding of a relationship among will, imagination, and language that I think is very important for Christian ethical reflection. Some recent works that are very suggestive in this respect are: Iris Murdoch, "Vision and Choice in Morality," in *Christian Ethics and Contemporary Philosophy*, edited by Ian Ramsey (New York: Macmillan Co., 1966), pp. 195-218; Donald Evans, *The Logic of Self-Involvement* (New York: Herder and Herder, 1970); Rollo May, *Love and Will* (New York: W. W. Norton, 1969); and Herbert McCabe, *What Is Ethics All About?* (Washington: Corpus, 1969).

develop such community.[39] Otherwise, our political activity, while working for the best of ends, may only succeed in making the achievement of such community more difficult.

After this long excursion into the wilderness of political ethics I should like to return briefly to the question of the church's relationship to the contemporary crisis. If this analysis has been correct, I suspect the church has little to offer in terms of political strategy. The church has no corner on political wisdom. In a deeper sense, however, I think that the church has a great deal to offer in terms of the necessity for us to achieve a wider community of discourse in our society. For I am impressed by the fact that early democratic society did not begin primarily from men adhering to abstract doctrines of the state or natural right, important as these were. Rather, the basis of democracy according to A. D. Lindsay in *The Modern Democratic State* arose from the experience of the Puritan congregations as a fellowship of equals.[40] I suspect that all truly significant political forms arise not from the speculation of the

---

[39]For a very suggestive article in this respect see David Kettler, "The Politics of Social Change: The Relevance of Democratic Approaches," in *Bias of Pluralism*, pp. 213-249. One of the greatest failings of contemporary Christian social ethics is the disregard for the interrelationship between political ethics or theory and political strategy. It has concentrated primarily on strategy around particular issues without such strategy being informed by a more fundamental stance concerning political society. Some regard this not just as an oversight, but as a positive good. Richard Schaull for example says, "The revolutionary finds himself caught up in an accelerated process in which he is confronted, at every moment, with a new configuration of facts and events. All schematic definitions of ethical responsibility tend to hinder him from dealing with concrete reality." "Revolutionary Change in Theological Perspective," in *Social Ethics,* edited by Gibson Winter (New York: Harper and Row, 1968), p. 248. I do not wish to deny that a theory can be used to blind us to reality rather than to help us see what is at stake, thus the constant requirement to test our conceptual apparatus by experience. However, if this position is taken completely seriously, I cannot understand how any political disucssion can rise higher than a journalistic or propagandistic effort to acquire power. This failure to try to evaluate one's strategy in terms of a fundamental framework also often results in inconsistencies. For example in radical literature there is often a critique of the power of the state in quite conservative terms while programs that only a strong government can perform are recommended.

I do not mean to imply by this criticism that if one's ethical stance is clear then a strategy is easily determined. It is of course true that men with the same ethical vision may disagree about strategy questions as they involve contingent facts over which men of good will may disagree. This difficulty only points to the importance of a more detailed investigation of the relation between stance and strategy. For some beginning suggestions in this respect see James Sellers, *Theological Ethics* (New York: Macmillan Co., 1966).

[40]Lindsay, pp. 117-121.

philosopher, but from the actual experience of people which provides a paradigm for their wider social experience. What we need in our contemporary context is not so much moral rhetoric but moral experiences of community.

If this is in fact the case, then the most lasting contribution the church can contribute to the contemporary political community is not to make more statements about particular issues—that is, to try to become an explicit political force—but its most important social function is to *be itself*.[41] This does not mean that it should not be concerned about particular issues, but such issues should be handled in a way that reflects the fact that the ground of the church consists in being the people of God. For it is such a people who can, through their diversity, find unity in their one Lord. It is only as we experience such community, in fact, that the possibility of our visions for political community will be expanded beyond the conceptual limitations in which we are now encased.

---

[41]The ecclesiology that I find most amenable to this position is George Lindbeck's description of the "church or the messianic pilgrim people of God, the sacramental sign of the kingdom which has begun and will be consummated in Christ." See his *The Future of Roman Catholic Theology* (Philadelphia: Fortress Press, 1970), p. 27. Such an understanding of the church does not presuppose the "incarnationalist" position that somehow the Christian responsibility is converting the world to make it Christian. Nor does it assume that the "secular" development of the world is the same as the development of God's kingdom. The social responsibility of the church is to prepare the way for such a kingdom by being the "sacramental sign" as the community of reconciliation. See also George Lindbeck, "Ecumenism and the Future of Belief," *Una Sancta*, 25, 1968, pp. 3-17.

13.

Theology and the New American Culture

The relationship of theology and the new American culture is a problem, I think, on many sides and various levels. The issue involves questions I do not even know how to ask meaningfully, let alone resolve.

First of all, I have all sorts of problems with a term so amorphous as "American culture." I know there is something distinctive about being American, that is, being heir of and participant in this nation's history and culture. Yet if forced to characterize that distinctiveness, I find myself either mouthing meaningless abstractions about democracy, freedom, and equality—or simply lost in the sheer diversity of people and experience which make up the country. So it is definitely problematic for me to attempt relating theology to something as hard to pin down as concepts like "American culture" or "the American character."

Moreover, the turbulence of the 1960's makes me suspect that America well may have undergone some fundamental changes which indicate the beginnings of a new culture. Yet I am even more puzzled about how to identify and properly characterize this "new American culture" than I am the old. Even from this time perspective it is still not clear what happened. Did we see the development of a new technological society, or did the "counterculture" signal a fundamental change in our society? Were these seemingly momentous changes at that time really "new," or only different ways of construing the familiar American pragmatic and individualistic spirit? In other words, is the so-called "new American culture" something different in kind or but one or several variations on traditional American values and institutions.

Finally, the relationship of these kinds of questions and theology is highly problematic. Today there are numerous "theologies of culture"—not least because it is so unclear as to what such an enterprise entails. Without broaching that thorny

241

matter, I can at least insist that the question of theology's relation to the "new American culture" be separated from that of religion's relationship to a culture. Theology is a normative discipline. In the context of the questions we are raising here, theology is concerned with how religious people *should be* related to culture, regardless of how in fact they are so related. Historically, of course, religion has played a decisive role in the formation of the American spirit. But such a descriptive account has no normative weight for the theologian. At best, awareness of religion's role will inform his enterprise since the theologian must have some idea as to what has been in order to know what should be.[1]

At least such has been the traditional view of theology as normative. One of the most striking aspects of contemporary American theology, however, has been its willingness, even avidity, to enter into dialogue with its culture. Today's theologians appear eager to rush in where historians and sociologists fear to tread. Or to change the image, American theologians no longer sit around the hearth of philosophy, but warm themselves with the cultural themes of the day. It is the leaping flames of cultural issues they contemplate, seeking to discern implicit or explicit "religious" significance in that fire.[2] And no longer is the theologian's handbook Aristotle's *Metaphysics,* but rather Reich's *The Greening of America.*

The difficulty with the resulting theology is, however, deciding why Reich's (or X's or Y's) account of modern American society should be accepted rather than Parsons' (or X's or Y's).

---

[1]For example, my own analysis below presupposes the kind of work done by Perry Miller in *Errand into the Wilderness* (Cambridge, Mass.: Harvard University Press, 1956) and H. R. Niebuhr in *The Kingdom of God in America* (New York: Harper, 1937).

[2]Harvey Cox's *The Secular City* (New York: Macmillan, 1965) is the classic example of this kind of theology. Many lesser lights continue the attempt over different aspects of culture they find more significant. For example, see Myron Bloy, "The Counter-Culture: It Just Won't Go Away," *Commonweal,* October 17, 1971, pp. 29-34, and Robert Johnson, *Counter Culture and the Vision of God* (Minneapolis: Augsburg, 1971). A summary of Michael Novak's work would make a fascinating account in this respect as he originally gave a theological blessing to the "youth movement" but then has begun to be more and more disenchanted with it. For a well-balanced assessment see his "American Youth and the Problem of God: A Theological Reflection," *Proceedings of the Catholic Theological Society* (New York, 1972), pp. 138-155. Many of the essays in this volume are of interest for the subject of this essay.

With such theology, the theologian's claims seem to be only as good as the cultural commentator he happens to prefer. Nor is it clear how such theology is to be distinguished from journalism.

I do not wish to deny many healthy aspects of the theologian's concern with contemporary culture; but in actual practice the development has tended to trivialize the theological task. An indication of this danger is the highly faddish and arbitrary nature of such theology. For example, in 1965 Harvey Cox in *The Secular City* gave an almost unqualified baptism to the new "secularity" with its pragmatic and technological style.[3] This was necessary, according to Cox, because theology is called upon to make religion relevant and responsive to the new forces of our society. (Thus reversing the ancient Christian assumption that the Christian's task is to make the world relevant to the gospel.) Yet only four years later we find Cox praising the emphasis on fantasy, play, and celebration in the antitechnology counterculture.[4] Perhaps Cox has begun to suspect that there is nothing more boring or pathetic than the irrelevancy of the "relevant theology" of the generation just past. Nonetheless, he has created a hard theological world to live in: the theologian must somehow keep up with every new movement the media decide to create.

Such criticism of the recent theology of culture, however, does not reach the basic difficulty. Often the implicit assumption in this kind of theologizing is that the prime duty of theology is to help create or reconstitute Christendom. Such a suggestion may appear odd, since the theology I am criticizing tends to be itself critical of past failures of the church to stand over against the pretensions of American righteousness. It vigor-

---

[3]The issue of the relation of religion and "secularity" is of course an important and significant problem for the theologian. The problem with *The Secular City* was the assumption that the meaning of "secularity" and its relation to our contemporary culture was clear. For an excellent collection of essays concerned with this issue see Childress and Harned, eds., *Secularization and the Protestant Prospect* (Philadelphia: Westminster Press, 1970).

[4]Harvey Cox, *The Feast of Fools* (New York: Harper, 1969). Cox explicitly denies that there is any conflict between his earlier and later books and calls the latter only a "companion piece" to *The Secular City*. However, it is extremely hard to see how he can have both worlds; the "festive radical" he calls for surely seems bent on tearing down a good deal that the pragmatic-technological culture wishes to preserve. He is right, however, that there is a continuity between the books as he continues to have a rather touching faith in the goodness of his fellow creatures.

ously opposes the willing domestication of the gospel to believing in belief. Such theology dissociates itself from the church's rather crude baptism of the "American way of life." And this theology insists that its perspective is not determined by the church's good faith, but rather by the bad faith of the church expressed in the acceptance of racists, capitalists, and a dehumanizing society. Thus for the theologians of the "new American culture" the counterculture movement seemed to offer the church a way out of its all-too-willing service to the old culture which has now revealed its true warmaking, racist, and technologically repressive character. Such a way out, however, leads through the same error of the past: confusing the demands of the gospel with the reigning idealities of culture. The New Left and the counterculture were in fact, no less aspects of the American phenomenon than the pragmatic-technological culture which they reacted against.

Thus theologians continue to foster the idea that the church's mission is to translate the gospel into the pieties of contemporary culture—that her mission is to spiritualize our civilization and our lives by identifying the current moralisms with the meaningfulness of salvation. The church's very success in the past now weds her to the continued bad faith that she is shepherd of the goodness of our culture.[5] But such a view of the church's mission, I would argue, is theologically askew. The church is not called to build culture or to supply the moral tone

---

[5]James Sellers says, for example, "Christian theology plays its role by seeking to identify those elements in the [American] tradition that express the gospel, while it is at the same time open to those new elements in our contemporary situation that express new challenges and call for new expressions of the gospel." *Public Ethics: American Morals and Manners* (New York: Harper and Row, 1970), p. 226. Herbert Richardson attempts to identify theology with what he calls the sociotechnic age. Thus, he says, "A sociotechnic theology must develop new ethical principles which will enable men to live in harmony with the new impersonal mechanism of mass society. This ethic will affirm the values of a technical social organization of life in the same way that earlier Protestantism affirmed the values of radical individualism and capitalism." *Toward an American Theology* (New York: Harper and Row, 1967) p. 25. Sellers and Richardson have the virtue of not being mesmerized by the "righteousness" of the counterculture but their theological difference with the counterculture theologians is only over which part of the culture they wish to make the engines of theology serve. To provide one final example, Leroy Moore suggests that the great unfinished theological task of the American church is to construct a theology to support the pluralism and freedom of the American culture. "From Profane to Sacred America: Religion and the Cultural Revolution in the United States," *Journal of the American Academy of Religion*, 39 (September, 1971), 322-324.

of civilization, old or new. The church is called to preach that the Kingdom of God has come close in the person and work of Jesus Christ.[6] It is only as the church becomes a community separate from the predominant culture that she has the space and rest from which to speak the truth to that culture.[7]

The church's task, then, is not to choose sides among the competing vitalities of the current culture, but to speak the word of truth amid warring spirits. For the truth it speaks is not any truth; it is the truth of the Kingdom which the bounds of this earth do not contain. That is the reason why the first word the church always speaks to its culture is a word of incompleteness and finitude. However, this is not a word men gladly hear. It is characteristic of our personal and national existence to claim that we have a hold on truth which gives security in this life. We indulge the illusion that we can and do imbue our life and culture with meaning that is not subject to the ravages of time and human perversity. This is the reason a society only confesses its past sins within a framework of later rectitude. To do otherwise would necessitate admitting that the society's call for loyalty and devotion can only be accepted with qualification, or perhaps not at all.

The theologically interesting aspect of the current cultural "crisis" is, therefore, the tension it reveals in the idealism of the American spirit. For, as Reinhold Niebuhr demonstrated in *The Irony of American History*, the great strength and great weakness, the great wisdom and great folly of America have been the assumption that her beginning and history somehow captured the ideal possibilities of man.[8] To be sure, America often

---

[6]Since I am primarily concerned in this context to criticize what I interpret to be a new form of the "Christ of culture" position, my understanding of the relation of "Christ and culture" may appear more negative than it is. A culture may offer many positive forms of life congruent with the demands of the gospel. My concern in this essay, however, is to deny that this congruence can be *a priori* asserted in the name of relevance or social reform, but occurs only because Christians first take a critical and discriminating stance toward the society in which they happen to find themselves.

[7]I suspect that this is also true for the university. However, it remains to be seen if the university's commitment to truth in the abstract is sufficient to withstand the temptation to become mistress to the reigning culture. For a position close to my own in this respect see James Schall, "The University, the Monastery, and the City," *Commonweal*, April 7, 1972, pp. 105-110.

[8]Reinhold Niebuhr, *The Irony of American History* (New York: Scribner's, 1962). Some may interpret this essay as a reassertion of Niebuhrian realism against the idealism and romanticism of the new politics. However, this would be a serious

betrayed her ideals for lesser goods; but her very hypocrisy proved but another aspect of her spiritual pride. For America's ability to see critically her shortcomings has been interpreted by Americans as another sign of her essential righteousness and distinctiveness among the nations. The theologians of the "new American culture" question no more than those before them that a righteous America is possible. The debate between the representatives of the old and the new cultures concerns only whether we have fallen, or to what degree the fall has occurred, so that the necessary nostrums may be applied.

The interesting "problematic relationship" for me in this essay is therefore the tension created by a necessary theological stance. As a theologian I must be a critic who somehow stands apart from his culture, while remaining at the same time part of it. In attempting such a task I am sure I will make some horrendous errors concerning my perception of the nature of the American culture, both old and new. However, such a risk must be taken, since the Word to which the theologian is first responsible does not go out to the world to come back empty. The theologian shares in the church's desire not to keep a place above the battle, but a place within it, so as to speak the truth about the human condition in its localized cultural dress. Relevancy is not the criterion of truth. It is, however, an obligation of the church and the theologian if they are to avoid narcissistic infatuation which breeds the self-righteousness of men who have forgotten that Christ belongs not to themselves but to the world.

In this essay I am attempting to suggest what I take to be pertinent theological aspects of the current crisis of American culture. For purposes of analysis, I will distinguish between the crisis associated with our institutions and the crisis of persons. I

---

misunderstanding for even though I continue to have deep sympathies with Niebuhr's insights I think much of the recent criticism of "Christian realism" as a position has been just. It would take me too far afield to go into this matter but generally I think Niebuhr failed to appreciate the positive nature of society, or, in more theological terms, he tended to continue to assume, admittedly in a more dynamic fashion, the Lutheran dichotomy between the orders of creation and redemption. However, even if that is the case many of Niebuhr's contemporary critics ignore his positive appreciation of community for the flourishing of the self. Moreover, the critics are wrong in their claim that Niebuhrian realism is essentially conservative. This appears to be the case due to Niebuhr's refusal to develop any principles of justice on which discriminating social judgments could be based. In the absence of a substantive view of justice, Niebuhr's realism was and is open to conservative distortion.

hesitate to employ such a distinction, for it separates the inseparable and tends to suggest a cleavage between the social and personal factors of our life. As a way of sorting out issues, however, I think the distinction will prove functionally useful.

The account of the crises of American institutions is a familiar litany. Our cities are decaying. They are filled with black refugees from the South, who must try to survive strangled by white insensitivity and stupidity. Integration of the blacks has proved more difficult than was originally envisaged; the blacks resist it for reasons of manhood and identity, while whites fight integration in order to preserve the "quality education of the neighborhood school." Then there is the continuing problem of poverty. We have discovered a poor in the midst of society's plenty whom the growth of a mixed-capitalist economy does not seem capable of reaching. On top of it all, we are becoming aware that we are callously destroying our environment, so that we can neither drink our water nor breathe our air without endangering health. And all these problems seem to be occurring at a time when our political institutions are not able to provide even the most basic services for society to keep running at a minimal level.

Brooding over these immense problems of course has been the war in Vietnam. Even though we have withdrawn from the fighting, the war continues to stand as sign and symbol that America has fallen from the ranks of the righteous. For many think that by our participation in that war we helped perpetrate an evil so terrible no possible rationalization can be offered to explain or excuse what we did there.[9] Our retreat from the war is not therefore sufficient to blot out the stain of our involvement.

These are extremely serious problems; taken together they pose a real threat to our society's current form of existence. What I am concerned about here, however, is how this common litany of our problems serves to substantiate the claim that we are living in an "apocalyptic" or "crisis" time. Such a proclamation is not a new phenomenon in American life. But framing the current revision of the claim reveals some of the basic illusions

---

[9] I do not mean this to be taken as my own ethical judgment about the Vietnam war. Rather, I am discussing the war insofar as it has become a cultural symbol. It is one of the marks of our ethos that it is so difficult to discuss the war as an issue of ethical ambiguity, for either one must think it a complete evil or a complete good.

associated with the American dream. For this apocalypticism is based on our prior claims to greatness and innocence. That is to say, our apocalypticism is a sign of a disease deeper than the actual problems which we Americans face. It is noteworthy that the radical critiques of American society as corrupt continue to presuppose, as their model of the good society, a purer and more perfect America which supposedly existed in the past. The American radical is not the born cynic but the lover who has discovered his beloved works part time in a brothel.

In a decisive way, then, our times render problematic the notion that America represents a new start and opportunity for mankind. We are not, were not, a nation conceived in inno- cence. The new Eden or the new Israel we have never been and will never be.[10] Yet many continue to presuppose the myth of innocence by suggesting that America's way out of her current crisis is to make a completely new beginning. We have betrayed the original covenant; our hope now lies in making a new contract which allows us to begin again, leaving behind our sin of the past.

This illusory quest for our lost innocence, however, only deepens our problem. It perverts the accuracy of how we describe our current situation. For example, Americans seem unable to believe that our present troubles may possibly be due to the very hardness of the issues, inadvertence, or sheer stupid- ity.[11] If we are in a mess, we prefer to explain it in terms of evil men conspiring to put us there. The war in Vietnam is brutally

---

[10]For a fascinating account of the idea of innocence in early American literature see R. W. B. Lewis, *The American Adam* (Chicago: Phoenix Books, 1955). John Barth's *The Sot Weed Factor* is a marvelous satire concerned with the myth of America's birth in innocence (New York: Grossett and Dunlap, 1966). See also Thomas Merton's *Conjectures of a Guilty Bystander* (Garden City: Doubleday, 1968), pp. 32-40.

[11]It never seems to occur to the current radicals that part of our problems is the result of the incompatibility of positive moral values. For example, the early S.D.S. manifesto, the *Port Huron Statement,* seems to assume that we can reduce poverty, provide better housing, destroy racism, and at the same time decentralize the governmental process and decrease our dependence on technology. Zbigniew Brzezin- ski is closer to the truth when he says, "Today's America has set higher standards for itself than any other society: it aims at creating racial harmony on the basis of equality, at achieving social welfare while preserving personal liberty, at eliminating poverty without shackling individual freedom. Tensions in the United States might be less were it to seek less—but in its ambitious goals America retains its innovative character." *Between Two Ages: America's Role in the Technetronic Era* (New York: Viking, 1970), p. 257.

painful to us. Even if one allows for the incredible deviousness associated with American involvement in Vietnam, the truth is that honorable men with good intentions tragically committed us to the present course. But to admit such a truth means that as a nation Americans must face the fact that we exist in a world of ambiguity. And within that world innocence is bought only at the price of illusion. Put differently, accepting the hard truth means that we must somehow learn that life is often neither good nor bad, but simply tragic. Even more difficult, we must learn how to embody that fact in our experience.

For example we need symbols in our political discourse that are rich enough to embody the tragedy of Vietnam. Good men died there because they thought it was their duty; good men refused to die there because they thought it was their duty. As a nation we need symbols that allow us to honor both, as Lincoln did in his "Second Inaugural." But such discourse is possible only if we are able as a nation to understand that we like other nations stand amid a history of sin and illusion.

In this matter of overcoming the myth of innocence, the crucial issue before Americans is whether we can include within the account of our history the reality of the black man's existence and struggle. I am not talking about whether we finally are able to integrate the blacks into the larger society, important and necessary as that is. (Integration, in fact, might well be a way of avoiding the hard problem which the black American raises for his white compatriots.) Nor do I mean that our white histories should be written to include the contributions blacks have made to our nation, though that also is necessary. Rather, I want to point up the fact that the black population stands in our midst as a people who have suffered the injustice and humiliation of being systematically oppressed and exploited. As such, black people are a constant check on the American presumption of innocence with its corollary of omnipotence.

As Vincent Harding has put it so well:

The black experience in America allows for no illusions, not even that last ancient hope of the chosen American people whom God will somehow rescue by a special act of his grace. America began with such hopes, but they were tied to the idea of a Convenant, that men would have to do God's will for them to remain as his chosen ones. Somehow, just as America forced black men to do so much of its other dirty but productive work, the nation evidently came to believe that whites could be chosen while blacks did that suffering which has always been identified with the chosen ones. Now that is over. The black past has begun to explode and to reveal to a hidden chosen people that to be the anointed one is to be crushed and humiliated by the forces of the world. So, for all who would see it, the Afro-American past illuminates the meaning of being chosen. Perhaps this is what white Americans must see: that they will either join the ranks of suffering and humiliation or there will be no chosen people on these shores. Either they will submit their children to some of the same educational terrors they have allowed black children to endure or there is no future for any. Either they will give up their affluence to provide necessities for others or there will be neither affluence nor necessities for anyone. Perhaps we were chosen together, and we cannot move towards a new beginning until we have faced all the horror and agony of the past with absolute honesty. Perhaps integration is indeed irrelevant until the assessment of a long, unpaid debt has been made and significant payments begun. Perhaps atonement, not integration, is the issue at hand.[12]

To speak of institutional crises as finally a matter for atonement may sound odd, since such crises are only solved by action and new programs. It is my contention, however, that while new programs and new institutional forms are certainly necessary in our society, they do not reach to the heart of our current problems. I suspect that as Americans we will find some way to "muddle through." The great tragedy will be if we do so in a way which keeps us trapped in the illusion that further action will free us from the past. A viable moral future for America is possible only if we embrace our sinful past not as an accidental sideshow, but part and parcel of what it means to be American. That may be asking far too much of any nation; but we can do nothing less if the moral substance of our society is ever to be based on truth rather than illusion.

Severe as it is, the crisis of institutions in America in some ways pales in comparison with the crisis of persons. For in the midst of the most affluent economy in the world and the freest political system, we find a quarrelsome and dissatisfied people. This disquietude appears in its most dramatic form among the youth identified with the New Left and the counterculture.[13]

[12]Vincent Harding, "The Afro-American Past," in *New Theology* No. 6 (New York: Macmillan, 1969), 175-176.

[13]I do not mean to imply that there are not often profound differences between those associated with the New Left and members of the counter-culture. However, for my purposes there is no reason to try to carefully distinguish between them. The

Common to these is a kind of conventional wisdom about contemporary society. These young people see themselves trapped in an increasingly and seemingly irreversible technological society which leaves nothing to chance. We each become cogs in a completely planned system. The bureaucrat and the expert are the new power brokers in this society. And their power is all the more secure because, with ideology now relegated to the irrational past, they no longer have to justify their position.[14]

In such a technological society, democracy becomes but a sham, since government manipulates the masses through the media. Freedom thus becomes but a word for submitting to the choices of those who run the technological machinery. Work becomes pointless and empty. Reich describes work in this society as "mindless, exhausting, boring, servile, and hateful, something to be endured while 'life' is confined to 'time off.' At the same time our culture has been reduced to the grossly commercial; all cultural values are for sale, and those that fail to make a profit are not preserved. Our life activities have become plastic, vicarious, and false to our genuine needs, activities fabricated by others and forced upon us."[15]

The greatest loss we feel in such a society is the loss of self. The system strips us of all personal uniqueness in order to make us productive members of the technological mass society. We tend to become our roles, and thus are alienated from our true selves. Moreover, in such a society all attempts at community are killed, for "modern living has obliterated place, locality, and neighborhood, and given us the anonymous separation of our existence."[16] Thus we are left as machines without souls; we

standard works describing this phenomenon are of course Theodore Roszak, *The Making of a Counter Culture* (Garden City: Anchor, 1969); Charles Reich, *The Greening of America* (New York: Bantam, 1970); Jacobs and Landau, *The New Radicals* (New York: Vintage, 1966); and for a good collection of Movement literature see *The Movement Toward a New America: The Beginnings of a Long Revolution,* edited by Mitchell Goodman (New York: Alfred Knopf, 1970).

[14]It is interesting that Roszak relies so heavily on Jacques Ellul's book, *The Technological Society* (New York: Vintage, 1964), for the implications of Ellul's analysis is that there is no way of opting out or fighting a technological society without becoming part of it. This is but one example of the failure of the New Left to find adequate intellectual positions that would make intelligible the profound dissatisfaction they feel.

[15]Reich, *op. cit.,* pp. 6-7. One wonders why Reich thinks work was otherwise in the past.

[16]*Ibid.,* p. 7.

are condemned to a life of meaningless consumption so that our technological society can continue to function.

Against such a system, American youth see the only hope in forming a counterculture based on love and friendship. It becomes a political act to "do your own thing," for "the system" cannot stand any form of deviation. Style thus becomes a matter of political substance as it embodies the "idea that an individual need not accept the pattern that society has formed for him, but may make his own choice."[17] Genuine participatory democracy must be made a reality, even if it means the violent overthrow of the current rule.

What is impressive about this position is not the analysis of our society associated with it, but rather the profound dissatisfaction to which it witnesses. The dissatisfaction, however, is all the more tragic because of its failure to perceive accurately and face the reality of our contemporary experience. The New Left and the counterculture are thus more interesting as a symptom of our times than as a herald of our future.[18] But these movements are indeed a significant symptom. The language of their protest reveals their profound commitment to traditional American values—the very values that are often the source of their dissatisfaction. What is so striking about Reich's description of Consciousness III, for example is not how new it is, but

---

[17]*Ibid.*, p. 395. The New Left makes no attempt to distinguish between a political and a cultural revolution. That is why it often appears totalitarian. It wishes to transform the political form of society to get at the general culture. In some ways Reich's naive view of the necessity of changing "consciousness" first is nearer to the truth, but that implies a far longer, harder, and more ambiguous process than many associated with the New Left want to contemplate. For that reason Reich is considered by many of the New Left to be dangerous, since he assumes social change can occur without a transfer of power.

[18]Brzezinski, *op. cit.*, p. 232. He goes on to claim that the New Left "is an escapist phenomenon rather than a determined revolutionary movement; it proclaims its desire to change society but by and large offers only a refuge from society. More concerned with self-gratification than with social consequences of its acts, the New Left can afford to engage in the wildest verbal abuse, without any regard for the fact that it alienates even those who are potential supporters. Its concern is to create a sense of personal involvement for its adherents and to release their passions; it provides a psychological safety valve for its youthful militants and a sense of vicarious fulfillment for its more passive, affluent, and older admirers." Though I am sure there is much truth in this kind of *ad hominem,* we must be careful not to let the excesses of the youth culture blind us to its importance. For without such protest, I suspect we would feel a good deal less the oddness of our everyday life than in fact we do.

how very American it is with its optimistic and individualistic assumptions about man.[19]

Undoubtedly many Americans do feel profoundly alienated. But this alienation is not necessarily due to an oppressive technological culture.[20] Nor is the estrangement due to a fundamental denial of the original promise of America. Rather the alienation is rooted precisely in the fulfillment of that promise—ironic as it seems. The current malaise of our people stems not from the failure of the American dream, but from the fact that we are now closer than ever to realizing it. And we are beginning to suspect that dream may be a nightmare. In America we have sought to create a society of individuals—autonomous, self-sufficient, and stable—and the criterion of our success was taken to be the progressive emancipation of the individual from the "irrational" social constraints of the past.[21] Such freedom, it was assumed, would allow for a breakthrough of creativity and universal brotherhood, for the particularistic ties of kinship and tribe were taken to be the barrier to human fellowship. But to our dismay, we now discover that this "freedom is accompanied not by the sense of creative release but by

---

[19]Reich, *op. cit.*, p. 338. The romantic element in Reich's account of our modern situation is unmistakable. He assumes that if we could just strip from our existence the old forms of consciousness and structures, we would find the naked-beautiful-creative-loving self. The *Port Huron Statement* also argues that men have "unfulfilled capacities for reason, freedom, and love," and "unrealized potential for self-cultivation, self-direction, self-understanding and creativity." The current attempt of theologians to identify with this understanding of man makes one wonder how deeply Reinhold Niebuhr's work is capable of penetrating the American spirit.

The contradictions in Reich are obvious but perhaps the most important is the tension between his stress on community and individuality. Though he insists that the self can only be realized in community (p. 417), it is a community only of autonomous, self-realizing individuals who must refuse to accept any group responsibility, for "the individual self is the only true reality" (p. 242). Thus the individual of Consciousness III rejects all general standards and classifications since each person is intrinsically different, and values are but the subjectivistic choice of our sovereign will. While we can use no person as a means, it is equally wrong to alter oneself for someone else's sake (p. 244). What makes Reich's position so ironical is he entirely fails to see that he has restated the bourgeois individualism of pluralist democracy in a new style. He has reaffirmed the ethic of the middle class in a form that its children will accept.

[20]Of course, I do not mean to deny that technology poses many different and complex problems for our society. But as it is often used in radical literature, technology is but a symbol for all that is wrong with our society. That makes the term descriptively about as interesting as saying, "We are all sinful."

[21]Robert Nisbet, *The Quest for Community* (New York: Oxford University Press, 1953), p. 4. My general debt to Nisbet's thought should be apparent in this essay.

the sense of disenchantment and alienation. The alienation of man from historic moral certitudes has been followed by the sense of man's alienation from fellow man."[22]

The freedom America gives the individual has occasioned the furious quest for community in our society. The attraction of many to the New Left lies in being given a sense of participating in a reality larger than the confines of one's own ego. But the amorphous and self-destructive nature of "The Movement" cannot be sufficient to supply the community required, without that community itself becoming totalitarian.[23] Groups and societies are not sustained simply because men desire to be together, but because they share common purposes and loyalties. The high failure rate of the communes currently being formed is due largely to the fact that no society, even very small ones, can sustain itself for the sole purpose of letting everyone "do his own thing."

The other side of the American quest for community is our search for the self or identity. Contrary to the New Left assertion that technological society robs us of our identity, the problem is that it leaves us free, or even forces us to choose what we shall be. It would take us too far afield to engage here in an extensive comparison of our modern legal-rational social order as compared to traditional societies; suffice it to say that all modern sociological analysis confirms that we live in a highly

---

[22]*Ibid.*, p. 10. In this paper I am concerned with the more general cultural aspects of this phenomenon. However in the previous chapter, "Politics, Vision, and the Common Good," I have tried to relate these individualistic and utilitarian assumptions to the nature of pluralist democracy and the resulting political problems.

[23]One of the striking things about the development of the New Left is how dependent it is on the paradigm of community and solidarity which many of its leaders shared while working in the early civil rights movement in the South. In effect, these people have moved from one cause to another in an attempt to preserve their original experience of community. Moreover, ther political ideal derives from this experience as they wish somehow to apply this experience of community to wider society. In a sense, the New Left is a sectarian community trying to make a church of society. For as the *Port Huron Statement* says, participatory democracy must provide the necessary "means of finding meaning in personal life"—that is, it must at least provide the opportunity for salvation. For an interesting but unsuccessful attempt to relate the New Left to traditional forms of Christian sectarianism see Arthur Gish, *The New Left and Christian Radicalism* (Grand Rapids: Eerdmans, 1969). In this context the New Left differs significantly from the adherents of the counterculture as the former continues to exemplify and embody the American faith in man's dominance over his environments, both political and natural, through work and activity. It may be that some form of the more passive counterculture is a significant alternative to the American spirit.

differentiated society.[24] Such a society is individualistic and voluntaristic, for it separates men from their communal or ascribed societal structures. Men no longer belong to groups that give them a place within the whole, but join associations built around specific goals and purposes. Such voluntary associations make no claim to supply a unified world view. Paradoxically, in such a society the more independence we achieve the more interdependent we become; but our interdependence is highly formal since we meet one another only in specific roles and functions.

Philip Slater characterizes our quest for independence by describing the kind of vicious circularity that results:

Technological change, mobility, and the individualistic ethos combine to rupture the bonds that tie each individual to a family, a community, a kinship network, a geographical location—bonds that give him a comfortable sense of himself. As this sense of himself erodes, he seeks ways of affirming it. But his efforts at self-enhancement automatically accelerate the very erosion he seeks to halt. It is easy to produce examples of the many ways in which Americans attempt to minimize, circumvent, or deny the interdependence upon which all societies are based. We seek a private house, a private means of transportation, a private garden, a private laundry, self-service stores, and do-it-yourself skills of every kind. An enormous technology seems to have set itself the task of making it unnecessary for one human being ever to ask anything of another in the course of going about his daily business. Even within the family Americans are unique in their feeling that each member should have a separate room, and even a separate telephone, television and car, when economically possible. We seek, more and more privacy, and feel more and more alienated and lonely when we get it. What accidental contacts we do have, furthermore, seem more intrusive, not only because they are unsought but because they are unconnected with any familiar pattern of interdependence.[25]

---

[24]For a good summary of this contrast see James Nelson, *Moral Nexus* (Philadelphia: Westminster Press, 1971), pp. 131-144. This sociological point is important for it makes clear why America was able to give actual institutional form to its basic value commitments. Every society emphasizes some values as peculiarly its own, but seldom have societies had the institutional means to make their "preferred" values dominate all other forms of values embodied in other social relations as has America. By characterizing America's stress on individualism I do not mean that other societies do not share this value nor that Americans do not share some values that tend to qualify their individualism. However, I have isolated the idea of "individualism" here because I think it illuminates the current American malaise.

[25]Philip E. Slater, *The Pursuit of Loneliness* (Boston: Beacon Press, 1970), p. 7. Slater's book is easily the most suggestive of the popular critiques of contemporary

Thus living in a highly pluralistic society means that we are called upon to make more choices every day, "with fewer 'givens,' more ambiguous criteria, less environmental stability, and less social structural support, than any people in history."[26] In contrast to traditional social orders, our public institutions no longer contribute to the formation of the individual personality. "Personal identity becomes, essentially, a private phenomenon."[27] Men are now free to construct their personal identity as we are left to ourselves to choose our

---

American society. For Slater, technology is not an evil in itself; the power of technology becomes perverse only when we attempt to regulate it with the assumptions of an individualistic society. It is extremely interesting to compare Slater's book with Reich's. On the surface they seem to be in agreement, since both find our society overcompetitive, impersonal, garish, and boring. Yet Slater's analysis is fundamentally antithetical to the naive individualism characteristic of Reich's book.

For an analysis that I find in many ways similar to Slater's, yet more profound, see Simone Weil, The Need For Roots (New York: Harper, 1952). For example, she says, "When the possibilities of choice are so wide as to injure the commonweal, men cease to enjoy liberty. For they must either seek refuge in irresponsibility, puerility, and indifference—a refuge where the most they can find is boredom—or feel themselves weighted down by responsibilities at all times for fear of causing harm to others" (p. 13). Even though this was written with France in mind, there is no better analysis of the difference between the American middle class and the young as the former retreats into the suburbs of uncare to avoid the moral agony of being alive in such times, and the latter rush to claim total responsibility to assure their moral righteousness. We no longer seem to have any way to appreciate the man that faithfully fulfills his limited duties in this time and this place. To quote Weil again, "Uprootedness is by far the most dangerous malady to which human societies are exposed, for it is a self-propagating one. For people who are really uprooted there remain only two possible sorts of behavior: either to fall into a spiritual lethargy resembling death, like the majority of the slaves in the days of the Roman Empire, or to hurl themselves into some form of activity necessarily designed to uproot, often by the most violent methods, those who are not yet uprooted, or only partly so" (p. 47).

[26]Slater, op. cit., p. 21. Contrary to the radicals' charge, Americans are not forced to conform by an oppressive system, but their very individualism produces uniformity. In a highly cooperative and traditional society variety and eccentricity can be tolerated. It is assumed the social order is a going concern. In a highly individualistic society, however, eccentricity represents to the individual the threat of societal chaos and anarchy that he cannot bear to contemplate. In other words, the conformist aspects of American society are a correlate of our inability to handle the freedom that society forces upon us. In America there is seldom a battle between individualism and conformity, but a conflict between antithetical styles of conforming. For a still provocative treatment of this theme, see Winston White, Beyond Conformity (Glencoe: Free Press, 1961).

[27]Thomas Luckmann, The Invisible Religion (London: Macmillan Co., 1967), p. 97. For similar analyses that have influenced my presentation see Peter Berger, The Sacred Canopy (New York: Anchor Books, 1969), and Berger and Luckmann, The Social Construction of Reality (New York: Doubleday, 1966).

friends, marriage partners, neighbors and even "ultimate" meanings. Our culture is "no longer an obligatory structure of interpretive and evaluative schemes with a distinct hierarchy of significance. It is, rather, a rich, heterogeneous assortment of possibilities which, in principle, are accessible to any individual consumer."[28]

But as we are thrown back upon ourselves, when we lose the sense of moral and social involvement, we become prey to sensations of anxiety and guilt. For we perceive the pain our aloneness causes others and our consequent guilt eats on our soul; but our only choice seems to be to call our self-hatred the pursuit of happiness. There appears to be no external reality strong enough to call us from the monad-like form of our existence, for value has become privatized. Morally, it is assumed that our ethical positions are but subjective preferences. The only way of establishing the best preference is by observing which are held by the largest number of individuals, or those that can be forced by power. Religion becomes a matter of voluntary choice and thus must be marketed in forms palatable to the pagan pieties of those who still feel they should be "religious." Thus, by relegating all values to subjective choice, we cut ourselves off from any resources that might call us out of infatuation with our aloneness. Even if religious institutions wished to speak critically to the American culture, they would find their resources spent by having already accepted the option of that privatized religiosity so amenable to the American spirit.

The new upsurge in religiosity among the young is but a variation on the individualistic piety of their parents. The rise of "Jesus groups" and the interest in Eastern mysticism are to be expected, for when "the institutional framework of religion begins to break up, the search for a direct experience which people can feel to be religious facilitates the rise of cults." [29] The religious search is one aspect of the kind of political immersion and/or drug experience shared by many today. Each in its own way is an attempt to fly from the self, to dissolve the self in "mystical" experience or political involvement.

---

[28]Luckmann, *op cit.*, p. 98.

[29]Daniel Bell, "Religion in the Sixties," *Social Research*, XXXVIII (Autumn, 1971), 474. In no way should what I am saying be taken as a denial of the religious integrity of many who share this kind of religious experience. The mystic has an honored position among the religions of the world.

Yet this flight from the self is not just the province of the young. Their experience in this respect is not more intense than that of their elders. For none of us has yet discovered how to live morally in our consumer society without becoming a collector of the seemingly endless array of goods constantly produced for our pleasure. In our aloneness we are tempted to think that surely our lives have more significance than increasing our wealth to buy more and different goods, or bequeathing to our children the ability to consume more than we ourselves were able to do. Even if we turn our attention to helping those in our society who have less, we are struck by absurdities. For example, the idea that helping the poor is to provide them with the opportunity to share the kind of life that the affluent now find so unsatisfactory. We are thus tempted to romanticize what it means to be poor. Some have even begun to play at being poor, in order to escape the self-hatred occasioned by the meaningless existence brought on by our wealth.

Put another way, the attempt to find our identity in this society inevitably seems to create a tension between becoming a useful member of society and a real person. For to be "useful" means we must be able to play well a repertory of roles; but to be a real person implies we possess a core of personal reality which controls the roles so that we are not swallowed up by our societal existence. But we live in a world that rewards those most adroit at completely identifying with their roles.[30] Yet the more adaptive we become to our roles the more we wish to deny ourselves; we can no longer distinguish who we are from our public appearance which, by the way, we cannot stand.

The wish we spoke of earlier—to return to a purer, more simple, innocent America—can thus be seen as the social form of our personal crisis. As Daniel Bell characterizes it, the desire is "to step outside one's social skin, to divest oneself of all the multiple roles which contain behavior, and to find a lost innocence which has been overlaid by rules and norms. The search for feeling is a search for fantasy and its unrestricted play."[31]

---

[30]For example, Alvin Toffler says, "What is involved in increasing the throughput of people in one's life are the abilities not only to make ties but to break them, not only to affiliate but to disaffiliate. Those who seem most capable of this adaptive skill are also among the most richly rewarded in society." *Future Shock* (New York: Random House, 1970), p. 105.

[31]Bell, *op. cit.*, p. 488. A topic I have not treated associated with the new culture is the rediscovery of the body and sensuality. I suppose one of the reasons for this is

Such a longing assumes that if we could just divest ourselves of our degenerate culture, underneath the decay we would find a self morally worthy and uncomplicated. But secretly we know that all we would find is the emptiness of a life that has no moral form, and that suspicion paralyzes our souls and we abandon ourselves to complete activity. What we flee in our alienation is not external structures but the internal guilt of our existence occasioned by living in a suffering world as rich men who have lacked for nothing except the meaning that makes life worth living. We have failed to understand that the only way to gain wholeness in such a world is to grasp and understand the suffering and the world's needs with a patience that refuses to create more suffering in the name of some who suffer.

Theologically it is tempting to grasp this search for the self as true religion. But such an interpretation is no more viable than the attempt to develop a new "civil religion," "story," or "myth" for the American ethos.[32] No doubt a renewed sense of national purpose would provide many a solution for the personal crisis of our times.[33] But such a purpose, I suspect,

---

my uncertainty whether the body has ever been lost. However, for an interesting analysis of religion and the "new American culture" written from this point of view, see Leroy Moore's article cited above.

[32]Robert Bellah's famous article, "Civil Religion in America," made respectable again the idea of a theology of support for American ideals. It is indeed a temptation hard to resist as so many of the values of the American ethos seem to have such a natural relation to the gospel. Bellah's article can be found in *Secularization and the Protestant Prospect*, pp. 93-116. To see the influence of Bellah, see Novak's suggestion of the need for a new American "story" and Richard Neuhaus' idea of the new American "myth." Novak, *Ascent of the Mountain, Flight of the Dove* (New York: Harper, 1971), and Neuhaus, *In Defense of People* (New York: Macmillan, 1971). Neither Novak nor Neuhaus makes clear the relation of theology to the development of such a "story" or "myth," or how such a "story" can embody the sense of the tragic I have tried to articulate above.

[33]Theologically, the attempt to alleviate our personal aloneness by constituting the American people, as such, as the primary group of our society must be resisted. Such an attempt inevitably runs the risk of imbuing the political order with more significance than it deserves. The greatness of realism, for all of its weaknesses, was its appreciation of the ambiguity of the political. A national purpose we need, but not at the cost of the development of the individual through groups less quantitatively extensive than the nation but qualitatively more substantive. Nisbet, I think, is quite right that the great danger of the current quest for community is the totalitarian potential of constituting the state as the one source of ultimate meaning for society. Politically the hard problem confronting America is how to embody at once a substantive sense of the common good as an alternative to interest group or pluralist democracy as an end in itself without destroying the authentic diversity that a healthy society must have.

would only create new myths which would create more persistent illusions about our capacities. For the flight from the self which I have been describing is not simply a flight from the peculiar difficulties of living in American society. Like the American dream itself, I fear it is an attempt to flee the human condition of finitude, limitation, and guilt. The radical and the nonradical have much to criticize about the American culture, but the very extent of their criticism is a clue that they seek an escape from the limitation of personal and social existence. In such a context the primary task for adherents of the gospel is to remind ourselves and others that such an escape is not possible or desirable. The gospel's primary thrust is not to provide the details for the development of a just society, but rather to give men the strength to see their problems and condition honestly and without illusion. Only on such a basis is it possible to establish social justice, for lasting justice can only be built and sustained by a people who have no fear of the truth. A justice not so grounded becomes but the injustice of the next generation for it has no defense against those that would claim it in the name of their peculiar version of the truth.

The hard struggle that the American people now confront is not a struggle to overcome external adversities, though there is still much to be done. Rather, it is a crisis of spirit. It requires we face honestly what we have been and what we must do in a world where death is the one sure reality. The problem of living in America is that there literally seems to be nothing worth dying for. We manufacture "moral-political" causes to hide this from ourselves but the emptiness of our lives cannot long be filled with such goods. For to be willing to die means our lives have significance yet without significance our self-hatred is so intense it must seek to destroy any significance we see in the lives of others. We fail to see that significance is only possible when we are able to accept ourselves, our nation, and our "crises times" as having less than an eternal form, or, in more traditional language, as standing under the judgment of God's eternal kingdom.

Index

Reeder, John, 86n.
Reich, Charles, 242, 251n., 252n., 253n., 256n.
Reich, Warren, 182n.
Reich, Wilhelm, 49n.
Reynolds, Charles, 85n.
Richardson, Herbert, 244n.
Robitscher, Jonas, 167n.
Roszak, Theodore, 223n., 251n.
Rules, 17-18, 35; context Vs, 48-49; in relation to stories 71-72; as constitutive of basic morality, 82; 87-88; in relation to reasons, 106-107; as interpreted by the new morality, 112.

Sanctification, 67.
Sayers, Dorothy, 120.
Schall, James, 245n.
Schaull, Richard, 223n., 239n.
Schutz, Alfred, 60n.
Sellars, James, 30n., 239n., 244n.
Simon, Yves, 219n.
Singer, Marcus, 61n., 84-85.
Slater, Philip, 255.
Snyder, Stephen, 223n.
Story, 3-4, black man's, 7-8; 71-76; 249-250; stories and rules 89; in relation to love, 115-116; and truth, 120.
Strauss, Anselm, 183n.
Strawson, P.F., 82-83, 84, 89.
Suffering, 43, 96; 191, 193, 259; as necessary for seeing truthfully,

104-105; 123; and abortion, 162-163.

Taylor, C.C.N., 85n.
Taylor, Charles, 56n., 58n.
Taylor, Richard, 56n., 58n.
Thorson, T. L., 236n.
Toffler, Alvin, 258n.
Troeltsch, Ernst, 119n.

Universalizability, 60-61, 84-89, 157.
Urmson, J.O., 84n.

Virtue, see character
Vision: relation to the self, 2; notion and vision, 19-20; and illusion, 31-34, 102, 249; and objectivity, 227n.
von Wright, G.H. 58n.

Weil, Simone, 39n., 41, 45, 256n.
Wesley, John, 67n.
White, Winston, 256n.
Wiesel, Elie, 116n.
Winch, Peter, 17n., 58n.
Winter, Gibson, 41n., 232n., 239n.
Wisdom, John, 72n.
Wittgenstein, Ludwig, 35.
Wolfe, Peter, 30n.
Wolff, Robert Paul, 229n., 230n., 233n., 234, 237.
Wolin, Sheldon, 224-225, 237n.

Yoder, John Howard, 6, 197-221.